HANDBOOK OF RESOURCE ROOM TEACHING

Contributors

Margo Neale
Gale Reiter
Rita Gordon
Sheldon Horowitz
Kathleen Joyce
Joseph Zacherman

Rochelle Simon
Gloria Wilson
Beverly Zimmerman
Joan Bossis
Elaine Schwartz
Ruth Gold

HANDBOOK OF RESOURCE ROOM TEACHING

Judith H. Cohen
Adelphi University
Garden City, New York

AN ASPEN PUBLICATION®
Aspen Systems Corporation
Rockville, Maryland
London
1982

Library of Congress Cataloging in Publication Data

Cohen, Judith H.
Handbook of resource room teaching.

Includes bibliographies and index.
1. Resource programs (Education)—Addresses, essays,
lectures. 2. Handicapped children—Education—Addresses,
essays, lectures. 3. Mainstreaming in education—
Addresses, essays, lectures. I. Cohen, Judith H.

LB1028.8.H36   371.9   81-20599
ISBN: 0-89443-653-8   AACR2

Library of Congress Catalog Card Number: 81-20599
ISBN: 0-89443-653-8

Printed in the United States of America

1 2 3 4 5

For Stuart with love

Table of Contents

Preface

In teacher education, finding the proper balance between theory and methodology is necessary. This textbook is intended to aid special educators in applying theoretical knowledge to the practical problems of creating resource room programs. The task of creating effective resource programs is enormous, and the knowledge necessary to be a competent resource teacher is multifaceted. I have therefore called on the expertise of a group of special educators who have actually faced the challenge of creating resource programs at different instructional levels in a variety of communities.

In deciding the format for this text, I asked each chapter contributor to focus on an aspect of resource room teaching that is essential for the development of resource room programs. The chapters were written independently of each other, and I hope that the reader will understand the small amount of redundancy that is the product of this type of format. In addition, I have provided a conceptual framework for understanding the resource room teaching strategy in Chapter One.

Following each chapter is a section that I have written and titled "At Issue." These minichapters expand upon, clarify, or raise a controversial issue associated with the content of each chapter.

Knowing fully that much of a teacher's education arises from actual experience and that a teacher's experiences are always unique for that person in a particular environment, I trust that this book will prove to be a helpful guide. I encourage each prospective resource teacher to read, question, explore, and ultimately test out the ideas presented.

JUDITH H. COHEN
Adelphi University
Garden City, New York

Acknowledgments

The impetus for creating this text originated with a graduate course in special education at Adelphi University entitled "Developing Resource Rooms in Special Education." I am grateful to my friend and colleague, Dr. Ruth Gold, who designed the course and invited me to participate in teaching it. Ruth has provided guidance and support throughout the development of this book.

The contributors to the text are all personally known to me as outstanding special educators. They have shared their knowledge and expertise. Without their contributions, this text would not have been possible.

I am also grateful to two other colleagues and friends in the Education Department at Adelphi University, Dr. Roberta Wiener and Dr. Sheila Hollander, who have assisted me with various aspects of this text. My editor, the late R. Curtis Whitesel, provided clarifying insights that greatly facilitated the development of this work.

Without the love, encouragement, and faith of my husband, Stuart, and the cooperation of my sons, Robert and Richard, no such work could have been accomplished.

Chapter 1

The Resource Room: A Real World Context

Judith H. Cohen

DEFINING RESOURCE TEACHING

The concept of resource teaching is multifaceted. Resource teaching or a resource room program is the attempt to provide special education services to children who need assistance in order to learn in a normal classroom. Such children most likely have been designated as needing special education, but the decision has been made to keep these children within the normal school program to the greatest extent possible. However, because these students have been identified as having specific learning problems arising from physical, mental, or emotional anomalies, they could not fully profit from regular education unless additional instruction or other supportive services are provided. These services are provided on a parttime basis by resource personnel working outside the child's regular classroom. The person whose job is to support the child's regular instructional program and to assist the child's learning becomes the resource teacher.

The resource teaching concept has originated from the current attitude that many children, who in previous times would have been educated in self-contained, special education classes, can derive greater benefit from being part of the normal school program. The term "mainstreaming" has come to mean the placement of children with special educational needs in the regular school program. Fully realizing that students with special educational needs are going to encounter difficulties learning in the regular classroom, support services need to be provided. Providing support services for these children falls to the resource teacher.

While the many services that resource teachers are responsible for providing will be fully explored later in this chapter, the resource teacher's duties can be categorized as those *directly* rendered to children and those that *indirectly* assist them. The resource room teacher directly supports

1

the learning of students when the teacher works with students in the following ways: diagnosing learning problems, remediating areas of deficit, tutoring in curriculum areas, or helping manage the students' behavior. Indirect services that resource teachers perform might include: consulting with classroom teachers, revising or modifying curriculums, advising parents, and working with administrators and other designated personnel who are involved in special education.

The variety of roles that the resource teacher takes develops from the type of resource program that has been created. The job description of a resource teacher and the method of providing services to children must originate from the profile of students' needs. Thus the concept of the resource program is probably one of the most flexible designations in the field of special education today; resource programs must be created to fit the needs of a particular group of children, and no one type of program can be unilaterally applied. Important decisions about the types of children needing support services, the number of children who would most benefit from resource teaching, the curriculum areas to be taught, and the kinds of consulting services to teachers all create the components of the resource program and thereby create the role for the resource teacher.

A resource program is only one means of providing special education to children in a school district. Many children in special education will still need to be placed in self-contained, special education classes for varying amounts of time during their school years. Others may profit only from home instruction. More severely disabled children might need placement in a facility designed to meet their special needs. Such a facility might exist within a child's own school district or be found in a nearby community, serving the needs of several school districts.

The resource teacher becomes a team member of the special education faculty, who support children needing special education who are mainstreamed in the regular school program. Within the spectrum of children needing special education, resource teachers work most effectively when resource programs are created to assist the more mildly handicapped child. The goal of the resource teacher becomes that of providing the proper kind and amount of services to children so that they can maximally benefit from mainstream education with their peers.

HISTORICAL DEVELOPMENT OF RESOURCE TEACHING

There have been profound differences in the way that children with special needs have been educated. Decisions about removing students from their classes to go to the special teacher or having the teacher provide special education in a self-contained setting must be based on a clear understanding of the needs of different kinds of children in special education. The development of resource teaching is an outgrowth of the educational theory requiring that instructional programs appropriate for students with special needs be designed. Historically, educating exceptional children has ranged from placing children in residential treatment facilities, most often isolated from their communities, to placing children in self-contained special education classes within their communities, to the most recent trend of placing children with special needs back into the regular school program. Thus the concept of resource teaching has developed from both history and philosophy.

In the United States the field of special education originated with an awareness for treatment of the physically handicapped. In the first half of the nineteenth century, particularly in the eastern region of the country, there was great concern for children with obvious handicaps, such as deafness, blindness, and mental retardation. Special schools dedicated to meet the needs of these atypical groups were established because it was felt that society had a moral and civic obligation to care for those with special needs. This period saw the development of the residential treatment facility, where those who were felt to be less fortunate because of their handicaps could be cared for in a beneficent manner. These institutions were most often located in isolated places outside the mainstream of community activities. However, the removal of the physically handicapped from their communities and their relocation to separate residences may have created some of the societal attitudes that have dominated the thinking of this country for many years.

Historically, the handicapped individual was not expected to be a functioning member in a community. In addition, because most people did not see and know handicapped people, distorted stereotypes and false impressions of the handicapped were created. The growth in residential treatment facilities was marked throughout the second half of the nineteenth century. Every state admitted into the union had to demonstrate provision for dealing with handicapped children.

In the early part of the twentieth century, large urban centers began to develop. As people grouped together in larger numbers, providing for the handicapped was no longer an isolated problem. Many families felt that removing handicapped children from their homes was inappropriate and sought different methods of treatment. In addition, the development of intelligence testing made it possible to assess levels of mental functioning and thus allowed for the grouping of the handicapped into various categories. This allowed professionals to differentiate treatment based not only on the kinds of disability, that is, deaf or blind, but on the severity of the disability. The technology for discriminating between the mildly handicapped and the severely disabled created differentiated placement in various treatment settings.

In 1904 Alfred Binet was commissioned by the French minister of public instruction to develop a technique for discriminating between the mentally retarded and the normal in school populations so that appropriate instruction could be based on a child's ability. Henry Goddard is cited as the first American psychologist to use Binet's early scales for evaluating mental functioning in the United States. Goddard saw the utility of an instrument that could be used to identify and separate different levels of the mentally handicapped, and he adapted Binet's instrument for use in the Vineland Training School for the mentally retarded in New Jersey in 1914. This was one of the first applications of a mental measurement to provide differentiated education in a school setting. It resulted in the development of categories of levels of atypical functioning.

Gradually, the prevailing social attitude of maintaining and caring for the atypical began changing to that of education rather than custodial care. The community began to assume responsibility for the education of disabled groups and, therefore, created a variety of educational programs for the handicapped.

Day schools for children with health problems and mental handicaps expanded rapidly in the early 1900s, and such schools could be found in approximately 200 cities by 1911.[1] Another significant change in special education occurred due to the compulsory enlistment of all males during World Wars I and II. Tens of thousands of men were rejected for military service after screening because of physical or mental deficiencies. In addition, the influx of soldiers returning from war with debilitating injuries focused attention on the practical problem of returning them to productive life. American citizens felt a moral obligation to assist the returning war veterans in adjusting to their injuries, and treatment programs had to be established to meet their specific needs.

The formation of the most potentially active and aggressive group in behalf of the handicapped came about with the parent movement. In 1940 an advertisement was placed in *The New York Times* by the parents of a child with cerebral palsy requesting that parents of similar children contact them.[2] The formation of this group of parents marked the beginning of an aggressive campaign to win equal rights for disabled children that reached its climax with the passing of special education legislation in the 1970s. Parent groups concerned with mental retardation and learning disabilities helped to establish the impetus for social change. Today judicial decision and legislative action have established that all children are entitled to equal opportunity under the law and therefore under the domain of educational institutions. Obtaining a free and appropriate education, regardless of a handicapping condition, is a child's legal right and not merely a product of a well-meaning society.

The change in educational patterns for the handicapped in recent years has been so marked that some have called it "revolutionary."[3] During the 1960s the attention of the country was focused on what had been called the "disadvantaged" child. Programs were developed through federal funding to enable school districts to help such children compensate for their cultural divergency and for what had been thought by some to be a conceptual and experiential deprivation. Yet, during the same time period, it has been estimated that one handicapped child in eight, totalling more than one million handicapped children, did not receive any education.[4]

In 1974 Congress passed Public Law (PL) 93-380, which acknowledged the handicapped child's right to education and due process under the law. The Education for All Handicapped Children Act, PL 94-142, passed by Congress in 1975, has been the milestone for the revolution in special education. The inherent provisions of this legislation have given impetus to the formation of resource programs throughout the nation. The law's provisions came into full effect in 1978, and guaranteed exceptional children and their families a kind of education that many would not have dreamed possible. Specifically PL 94-142 provides that:

- Every handicapped child shall have an Individualized Education Program (IEP) that has been designed by parents, teachers, administrators, and specialists to meet the specific educational needs of the child regardless of availability of services.
- Every handicapped child shall have access to the same variety of services and programs, that is, art, music, physical education, extracurricular activities, and so on, available to nonhandicapped children.
- Every handicapped child should receive education in the "least restrictive environment" possible.

The passage of this law makes the dream of many a reality in schools today. As had been previously discussed, the origin of special education services was at the outset in the most restrictive environment of the residential setting. Today, special education services extend to the least restrictive environment of the mainstream program, supplemented by resource teaching.

What is now considered the newest form of special education teaching— resource services—can be traced to 1913 in a resource program created for the visually and hearing handicapped child who was educated in a normal school setting.[5] However, throughout most of the twentieth century the trend in education has been that of isolating the special education student to a self-contained classroom. Resource programs that were in abundance during the 1950s and 1960s were designed to provide education for remedial learners in such curriculum areas as reading, mathematics, and speech, and were not part of the typical pattern of special education programs.[6] An important and controversial group of research studies that had been conducted in the late 1960s and early 1970s documented the disadvantages of the restricted placement of children in special education classes and clearly demonstrated that there were inherent weaknesses in the self-contained special education setting.[7] The researchers could not find evidence to substantiate that the restrictive, self-contained, special education class created a better learning environment for children of special needs than did other arrangements. In fact, all too frequently restrictive placements were disproportionately registered with minority group and economically disadvantaged children.

Thus began the brave experiment to create mainstreaming programs for handicapped children that would be supplemented by special education services provided through resource programs. This new model for delivering services to atypical learners would enable such children to benefit from all of the variety and stimulation that their nonhandicapped peers had always been privileged to have.

PATTERNS OF RESOURCE TEACHING

With the mandate of PL 94-142 to place handicapped children in the least restrictive environment, a method for delivering support services to these children in the regular school program had to evolve. Thus developed the concept of resource programs. Mildly handicapped children would be returned to the regular school program but would be required to attend a special education class on a parttime basis. The general function of this parttime special education class, now called the resource room, would be to provide basic remediation in students' areas of deficit and in general to help support the program the students received in the normal classroom setting. Regardless of whether the students exhibited handicaps of physical or emotional development, or had primary problems with learning, resource programs would be created to adapt to the various and specific needs of children in need of parttime special education.

Many now consider that the resource concept is the best alternative in a public school setting for the education of the mildly handicapped child. However, this model of teaching should not replace other kinds of special education programs. The resource program is simply one alternative in a list of possible placements for handicapped children. It is a vital component in the range of special education services that can be provided for children.

From the most restrictive environment of the residential or nonpublic school setting through other options, such as home instruction, special schools, and fulltime special classes within the regular school setting, to various degrees of mainstream programs, the child's needs must be the first priority in deciding on the best educational environment. Lerner puts the resource concept into clear perspective when she says:

> In summary, a resource room is simply an administrative arrangement. Its success depends upon many factors, including the competence of the resource teacher, the support and cooperation of all levels of administration and the availability of adequate space and materials.[8]

Resource programs work best when they become an integral part of a team approach to providing services for mildly handicapped children. School resource personnel who do not normally provide services within the confines of the resource room environment are nevertheless essential to its success. Personnel to be considered as members of the resource team should include school district administrators (for example, the superintendent, assistant superintendent for instruction, coordinator of special education, director of pupil services, building principals, and department chairpeople), school psychologists, school nurses or health teachers, speech and language specialists, reading and math specialists, classroom teachers, guidance counselors, librarians and media specialists, social workers, and special education teachers.

To some extent the overlapping of roles between the remedial specialist and the special education teacher presents a source of potential conflict. Before the imposition of PL 94-142, handicapped children were taught by special education teachers, whereas students with learning problems were taught by curriculum specialists, usually in the fields of reading and math. Sawyer and Wilson correctly point out that politicians, not educators, are responsible for the current laws governing delivery of services in education and thus paradoxically may have created unforeseen role conflicts.[9] If resource programs have been established to service children classified as ''handicapped'' and are thus financed through PL 94-142, then such programs must be staffed with certified special education teachers. However, if resource programs are funded through regular school district allotments or with Title I funding (The Elementary and Secondary Act of 1965), then teachers not certified in special education, such as reading specialists, may staff such programs. Because many, if not most, learning disabled children demonstrate problems in such primary curriculum areas as reading and mathematics, a controversy has been created. Frequently reading teachers express concern that those in special education do not have sufficient in-depth training in the field of reading development to instruct children with severe reading disabilities. As a counterpoint, special education teachers express concern that reading teachers have not had the training to integrate teaching in a multitude of curriculum areas and cannot adequately instruct the child who has primary learning process problems.

A simple solution to this complex problem is not readily available. There is truth on both sides of this controversy, but it is the special education teacher who is legally responsible for the education of any child certified as needing special education. However, in a child's IEP a written commitment to deliver services by specified personnel must be enumerated, and the reading teacher and other learning specialists can be incorporated into the resource team. In many universities, teacher educators have responded to this dilemma by counseling teachers to be dually certified in special education and reading, or to choose electives relevant to the learning needs of children who show both reading problems and learning disabilities.

The following five basic patterns of resource programs for handicapped children in current usage have been summarized by D'Alonzo, D'Alonzo, and Mauser:

1. categorical resource programs
2. cross-categorical resource programs
3. noncategorical resource programs
4. specific skills resource programs
5. itinerant resource programs.[10]

The most traditional model of delivering education to handicapped children in special education classes has been the categorical concept. This can be defined as grouping children in terms of their disability, that is, mentally retarded, emotionally disturbed, physically handicapped, learning disabled, and so on. Children with the same type of disability are taught in one setting under the categorical concept. The categorical resource program parallels this model by developing programs specifically tailored to the needs of children within one area of exceptionality. Therefore, a school or school district would need to establish separate and distinct resource programs to provide services for each area of exceptionality evident within its pupil population.

Many university programs providing teacher certification in special education have focused the training of teachers on a chosen area of exceptionality. Their graduates tend to support the categorical resource program. These teachers feel that children in special education are best educated in a homogeneous setting taught by an appropriately trained specialist. They feel that this is true regardless of whether the special education class is fulltime or parttime.

The categorical resource room program appears to be most effective with the mildly disabled youngster who can benefit from mainstreaming. The more severely handicapped child would still most likely be placed in a self-contained special education class. However, even the moderately impaired child can be programmed into the categorical resource program fulltime, and then slowly and selectively be mainstreamed for particular subjects or experiences as the child is ready.

The cross-categorical resource program is designed to serve mildly handicapped children in more than one category of exceptionality. Wiederholt, Hammill, and Brown point out that the main advantages of the cross-categorical resource program are dual. Such programs can be used when the number of handicapped children in one area of exceptionality is not large enough to create a categorical program. Also, within the cross-categorical program children can be grouped according to their instructional needs rather than by the etiology of their disability as it exists under the categorical model.[11] Resource teachers using the cross-categorical model may choose to instruct children based on their learning deficits and thereby integrate different groups of children into one instructional setting. Other resource teachers may prefer to schedule children into the resource room in homogeneous groups by area of disability, but can develop a program that can meet the needs of children with diverse disabilities.

The noncategorical resource program is designed to provide services for students who present learning and or behavior problems, whether they have been classified as handicapped. Admission into the noncategorical program depends upon the type and extent of the child's learning problem and record of achievement in the normal classroom. Students who have gone through the legal process of diagnosis by a Child Study Team (CST) and who have been judged to be handicapped according to legal definitions by a Committee on the Handicapped (COH) can be scheduled for the noncategorical resource program, along with those children who have not been evaluated as handicapped but who simply need additional small group or individualized instruction. Wiederholt, Hammill, and Brown estimate that 70 to 80 percent of children in noncategorical resource programs are not handicapped according to the legal definitions.[12] Therefore these children would not normally receive special education services. Financial support for the noncategorical resource program cannot come solely from the funding created by PL 94-142. Thus the allocation of regular school district funding is needed to support such a program. In the noncategorical resource program, meeting the instructional needs of children is emphasized without attempting to label areas of exceptionality. Through the heterogeneous arrangement of teaching handicapped with nonhandicapped students in the noncategorical model, the potential stigma created by isolating children in special education can be avoided.

The specific skill resource program has been created to remediate problems within a specific curriculum area. Most frequently the specific skill program focuses on the areas of reading, mathematics, and speech and language development. Specific skill programs closely resemble the remedial resource programs that proliferated during the late 1960s when Title I funding was available for supplemental instruction. The traditional "pull-out" program of remedial instruction in reading can be retitled a specific skill resource room program in reading. Most specific skill resource programs work with children who have not been evaluated for handicaps. These children fall into the category of remedial or corrective learners, and they have primary learning deficits in one or more curriculum areas. Specific skill centers are particularly important in schools where categorical or cross-categorical resource programs have been established, because these programs would exclude nonhandicapped students in need of remediation.

The itinerant resource program may be any one of the four previously described models, but by definition it is mobile. In areas where the population of disabled youngsters is small and does not warrant a fulltime resource teacher in one location, an itinerant teacher may establish resource programs in more than one school. This type of program has several drawbacks, and the role of the itinerant resource teacher is the most difficult. Itinerant teachers rarely become accepted as part of a school faculty because their service and allegiance are divided between schools. Itinerant teachers are available only on a limited basis, and this makes the problems of scheduling consulting and advising sessions burdensome. Because of their itinerant schedules, these teachers are often perceived to be inaccessible both by classroom teachers and parents. Itinerant teachers confess that at times their instructional roles seem dictated by schedule rather than by choice. In addition, the physical burden of equipping and transporting materials between resource rooms, sharing locations with other parttime school personnel, and the general feeling of isolation make itinerant teachers frequently question their contribution to a school's program.

DEFINING THE RESOURCE TEACHER'S ROLE

The role of a resource teacher is multifaceted. It depends on the kind of resource program that is being taught and on the variety of direct and indirect services that resource teachers are expected to perform. When resource teachers are involved in direct teaching services to children, they may be called on to use analytic skills involved in diagnosis and assessment of learning problems through formal and informal testing. Direct services also involve the development and implementation of programs in a variety of curriculum areas, not only to remediate areas of deficit, but to support and coordinate with the instructional program in the child's regular class. Therefore, the resource teacher must function both as remediator and tutor so that children can be helped to strengthen deficit areas while they are given the opportunity to profit from instruction in the normal school program.

At the secondary level, with a full departmentalized program, this problem becomes acute. Each student in the secondary school resource program is also a student of other content teachers. The secondary school student needs a great deal of assistance in maintaining satisfactory work in diverse curriculum areas under the supervision of teachers who may differ greatly in their demands and expectations.

Additional direct services performed by resource teachers include behavioral management. Handicapped children often suffer from psychosocial adjustment problems that create behavior problems in the normal classroom. Whether the problem is short attention span, distractibility, poor concentration, inability to follow directions, or more disruptive behavior, such as hyperactivity or belligerence, resource teachers are expected to assist children in developing age-appropriate social skills. If the handicapped child is to benefit fully from being placed in the mainstream program, the child must be helped to develop self-control. Some of the behavior patterns that special education teachers can tolerate in the self-contained special education setting must be phased out when the handicapped child is placed in a busy, congested, normal classroom. Such simple actions as leaving an assigned seat or calling out in jest could create disruptive situations in a crowded classroom.

Resource room teachers are often needed to act as teachers, counselors, psychologists, and friends to the children they teach. They may in fact be needed as mediators or advocates for children when conflicts arise. The direct services they perform for children are multitudinous.

Indirectly, resource teachers assist children in their programs through services rendered to classroom teachers and to parents. Resource teachers must work in close conjunction with regular classroom teachers and school personnel to advise and consult on children's learning styles, problems, and achievements. Classroom teachers will frequently call on the resource teacher to help plan instructional programs for the handicapped child in the normal classroom. The resource teacher must therefore be up-to-date on all curriculum areas taught at the various grade levels, as well as cognizant of methods and materials that can be used in the regular classroom setting. Resource teachers should be able to appraise instructional materials critically and be able to plan and implement IEPs. The ability to analyze and interpret critically test data on a variety of cognitive processes and achievement tests is essential to the functioning of a resource teacher. In addition, resource teachers may be expected to provide inservice education through workshops and demonstration lessons to aid the professional growth of their colleagues.

PL 94-142 makes the handicapped child's parent a legal partner in the responsibility for educating that child. Therefore, parents are required to take on a more active role in the decision-making process of special education. It is the resource teacher's primary responsibility to assist parents in understanding their child's strengths and weaknesses, and in formulating relevant and appropriate educational goals. The resource teacher can also facilitate the parent's communication and cooperation with the mainstream teachers by being a coordinator and liaison with the child's home. Never before have parents of handicapped children been so assertive in partaking in the educational process for their children, and it is incumbent upon the resource teacher to facilitate this team approach between home and school. The role of the resource teacher does seem awesome, but it can be the most potent and effective role in special education today.

EVALUATING THE RESOURCE PROGRAM CONCEPT

Every model of educational program in use today carries with it inherent advantages and disadvantages. So too does the concept of the resource program. How can the resource program adequately serve the needs of mildly handicapped learners?

In terms of the child's socialization and ability to function in the world of normal children, the mainstream program with resource support lends itself to the development of better interpersonal skills than does the self-contained, special education environment. This model allows the child to spend as much time as is appropriate for his or her development with nonhandicapped peers while receiving the benefits of supportive special education services. The integration of mildly handicapped children with their nonhandicapped peers is an advantage both to the disabled and nondisabled child. There can be no question that the isolation of disabled children in self-contained classes gravely lowers their self-esteem and creates debilitating stigmas associated with their impairments that can never be overcome. In a recent work on the handicapped, Gliedman and

Roth say, "Most teachers recognize that stigma and prejudice are often far more constricting to a child than the strictly biological limitation of his handicaps."[13]

In addition, the awkward behavior and distorted stereotypes that normal children often develop toward the handicapped can be attributed to their isolation from handicapped individuals. The humanistic advantages of the integration of special education children into the mainstream program cannot be overemphasized. The resource model will help future citizens understand more clearly the legitimate rights that the handicapped have and the potential contributions they can make in today's world.

In learning to accept and deal with the special needs of their disabled children, parents are more likely to look favorably on the resource concept as compared to placement of their children in self-contained special education classes or schools. Parents of handicapped children frequently carry a burden of guilt and may react in such diverse ways as denying that problems exist, blaming others for the child's disability, or passively relegating all decisions to the school's professional staff. The diagnosis that a child has been found to be "handicapped" is a harsh label that parents frequently have difficulty dealing with. However, the placement of the mildly handicapped child in the mainstream program with additional support services provided by the resource program can be seen by parents as a good compromise in the range of all possible special education settings. Reger confirms this when he says, "A parent with a child who displays moderate problems is going to be much happier about resource room placement than about a special class placement."[14] When parents are made an active part of the planning team for their handicapped children, they can more easily see the contribution that the resource program makes toward fulfilling the educational needs of their children.

Resource programs can provide instruction to more children than would normally be instructed in self-contained, special education classes. This increases the capacity of the trained special educator to assist with the instruction of more of a school's total population. By removing the mildly and more moderately disabled youngsters from self-contained special education, more placements become available for the severely disabled children. Resource programs are less costly to the school district than would be the instruction of a similar number of children in self-contained classes.

Children in resource programs can profit from a diversity of instructional styles, methods, and materials as they move from the mainstream class to the resource room. Students benefit from individual or small group instruction in the resource room and larger group or whole class instruction in the regular program. Together the resource teacher and the classroom teacher can develop the best instructional program to meet the individual needs of a mildly handicapped child. The resource program format is flexible enough to accommodate the needs of students in a more relaxed and informal environment than might otherwise take place. Resource teachers quickly learn that their students' success depends not only on the quality of instruction in the resource room itself, but on the resource teacher's ability to support the instructional program in which the students participate during the rest of the school day.

Resource teachers can also provide an informal support system for regular classroom teachers. All too frequently teachers must deal with instructional problems in an isolated fashion. With budget restrictions and increasing class size, the days of team teaching are long gone. There are insufficient resources in most school systems to provide assistance to classroom teachers, and frequently classroom teachers are unwilling to discuss their concerns with those in supervisory or administrative positions. Resource teams can serve the dual purpose of providing support for children with learning problems and for their teachers.

Finally, resource teachers take on the ultimate responsibility for overseeing the education of the mildly handicapped children assigned to their program. Such a role incorporates becoming a child advocate so that every handicapped child has a professional spokesperson who is intimately aware of that child's personality, characteristics, social adjustment, and learning problems.

Disadvantages that arise from the resource model stem primarily from the complexity of the resource program and from the diversity of roles that the resource teacher must fill. It is easy to enumerate such obvious problems, including scheduling large numbers of students with diverse needs, learning to advise and consult with a wide range of other professionals, keeping records that may become legal documents, and becoming familiar with a vast array of curriculum areas and approaches. In addition, resource programs are parttime special education, and therefore the resource teacher is challenged to conduct a quality educational program in a limited amount of time. Resource teachers frequently report that while they do see improvement in the learning that their students are making, they often feel frustrated at not having more time to work intensely with individual students. Even the mildly handicapped child has a complexity of learning problems that cannot be simply eradicated by seeing even the most competent resource teacher for a limited amount of time on a daily basis.

Other problems may result from the acquisition of an appropriate budget, allocation of space for the resource room, and obtaining and storing materials. However, the most formidable problem with the resource concept originates from classroom teachers who feel ill-equipped to meet the needs of mainstreamed handicapped children. If mainstream education is to be a viable placement for handicapped children, regular classroom teachers must be helped to meet their instructional and social needs. The resource teacher most often assumes the burden of ensuring that an appropriate educational program is maintained for the mainstreamed child. Obviously, this is not an easy task. Commenting on this problem Lerner says, "Dynamic human relations and an understanding of the entire school organization is required of the person serving in the role of resource teacher."[15]

Many educators today debate the appropriateness of mainstreaming. Cruickshank, a prominent expert in special education, has gone so far as to state that a child's placement in the least restrictive placement of a regular class "may more often be the most restrictive place for learning disabled children to receive their education."[16] Cruickshank focuses on a multitude of frustrations created for the handicapped child if the child is placed into a mainstream classroom without considering the classroom teacher's preparation, desire, and ability to educate a handicapped child. He also feels that administrators' deep understanding of the nature of learning disabilities is vital if ample assistance for the classroom teacher is to be obtained from experts who know how to instruct children with learning problems.

Reger continues the debate about the appropriateness of resource programs when he cautions that resource programs must serve as "change agents" in special education today.[17] He says that resource programs can unintentionally perpetuate and protect an unfortunate status quo by limiting the responsibility of educating handicapped students to the special education teacher working in an isolated environment—now to be called the resource room—instead of the special education class. Resource programs, he feels, must not be separated from the general school program and become relegated to the narrow role of educating "problem children" outside of mainstream education. Sending children off to the resource room may continue the problem of removing those with learning problems from their rightful place in the normal classroom. This in turn takes the responsibility of dealing with a child's problems away from the classroom teacher and places the instructional burden once again on the special educator. Reger feels that resource teachers assist a school's general program through the prevention of learning problems by developing appropriate curriculums, destroying stereotypes about exceptional children, and providing advice and assistance for the mainstream faculty.

In a later work Reger continues his appeal for the role of the resource model as a change agent in education, although he cautions that change in the general school program may take many years.[18] He feels that resource teachers can affect a school's general program when they work as exemplary models and by the techniques of subtle persuasion. Resource teachers must become an integral part of general education, or they will simply be teachers of self-contained, special education classes working parttime with new labels.

Reger suggests the following excellent guidelines to help resource programs be effective:

- Resource teachers must be assigned to only one building.
- Administrators, not resource teachers, should be responsible for the placement of children in resource programs to avoid undesirable feelings about favoritism on the part of teachers or students.
- Ten to fifteen percent of a resource teacher's time must be specifically reserved for consultations with other teachers.
- A half-day per week should be designated for inservice training for both the resource teachers and the mainstream teachers.
- The size of a resource program should be no more than 15 children at the elementary level and 20 children at the secondary level.
- Resource teachers should work with no more than three to four children at any one time.
- No child should need a resource program for more than three hours a day, or the child is improperly placed.
- Resource teachers should not be used as crisis teachers.
- Resource programs should not replace all self-contained special education classes.
- The resource room should be the same size as a regular classroom or at least approximately half the size of a regular room.
- An initial resource budget should be at least $1,500 to $2,000, and at least $1,000 annually in subsequent years.[19]

In spite of the demanding role of the resource teacher and the complexity of problems that may arise from resource teaching, resource teachers claim that their personal satisfaction far surpasses what some might view as overwhelming frustrations. The resource concept is still a fledgling in the education for the handicapped, and years of refinement and improvement will be necessary before this new model of education is fully accepted and operating with great efficiency.

THE EFFECTS AND IMPLICATIONS OF RESOURCE PROGRAMS

Every teacher of special education and every parent of handicapped children, as well as those interested in education, should read a masterful work entitled *The Unexpected Minority* by Gliedman and Roth. This work constitutes an extensive report about the status of handicapped children in America and was conducted under the auspices of the Carnegie Council on Children. The authors contend that "over the past decade special education has witnessed a set of changes that can only be called revolutionary," and that "every revolution changes our moral and intellectual vision of the world."[20,21] Therefore the impact of resource programs and mainstream education of the handicapped must be viewed not only as important progress for handicapped children, but as a force that has implications for all education.

Gliedman and Roth feel that "perhaps for the first time in the history of the handicapped in America, a climate of growing optimism and rising expectations among parents, professionals, and handicapped adults prevails."[22] They continue, "And while traditional modes of thought continue to dominate the practice of special education, it must be said on the schools' behalf that never before in their history have they been more disposed to reconsider their aims and programs for children with handicaps."[23] Reordering their priorities due to the mandate of PL 94-142, schools all over the country are establishing methods for identifying previously undetected handicapped children in their districts, evaluating the needs of these children, and then creating and staffing special programs designed specifically for their needs. Commenting on the growing number of new resource programs that have thus proliferated, Lerner cites that "while there is little research data to indicate the superiority of this type of educational service over the others, it appears to be the most prevalent type at present."[24] The number of new resource programs continues to multiply on a national scale, and one New York City administrator has estimated that by 1982 there will be resource room programs in all 1,000 city elementary and secondary schools.[25]

Perhaps the greatest good to come from this revolution in special education will be the social benefits derived from the return of the handicapped to the mainstream of society. Gliedman and Roth review the current movement in special education as a force that may disrupt what they have labelled as the "social pathology" model for the consideration of the handicapped. By this the authors mean that society has treated the handicapped as an oppressed social group in much the same manner that any minority group has been victimized and deprived of its full rights. They call for a new pluralistic approach to the treatment of handicapped children:

> . . . to bring the handicapped child into the mainstream of childhood. It is to end his exclusion from social experience appropriate

to children his age. It is to provide him with an education that no longer reinforces—however inadvertently—society's traditional misconceptions and stereotypes about the abilities of handicapped individuals. It is the same vision that informs school desegregation for minority children: to improve education by breaking down the barriers of prejudice and misunderstanding that have excluded the handicapped from the mainstream of American life for so long.[26]

Gliedman and Roth continue their persuasive argument by looking at the role of the school today. They feel that if the schools are to break with the mistakes of the past to treat the handicapped in a truly equitable fashion:

They must provide curriculum materials that connect with the handicapped child's experience and do it in a way that attacks society's conventional stereotypes about disabled people, the fears aroused by the disease diagnosis of handicap, and the misguided notion of tolerance that is embodied in the handicapped role.[27]

Calling the schools of the past that have segregated handicapped children "factories of failure," Gliedman and Roth look to the research that has been done in the area of minority group race relations to cite specific techniques for successful mainstreaming. They say that teachers:

- must learn to establish friendly interactions in the classroom between handicapped children and their peers;
- should assign group projects to integrate handicapped children into classroom activities accomplished through direct contact and cooperative efforts, and with equal responsibility;
- make every effort to ensure that handicapped children are assigned and elected to the typical positions and roles that are expected in the normal classroom;
- should facilitate all informal contacts between handicapped and nonhandicapped children in the school setting.[28]

In summary, the writings of Gliedman and Roth reinforce the concept that handicapped children in society must be treated in an individual manner, not categorized and stereotyped by their disability diagnosis. They state:

Handicapped children are individuals. Because of the almost endless ways that different facts can interact in shaping the experience of a handicapped person, it is possible that as a group, handicapped children show an even greater range of individual variation in their learning strategies than able-bodied children of similar background. A pluralistic approach to the disabled should not be wedded to any specific set of diagnostic or educational procedures.[29]

Another fascinating and vital report for educators to know is *Exceptional Teaching for Exceptional Learning,* prepared by a panel of special educators for the Ford Foundation in 1980. Reviewing the function of schools in America, the writers conclude that much of American education has been a "watershed" approach whereby education has been provided *en masse* without regard for the learning needs and characteristics of the individual student.[30] What general education can derive from special education is clear regard for the education of the individual child, because: "What special educators have to offer springs largely from their intense experience with individuals or small groups of children whose special problems demand diligent and imaginative application of what is known about teaching and learning."[31] The report continues, "Whatever the field of special education has contributed in the past to the reformation of regular education seems likely to be surpassed by what is presently emerging."[32] Hopefully, what is emerging, which will have dramatic impact on all education, is greater emphasis on the individual student. While at the present time PL 94-142 mandates that IEPs are required only for those classified as handicapped, there are indications that the concept may be applied to all children.

There has been recent and renewed interest in the area of individualization of instruction. Certainly the necessity for specifying definite instructional goals and the consideration for pluralistic teaching strategies inherent in the creation of an IEP have become more obvious in all of education today. Performance testing, criterion-referenced diagnosis and prescriptive teaching for specific skills, continual and nongraded pupil placement, computer-assisted instruction, and mastery level learning are all evidence of new forms of individualized instruction.

The report indicates a significant change in the responsibility for educating children who experience failure.[33] It states that the once prevalent attitude that if a child is taught and does not learn then the responsibility for failure falls to the child and not to the instructor or school system is an attitude that is slowly changing. Teachers now recognize the many reasons why children may not learn successfully, and they have attempted to differentiate instruction to accommodate the individual learning styles of children in their classes.

There are other important principles to be derived from special education. The report enumerates and describes the following factors that should affect the education of all children:

- reemphasis on building a trust relationship with children to enhance their self-confidence;
- setting realistic and appropriate goals for learners so as to encourage and not frustrate them;
- varying the amount of time needed to complete work based on the learning abilities of the student;
- emphasizing the strengths rather than weaknesses of the child to develop a feeling of competence;
- shaping appropriate behavior through techniques of reinforcement instead of punishment;
- using teachers as role models for children;
- enlisting the cooperation and support of parents and peers in the education process;
- viewing education as what takes place in the child's total environment rather than solely within the confines of the school classroom;
- building a support system for teachers through staff development, technical assistance, and teaming;
- developing educational programs based on children's learning needs instead of anachronistic classification by disability category;
- realizing that learning takes place when the child has a healthy body, so that emphasis is placed on proper nutrition, physical education and exercise, and the maintenance of healthful living habits;
- emphasizing the role and purpose of education to children in an atmosphere that presents challenges with a sense of adventure and joy.[34]

The quiet revolution that has occurred in special education because of recent legislation is clearly an indication of the waves of change that can take place in schools to ensure the success of all learners.

The growing focus on competency-based education and testing of minimal competency in reading, writing, and mathematics has no doubt resulted from the impact of the general public's concern about the functioning of schools. The political action of parents of special education children has demonstrated that the public's voice can be heard, and dramatic changes result when parents question what have been traditional attitudes and methods of education. Certainly the new focus on the education of the gifted child has resulted from the model of education created by PL 94-142. The parents of gifted children have spoken eloquently about their concern for the exceptional needs of children defined as gifted. Classifying the gifted child as an "exceptional learner" has enabled school systems to obtain special funding for the creation of resource programs for the gifted child. While the originators of PL 94-142 may not have viewed the needs of the gifted child as falling under the domain of special education, this law has gone further than any other to provide for the needs of such diverse groups as the mentally retarded and the intellectually gifted.

Children have innate individual assets and liabilities in terms of their cognitive skills, social adjustment, and emotional adaption. To encourage the potential of each child and to demonstrate to each child that he or she is a worthwhile human being must surely be the goal of classroom teachers, special education resource teachers, and parents. Together, functioning as a team, they can only improve education and make the world a better place. The resource concept is a remarkable attempt to provide for the needs of all children, regardless of their diversity or exceptionality, in a humanistic fashion.

NOTES

1. William Cruickshank and G. Orville Johnson, *Education of Exceptional Children and Youth* (Englewood Cliffs, N.J.: Prentice-Hall, 1975), p. 14.

2. Ibid., p. 17.

3. John Gliedman and William Roth, *The Unexpected Minority* (New York, N.Y.: Harcourt Brace Jovanovich, 1980), p. 236.

4. Ibid., p. 173.

5. J.L. Wiederholt, Donald Hammill, and Virginia Brown, *The Resource Teacher: A Guide to Effective Practices* (Boston, Mass.: Houghton Mifflin, 1976), p. 4.

6. Ibid., p. 5.

7. Margaret Hawisher and Mary Lynne Calhoun, *The Resource Room* (Columbus, Ohio: Merrill, 1978), pp. 9–10.

8. Janet Lerner, *Children with Learning Disabilities* (Boston, Mass.: Houghton Mifflin, 1976), p. 376.

9. W. Sawyer and B. Wilson, "Role Clarification for Remedial Reading and Learning Disabilities Teachers," *The Reading Teacher* 33, no. 2 (November 1979): 162.

10. Bruno D'Alonzo, Rosemarie D'Alonzo, and August Mauser, "Developing Resource Rooms for the Handicapped," *Teaching Exceptional Children* 11, no. 3 (Spring 1979): 91–92.

11. Wiederholt, Hammill, and Brown, *The Resource Teacher*, p. 7.

12. Ibid., p. 8.

13. Gliedman and Roth, *The Unexpected Minority*, p. 218.

14. R. Reger, "What Is a Resource Room Program?" *Journal of Learning Disabilities* 6, no. 10 (December 1973): 614.

15. Lerner, *Children with Learning Disabilities,* p. 354.

16. W. Cruickshank, "The Least Restrictive Placement: Administrative Wishful Thinking," *Journal of Learning Disabilities,* 10, no. 4 (April 1977): p. 5.

17. R. Reger, "Resource Rooms: Change Agents or Guardians of the Status Quo?" *Journal of Special Education* 6, no. 4 (1972): 355.

18. R. Reger, "What Is a Resource Room Program?" *Journal of Learning Disabilities,* December 1973, p. 611.

19. Ibid., pp. 611–13.

20. Gliedman and Roth, *The Unexpected Minority,* p. 236.

21. Ibid., p. 173.

22. Ibid., p. 234.

23. Ibid., p. 235.

24. Lerner, *Children with Learning Disabilities,* p. 374.

25. D. Kleiman, "Program Attacks Inability to Learn," *The New York Times,* 8 May 1979, p. III 5.

26. Gliedman and Roth, *The Unexpected Minority,* p. 218.

27. Ibid., p. 226.

28. Ibid., pp. 230–31.

29. Ibid., p. 201.

30. Nicholas Hobbs et al., *Exceptional Teaching for Exceptional Learning* (Naugatuck, Conn.: Ford Foundation, 1980), p. 4.

31. Ibid.

32. Ibid., p. 10.

33. Ibid., p. 16.

34. Ibid., pp. 18–66.

BIBLIOGRAPHY

Creating the Least Restrictive Learning Environments. New York, N.Y.: Board of Education, N.Y.C., 1978.

Cruickshank, W. "The Least Restrictive Placement: Administrative Wishful Thinking." *Journal of Learning Disabilities* 10: 5–6.

Cruickshank, William, and Johnson, G. Orville. *Education of Exceptional Children and Youth.* Englewood Cliffs, N.J.: Prentice-Hall, 1975, chapters 1, 2, and 3.

D'Alonzo, Bruno; D'Alonzo, Rosemarie; and Mauser, August. "Developing Resource Rooms for the Handicapped." *Teaching Exceptional Children,* Spring 1979, pp. 91–96.

Gliedman, John, and Roth, William. *The Unexpected Minority.* New York, N.Y.: Harcourt Brace Jovanovich, 1980.

Hammill, Donald, and Wiederholt, J. Lee. *The Resource Room: Rationale and Implementation.* New York, N.Y.: Grune and Stratton, 1972.

Hawisher, Margaret, and Calhoun, Mary Lynne. *The Resource Room.* Columbus, Ohio: Merrill, 1978.

Hobbs, Nicholas; Bartel, Nettie; Docecki, Paul; Gallagher, James; and Reynolds, Maynard. *Exceptional Teaching for Exceptional Learning*. Naugatuck, Conn.: Ford Foundation, 1980.

Kleiman, Dena. "Program Attacks Inability to Learn." *The New York Times,* 8 May 1979, p. III 5.

Lerner, Janet. *Children with Learning Disabilities*. Boston, Mass.: Houghton Mifflin, 1976.

Reger, Roger. "Resource Rooms: Change Agents or Guardians of the Status Quo?" *Journal of Special Education* 6, no. 4 (1972): 355–59.

Reger, Roger. "What Is a Resource Room Program?" *Journal of Learning Disabilities* 6, no. 10 (December 1973): 609–14.

Sabatino, David. "Resource Rooms: The Renaissance in Special Education." *Journal of Special Education* 6, no. 4 (1972): 335–47.

Sawyer, Walter, and Wilson, Bonnie. "Role Clarification for Remedial Reading and Learning Disabilities Teachers." *Reading Teacher* 33: 162–66.

United States Public Law 94-142, 94th Congress. *Education for all Handicapped Children Act of 1975*.

Wiederholt, J. Lee; Hammill, Donald; and Brown, Virginia. *The Resource Teacher: A Guide to Effective Practices*. Boston, Mass.: Allyn and Bacon, 1978.

Chapter 2

The Resource Teacher at the Interface of School and Family

Margo Neale

To say that schools must involve parents as fully as possible in the education of their children has almost become a truism. This follows closely, however, on a time when the functions of school and family were seen as separate and different, and when the school considered itself the authority in its own domain. The boundaries of function and authority, however, have given way under the pressure of modern life. Schools now know, as do families, that neither can solely help children become responsible and contributing adults. There has to be some interface of the school and family systems that promotes change and growth in the child.

HISTORICAL FALLOUT

In 1977, the Carnegie Council on Children, directed by Kenneth Kenniston, produced an important report called *All Our Children,* which documented the effects of economic and political changes in history on the conception and functioning of the American family.[1] The report described how the intense individualism of the seventeenth and eighteenth centuries was translated into a myth of the self-sufficient family by the early nineteenth century. This myth defined the family as a special and protective place where humane values could be maintained over and against the raw aggressiveness of the early industrial society. In the myth, the father was held responsible for the economic self-sufficiency of the family. Only he was expected to risk corruption by contact with the outside world. The other members of the family were embraced securely within the home, where the mother was expected to be responsible for the intellectual, social, and moral education of the children.

Even as it was being formed, this myth represented an ideal more than an actuality for most families. Well-to-do upper middle class families could

25

afford to live out the myth, but families of immigrants and factory workers could not. Because it was the prevailing myth or ideal, families who could not live accordingly saw themselves and were seen as inadequate and needy. The idea of the public school rose in the midst of the discrepancy between the ideal and the reality, and was seen as a way of equalizing the possibility that all might live more or less self-sufficient and independent lives.

From the mid-nineteenth century on, the responsibility for education became less a responsibility of the home and more one of the public school. A functional split developed that widened until the schools were considered the experts on children and the ways in which they learned. Families wanting to maintain some control over the process needed to become skilled in dealing with schools. Many families either did not or could not develop such skills. Schools, on their part, kept hands off anything about the child not immediately related to learning. This was done out of respect for the myth of the private and protective nature of the self-sufficient family.

Recently, the split between family and school has begun to mend. This is probably part of a larger shift in outlook that pervades society. It might be characterized as a shift from the independent functioning of separate parts of a whole to interdependent functioning of related parts of a whole. It is represented by such ideas as the conception of gestalt in psychology, relativity in ethics and physics, process in history and theology, systems analysis in technology and business, and the "whole child" in education. The net result is that the points at which family and school touch have become highly activated, and a resource room is surely one of these.

However, even at such an interface of family and school as a resource room, residue from history is still encountered. For example, strong feelings of inadequacy, guilt, fear, and confusion often exist in parents whose children are not doing well. It is as if they thought they were still personally and privately responsible for their children's success in school. This relates back to the early myth of the self-sufficient family, which never was a reality and which has long since been layered over by public school functioning. However, when a person works with such families it becomes clear that the feelings are real and can cripple efforts to relate to them. The feelings are sometimes intensified by various circumstances. For example, if a child of a working mother is not doing well in school, the mother will often assume it is because she is working. Her working does not fit into the old myth of the self-sufficient and protective family in which she was expected to be at home. Similarly, if a child in a single parent family is not doing well, the parent will often assume it is because of the singleness, which again does not fit into the early myth that assumed a tight cooperation between two married partners.

Unfortunately, educators have often fed the feelings of guilt and inadequacy in some families rather than minimizing them. There are several reasons for this, the most crude being that if the family is to some extent responsible for school failure, then the school is, to the same degree, less responsible. In addition, there is a part of history that enhances the power of schools *vis-à-vis* families. That is, in the nineteenth century, when functions were split and schools got the job of being educational experts, they assumed an authoritative stance that makes families of children doing poorly in school feel even more inadequate, guilty, and fearful, rendering them less capable of advocating effectively for their children.

Both families and schools have been bound by the same historical and cultural myths, and are similarly challenged by the new and more holistic view of reality. Children who experience difficulty in school intensify the need for families and schools to relate somehow for their benefit. Because many of these children arrive in a resource room, the resource teacher needs to develop a good working relationship with the family.

RESOURCE TEACHERS AND THE SCHOOL PROCESSES

One of the immediate needs of a resource teacher is to clarify the nature of a child's difficulty. In order to do this, the teacher must meet with the child several times. Some of the meetings will consist of informal interactions and assessments. Other meetings should be more formal testing situations. To some extent, teachers should establish their own understanding of the nature of the difficulty. In addition, they should consult with other professionals in the school and have some understanding of others' views of the child's problem. To fill out the picture of the child, the teacher should also confer with the child's family. If the child is failing in school, family members may be aware of great difficulty at home and may be able to add to the understanding of the child.

In the past, most resource teachers have not been impelled either by school structure or by their own sense of appropriateness to seek information and interpretation from the family. They, or someone at the school, have usually called the mother in when they were ready to describe the problem and the solution. Federal and state laws regarding the education of the handicapped require, however, that at least the responsible parent or parents be drawn into the process at a much earlier point. Before any assessment can be undertaken by the school, parents must give their written consent, and this means that they must share with the school the view that there is a problem and must have some understanding of the nature of the problem, at however simple a level. Schools and resource teachers often regard this legal requirement to obtain written permission as a rather perfunctory matter, and they approach it casually. Others see the need to obtain written consent as a challenge and use almost any means to get the parents' signatures on a piece of paper. The requirements of the law, however, create an excellent opportunity for arriving at a common and detailed understanding of the child's difficulty at an early point in the process. A commonly held view of the nature of the difficulty is more critical to subsequent efforts on behalf of the child than the signature, and the whole process of obtaining the signature ought to be extended until there truly is consent from the family and a willingness to share its perception of the child. Resource teachers can, thus, use the process for obtaining consent to build a cooperative relationship with the child and family members, and as a time when they can fill out the school's view of the child with the family's view.

Another clear need and responsibility of the resource teacher is to establish a program for the child who is experiencing difficulty. After everyone agrees on what the child's needs are, the resource teacher usually must make concrete plans as to how the child's needs will be met. In the past, the planning has been done in some form of conference with the other professionals in the school and later communicated to the family. However, the new laws require the presence of the parent or parents at planning conferences. Many schools still call the parents in to agree *pro forma* to plans already established by the school, but the law again provides a wonderful opportunity for cooperative planning by family and school. Such planning should not be an issue if a common understanding of the child's problem has been previously established and if parental consent has been given.

There is enormous impact on the child's home behavior if he or she is experiencing failure at school. Similarly, the child who is experiencing difficulty at school often exhibits a set of behaviors at home, such as hyperactivity, distractibility, poor organization, and limited language interaction. These behaviors are part of the total syndrome that causes school failure in the first place. These behaviors often make the child extremely difficult to manage and to live with. Part of the planning for meeting such a child's needs must deal with what goes on before and after the school day, and before and after the school year. This kind of planning cannot be done by the school or family alone, but must be part of a cooperative effort on behalf of the child.

Resource teachers generally work intimately with the children who are included in the program. They usually see them individually or in small groups, and schedule them frequently. Teachers, therefore, are aware of the great fluctuation in behaviors and attitudes that affects learning, and this creates another need. Resource teachers need to find some ways of stabilizing useful behaviors and attitudes on a day-to-day basis. In order to do this they must establish a more or less elaborate feedback system, which ought to include the family. The feedback system runs something like this: Teacher reports to family→common speculation about origins of behavior→modification of family, teacher, or child behavior→instruction. There is nothing formal about this feedback system. It may be a simple phone call. Yet it reflects the special needs of resource teacher functioning, which again places resource teachers at the interface of family and school.

Finally, resource teachers usually work with children over a longer period of time than other professionals in the school. Therefore, they have a better opportunity to become acquainted with the family. They can also evaluate progress in a larger perspective. Resource teachers have the opportunity then to become the spokesperson for the family to the school and to become the interpreter of school policies to the family.

Being the interface of family and school was not even conceivable within the old mythology. However, the job of resource teacher creates a special situation that demands that resource teachers heal the split between family and school by becoming involved in seeking and sharing information and feelings.

In the process of working with a child where there is a particular need for the resource teacher and the family to relate, there first must be an agreed-upon definition of the problem. Second, there must be some cooperative planning. Third, there must be long-term commitment to working out the plans.

There is a parallel between this process and the grief process as described by Kubler-Ross and others.[2] In this parallel, when the parents receive news that their child is experiencing such difficulty in school that he or she may be considered handicapped, they must abandon old views of their child which might include negative qualities such as stupid, lazy, sick, poorly behaved, or "slow," and adopt a new view. It is almost as if the old, unhandicapped child dies, and a new kind of child emerges. This is particularly so in the case of a young child in a young family where there is little experience with either children or schools, and where the highest and most innocent hopes are put on the first child. It is useful, therefore, to examine the grief process, to translate it into family-school terms, and to juxtapose it against the process for working with a child in the resource room.

Although parents often do not know until they are told by someone at school that their child may be handicapped, this is clearly not always the case. Older and more experienced parents often do know. Sometimes, however, if they have had other children with serious problems, they may perceive the child under discussion as being "better than" or "different from" their other children, and they may be totally unaware that this child may be handicapped too. Parents of children who are severely handicapped usually know. The impact of the handicap on their lives is so immense that they do not need the school to tell them that there is a problem. The resource teacher will rarely deal with this kind of family, however, because, by definition, a severely handicapped child is usually not mainstreamed. So the resource teacher or someone in the school is often in the position of telling parents for the first time that there is a serious problem, and the first reaction on the parents' part is often one of denial.

Denial is an important first step in the grief process, for it allows parents to gain time to gather their resources to deal with the problem. While they are doing so, the resource teacher may hear them say things like, "We don't see Mary like this at home," or "Johnny doesn't like his teacher this year," or "The other kids have been picking on Sandy and making her miserable," or "Sean was sick on the day he took your test." Resource teachers have the option of countering all comments of this sort in an effort to persuade the parents that there really is a problem with their child. If they do this, however, it produces an unnecessary confrontation, which may set the tone for subsequent interaction. It is much better to simply back off from conflict at this point and give the parents the time they need to get their thoughts and feelings in order. Also, their responses often provide openings for gleaning useful information about the child. So, for example, when parents say, "We don't see Mary like this at home," the resource teacher can say, "Will you tell me something about how you do see her at home?" When parents say "Johnny doesn't like his teacher this year," the resource teacher can say, "What is there that is different in this teacher that Johnny doesn't like?" Thus, the teacher may gain information, and the tenor of these responses is respectful of parents' feelings and cooperative in character. This may suggest a pattern for working together in the future.

The second step in the grief process is the expression of feelings. These may range from anger (directed at the presenter, the teacher, the school, the spouse, or the child) to disappointment, guilt, shame, and expressions of loyalty and protectiveness. Resource teachers clearly have the option of responding to any or all of these feelings, and may have a great need to defend against the anger. To defend against the anger sets up a confrontation and should be avoided if possible. To respond to some of the other more negative feelings often involves laying blame on the parents. Probably the most constructive response is to acknowledge their feelings and join with them in some of their positive feelings about the child, and thus to communicate a sense of alliance in the future.

The third step in the grief process is adjustment to the new reality about the child. Parents in this stage are often depressed. At this point, parents will often start walking the child back and forth to school. They may linger around the door of the classroom. They may come to the resource room with no apparent purpose other than to just talk. They will often reminisce about the child and their family. It is useful at this point to give whatever time seems needed by either parent. This may feel like a vague and pointless use of time, but it stabilizes the alliance begun in the previous step. It is also possible to get a permission slip signed at this point and to begin to make some tentative plans together.

The fourth stage of the grief process is one of commitment. This is an active stage for the parents, as opposed to the third stage. The resource teacher will hear many questions, such as "What is going to be done to help my child?" "What more can be done?" "What can I do?" "How can I learn more about . . . ?" These questions indicate the parents' readiness to participate actively in planning. This is the time to move in strongly with recommendations. The resource teacher can expect some vigorous discussion, mutual input in planning, and full cooperation in implementing the plans. This stage is worth waiting for. The resource teacher can plan before this, but early plans will not carry the weight that plans made in this fourth stage do.

By attending to the parents' passage through the grief process, resource teachers can facilitate their own process needs and build a strong alliance that will serve the child positively during years in a resource program.

RESOURCE TEACHERS IN SCHOOL STRUCTURE

If resource teachers take the demands inherent in the work for conciliation and cooperation with families (and other professionals) seriously, they need to define where they stand on structural and theoretical issues as well as to locate themselves within a process. There is great shift and change in the field of special education, both at a structural level and a theoretical level. In the absence of stability, each person, including family members, brings to any given situation a version of reality highly colored by his or her own familial, educational, and vocational experiences. Since these are extremely vital and highly idiosyncratic, many issues tend to reverberate in a school until each person recognizes his or her own biases for what they are and can work with the biases of the other people involved. Resolution of certain issues, therefore, requires the development of self-awareness and some degree of negotiating skill.

Resource teachers must understand the organization within their own school for meeting the needs of children who are experiencing learning difficulties and know how they fit into that structure. Following are some possible models of organization:

- *Model A:* Classroom teachers are primarily responsible. They determine which children will be included in the resource program, define the nature of their needs, and design and coordinate programming, which is based on the needs manifested in the classroom. They report to parents. The resource teacher is essentially the classroom teacher's tool. This model is becoming less prevalent as the impact of laws regarding the handicapped are felt, but resource teachers are still often requested to go over whatever classroom teachers are currently trying to teach or to include a given child informally for "just a little help."

- *Model B:* School psychologists are primarily responsible. They receive and screen referrals from teachers. They define needs according to the results of their testing and prescribe for both classroom and resource teachers. They report to parents. The resource teacher functions as the expert implementer of the program designed by the psychologist. This model is very much alive where there is an active and highly respected school psychologist or where the district structure is such that the "chain of command" is from the district pupil personnel director through the psychologist.

- *Model C:* Resource teachers are primarily responsible. They receive and screen referrals. They define needs according to their testing and conferences with other professionals and the parents. They plan the program and report to the parents, and are clearly the experts on learning. This model exists in places where resource rooms were established before the laws regarding the handicapped came into effect. Where this still exists, it is in the process of modification to meet the demands of the new laws.

- *Model D:* A pupil personnel team is primarily responsible. It receives and screens referrals. It collects data of various kinds from various sources to determine needs. It recommends action by various members of the team and the family. It appoints one of its members to relate to the family and to the classroom teacher. The resource teacher is a contributing member of the team. This model is becoming more prevalent because it is an efficient way to meet the demands of the law, and because it has become clear that a high degree of cooperation among school personnel results in better service to the child.

Most resource teachers will find themselves functioning somewhere between the four models, but perhaps the preceding clarification will help resource teachers define how they function and how they would like to be functioning. Perhaps, also, it will help minimize the reverberations around certain issues in a school situation.

The kinds of issues that flow from a lack of understanding and agreement on structure include the following:

- Who calls parent conferences?
- Who attends parent conferences?
- Who deals with varying degrees of conflict with parents?
- Who interprets various programs to parents?

Failure to resolve these issues can produce feelings of exclusion and inadequacy among professionals in a school. It also invariably leaves parents feeling bewildered and confused. It is unnecessary for such issues to continue provided that those involved recognize their own biases about structure and make some attempt to deal with each other in an inclusive and conciliatory fashion.

RESOURCE TEACHERS AND THEORETICAL ISSUES

After questions of history, process, and structure, there are other issues related to theory about educating the handicapped. Because the theories are still evolving, biases again affect a person's behavior significantly, and these issues also tend to reverberate endlessly and needlessly. Some of the theoretical issues are described briefly below:

- *Etiology and prognosis of a learning difficulty*—The first level of this issue is usually whether the child's difficulties have an organic, emotional, or intellectual basis. Beneath that there may be the question of whether it makes any difference in educational terms what the etiology is. Finally, if it does make a difference, the question of how it affects planning and prognosis arises.
- *Medication in dealing with a learning difficulty*—Ultimately this issue will not be settled by a teacher, but this represents the first level of decision making. The issue is whether some medications do improve learning behaviors without undesirable side effects. Furthermore, there is often the issue of whether it is the child's behavior or the

school and family behaviors that need change. Further, for some people, there is the issue of whether drugs of any kind ever represent an optimal solution to a learning problem.

- *Grade retention in dealing with a learning difficulty*—Does retention do any good? If a person believes that it is effective, there are further questions of when it works best and whether the duration of the good effect is long enough to make it a useful approach. Underlying all of these questions is the larger issue of whether learning difficulties are understood as delays in normal development or whether they are best seen as specific aberrations in normal development. If a person believes that they are delays in normal development, then that person will be more likely to opt for "another year in which to grow."

- *Special class placement for children with learning difficulties*— Should children be scheduled into a resource room in their local school and among their neighborhood friends, or would they be better served if they were placed in a special class where they might get more service but are more separated from the mainstream of their daily lives? Underlying this issue is the further question of the degree to which the child is handicapped. This is often difficult to establish in resource room children. A further issue is the degree to which professional staff members of a school are willing to relinquish control over the education of a given child and the feelings that they have about doing so.

These issues, both structural and theoretical, arise continually and usually generate intense feeling. Resource persons should make an explicit effort to recognize and develop their own point of view and to develop skills in decision making with professionals and family members who have equally strong points of view. While some of the issues mentioned are being resolved, there is a simple truth that most people who relate to a child are trying to do what they think is best for that child. If the child's welfare can be kept at the center of concern, various disagreements can be more affably resolved.

RESOURCE ROOM PRACTICE

The practical suggestions for relating to families that follow are arranged in order of effectiveness in establishing closer relationships in the school with families. In practice, however, families respond differently, and what may be of use and interest to one family is less helpful to another.

An open house in the resource room is a simple way of accomplishing several things at once. Its best value is that it acquaints parents with the environment in which the child will be working and with the materials that will be used. Parents are usually impressed with the quiet of the room and with the potential for one-on-one interaction. They are also impressed with the materials because they look different and imply a different approach to education. A byproduct of the open house is that parents can begin to get acquainted with the resource teacher and with each other in a comfortable and relaxed way. Later interactions will take on a similar character. The open house is best held in the fall, as soon as the resource teacher's caseload is established.

The open house is a good time to raise the possibility of an ongoing parent talk group. The purpose of this group is to provide an opportunity for parents to share experiences related to the special issues that children with learning difficulties present at home. This is done with the thought that their collective experience is tantamount to a kind of expertise on which individual members of the group might draw. If the group is slow in getting oriented as to how it might want to function, or if the resource teacher is totally inexperienced in group processes, a book such as *Workjobs for Parents* can be used as a take-off point.[3] This book models a view of education that is consistent with good resource room practice. It also has the potential for giving parents something to do with their hands while they talk, which often makes the talking easier. Finally, the materials suggested in the book when used at home present some possibilities for parents and children learning together, which will be instructive for the parents, at least.

Resource teachers may want to consider visiting the homes of some of the children they serve in the resource room. The advantages of such a visit can be significant. Resource teachers can meet the parents on their own territory, which is often more comfortable for them. This can indicate to the parents an acceptance of their circumstances and a desire to form an alliance. Resource teachers may meet the other members of the family, who are certainly systemically involved with the learning difficulty. Finally, teachers can learn something about how the household is organized, which is often useful in prescribing for a child. There are a few problems connected with visiting families, however. The family may feel overwhelmed by the possibility of such a visit, in which case the resource teacher will want to find a way to play down the visit and to make it as informal and casual as possible. Also, the school district may discourage anyone, except the district social worker, from visiting homes. Resource teachers may want to tackle district policy on this point if they feel strongly about visiting some of the children.

Letters to the home can be distancing for families if they are not set in the context of a closer relationship. However, even simple notes sent home on a continuing basis can strengthen a partnership. The note should consist of a simple statement of what is being done by the child on a specific date and why. The why probably has more educational value for the parents, and care should be taken to state the rationale for any activity clearly and simply. The resource teacher may experience great difficulty in doing this, and it is often rather instructive to consider why a certain activity is chosen over others. Some comment about the quality of the child's effort and accomplishment should be included in any communication. Finally, the note should indicate that communication is not a one-way street from school to home. The note should provide an opportunity for response from the parent. This can be in the form of a question such as, "Have you noticed this behavior at home?" "Can you suggest a way we might deal with this behavior?" or a directive such as, "Would you please try this (activity) and let me know how it works?" A list of activities might be enclosed. The kinds of letters home to avoid are those isolated legalistic letters intended to meet the requirements of the law, letters summoning parents to school for a conference over a problem, and letters simply reporting poor behavior. Out of personal context, these letters will only create distance between school and home, and undermine any sense of alliance that might have been established.

Bibliographies and reading materials can also be distancing if they are a resource teacher's primary response to questions and concerns on the part of parents. Many parents simply want to talk with someone about their children, and they formulate questions because they perceive that the question and answer format is easier and safer for them. This is particularly true at certain stages of the grief process described earlier. Therefore, resource teachers should spend enough time with the parents so that they know whether the parents are actually seeking information or whether they want to talk. If they want to talk, then handing them a bibliography or a book is clearly off-putting. However, if the parents want information and seem to be able to draw it from the printed page, then a bibliography or a book can be extremely helpful, especially when given with an invitation to return and discuss whatever was read. One caution should be observed when giving reading references to parents. The material offered should not discuss children with problems markedly more severe than their own child's. For example, in attempting to answer questions about what a "slow learner" would be, the resource teacher should not offer a reference on retardation. This might do for professionals who can dispassionately draw inferences, but parents are sensitive. They may conclude that the prognosis for their child is terrible or that the teacher is trying to tell them something not explicitly stated before. A bibliography for parents is offered at the end of this chapter.

The historical moment may have arrived when it is possible to conceive an equitable partnership between school and family on behalf of children who are experiencing learning difficulties. The resource teacher is in an ideal position to contribute to such a partnership and to extract the greatest value from it. In order to function effectively at the interface, however, resource teachers must develop skills and concepts that go beyond teaching a child. These skills should include an understanding of group and family dynamics. Resource teachers must begin to think of their position, not as individual teachers, but as a unit in a system composed of highly interdependent and interrelated parts functioning together for the benefit of the child involved.

NOTES

1. Carnegie Council on Children, *All Our Children* (New York, N.Y.: Harcourt, Brace, Jovanovich, 1977).
2. Elizabeth Kubler-Ross, *On Death and Dying* (New York, N.Y.: McMillan Publishing Company, Inc., 1970).
3. Mary Baratta-Lorton, *Workjobs for Parents* (Reading, Mass.: Addison-Wesley Publishing Company, 1975).

REFERENCES FOR PARENTS

Free Publications

Closer Look
The National Information Center for the Handicapped
P.O. Box 1492
Washington, D.C. 20013
Practical Advice to Parents: A guide to finding help for handicapped children and youth.

The University of the State of New York
The State Education Department
Office for Education of Children with Handicapping Conditions
Albany, New York 12234
Your Child's Right to an Education: A guide for parents of handicapped children in New York State.

Newsletters and Brochures

Exceptional Parent: Practical Guidance for Parents of Exceptional Children, Lewis B. Klebanoff, editor. Psych. Ed. Corporation, 264 Beacon Street, Boston, Massachusetts, 02116.
Packet (or reprints) *for Parents*. The Orton Society, 8415 Bellona Lane, Suite 113, Towson, Maryland 21204.

Books

Mary Baratta-Lorton, *Workjobs for Parents* (Reading, Mass.: Addison-Wesley Publishing Company, 1975).

Helen Feathersone. *A Difference in the Family.* (New York: Basic Book Publishers, Inc., 1980).

Helen G. Weiss and Martin S. Weiss. *Home Is a Learning Place. A Parents' Guide to L.D.* (Boston, Mass.: Little, Brown and Co., 1976).

At Issue

THE ROLE OF THE PARENT OF THE SPECIAL EDUCATION
CHILD: PARTNER IN THE EDUCATION PROCESS, ADVO-
CATE FOR THE CHILD, OR ADVERSARY TO THE SCHOOLS?

*Judith H. Cohen**

Chapter 2 clearly describes the relationship between the parent of the special education child and the child's school. However, the dimensions of this role are undergoing rapid and diverse changes. There is no question that the changes in special education today have been created in large measure by direct action from the parents of handicapped children. Incorporating the parent into the educational team for the identification and placement of handicapped children is an integral part of PL 94-142. Indeed, this role for the parent is detailed throughout the legislation where parents' rights and a system of challenges that parents may undertake are described. Therein lies the dimension of the parent taking on the role of a child advocate and sometimes becoming an adversary to the schools.

In a recent newspaper article, a president of the coordinating council of 31 special education Parent-Teacher Associations (PTAs) declared, "Parents are the only ones in a position to challenge committee (on the handicapped) findings. . . . They are the ones with the right to request a hearing if the school doesn't identify their child or the right to challege the committee's findings. Yet only about 50 parents in any school know their rights."[1]

As parents grow in sophistication about special education law, so do the number of challenges to the schools. In New York state the only quantitative standard for the identification of learning disabled children was overturned during the summer of 1980 when a parent group challenged the discrepancy formula that was in common use. A U.S. district court judge ruled as invalid the state education department's working definition that a learning disabled child is one whose classroom achievement is 50 percent below the norm for the child's own age and grade. Instead of this quantitative discrepancy definition, a qualitative definition of the existence of a "severe" disability was substituted. Such a ruling was seen to have far-reaching ramifications for the schools as many more children can now be identified as learning disabled.

---

*This and all subsequent "At Issue" sections were written by Judith H. Cohen.

Other challenges to the schools have resulted from the fear by some parent groups that during a period of fiscal austerity school districts may identify and place children not according to children's needs, but with mind to the cost and availability of existing programs within a school district. One prominent attorney, specializing in this area of litigation, has gone so far as to say, "If they have an LD program, they'll put the child in one. If they don't, the school may offer instruction inappropriate for the child, classify the child incorrectly or not classify him at all."[2] Indeed, some school districts find that complying with special education legislation has created both a financial burden to the district and an angry backlash on the part of parents whose children are not involved in special programs. A lawyer representing one school district has said that "mandates concerning the handicapped are becoming financially overwhelming for school districts,"[3] and it has been documented that in large, urban districts where many children can be identified as needing special education, budgeting priorities have had to be shifted with reallocation of funds, materials, and staffing for special programs. Commenting on the trend toward fiscal conservatism on the part of the schools, another lawyer advocating the rights of handicapped children he represents has said, "Prior to the 1970s, the handicapped were excluded from public schools. Now the school district is attempting to roll back rights the handicapped have gained over the last decade."[4]

As the stigma for having a handicapped child diminishes, and as the services for the handicapped child increase, many parents request the smaller classes and individualized instruction that come as a result of a child's classification as being handicapped. Self-help groups for parents are developing as a means of ensuring that parents become aware of the rights for handicapped children. A guide entitled *Working With Your Schools* has been prepared by the southwestern office of the United States Commission for Civil Rights after it was inundated with requests from parents for legal aid.[5] Other groups, such as the American Civil Liberties Union, have assisted parents not only with litigation, but have represented the interests of parents and children in a process of mediation with the schools. The National Committee for Citizens in Education has prepared a billfold-sized card on which parents' rights in every state are listed. This consumer activism on the part of parents is a dynamic, new dimension in their relationship with the schools.

In New York state, the state education department has prepared a publication for parents of handicapped children entitled *Your Child's Right to an Education,* which is available to parents through local school districts or centralized state offices at no charge.[6] Such efforts as these are to be commended, for school districts must acknowledge the rightful role of the parent in the special education team and incorporate parental counsel into the decision-making process.

Another complete source of information about parents' rights and the education of their handicapped children is entitled *An Education Handbook for Parents of Handicapped Children.*[7] This reference provides worthwhile information for parents and teachers alike.

While there is no simple answer to the query as to what is the proper role of a parent with relationship to the schools, the issue is likely to persist. Schools must comply with the legal mandates of PL 94-142, and responsible school districts should assist parents in understanding the nature and needs of their disabled children. School districts must provide for children with special needs rather than passively waiting for referrals and challenges from parents. The ultimate responsibility for decision making with regard to the special child falls to the COHs constituted by each school district. These committees must function in the most professional and objective manner so that a child's best interests are met. However, throughout the 1980s many decisions regarding the placement and education of children with special needs will be decided by the courts.

NOTES

1. *New York Times,* 23 November 1980, p. 16.

2. Ibid., pp. 16–17.

3. *New York Times,* 23 November 1980, p. 15.

4. Ibid.

5. *New York Times,* 16 November 1980, p. 3.

6. Further information and a sample of the guide can be obtained from Nassau County BOCES II, 1196 Prospect Avenue, Westbury, N.Y. 11590.

7. Stanley Mopsik and Judith Agard, eds., *An Education Handbook for Parents of Handicapped Children* (Cambridge, Mass.: Abt Books, 1980).

Chapter 3

The Process of Diagnosis: The Work of the Child Study Team*

Rochelle Simon

THE MAKEUP OF THE CHILD STUDY TEAM

The Child Study Team (CST) is composed of a group of specialists who meet to discuss, diagnose, and evaluate children in a specific school. Each team member is also a working specialist in that school and, therefore, performs dual roles. The team consists of: the school's principal; the school's psychologist; the language, speech, and hearing (LSH) teacher; the resource room teacher; a reading teacher; and the school nurse.

The principal is the case convenor, who calls together the team when a referral is to be presented. For the sake of each member's schedule, the meeting usually takes place on a regularly scheduled day and time. The school psychologist is the case controller, responsible for distributing the evaluation forms and making sure they are completed and returned by a specific date. The psychologist then fills out the cover sheet of the evaluation packet and sends the packet to the Committee on the Handicapped (COH). The COH determines whether a handicapping condition exists.

The basic function of the CST is to engage in "Operation Child Find." The individual members of the team will combine their knowledge to make as clear, concise, and cohesive an evaluation of the child as possible. They can do this evaluation because they have learned to operate as a team and share their information. They have also learned enough about each member's specialty to understand test results and protocols.

---

*This chapter discusses the methods and procedures of "Operation Child Find," as implemented in the Baldwin Union Free School District, Baldwin, New York. The discussion of the evaluation packet and reproduction of the CST forms are done with the permission of the Baldwin Schools.

HOW THE CST OPERATES

To get a better understanding of the way in which the CST operates, a hypothetical case study will be used. Mrs. Jones is a third-grade teacher. She is distressed over the apparent lack of progress in one of her students, Johnny. Although it is only November, she feels that Johnny is falling further and further behind. He is having much reading difficulty. His reading level is far below others in the class, and even his remedial program does not seem to be helping him. He seems to lack the ability to concentrate on what he is doing, especially if he has to work independently. His word attack skills are poor, although he does know initial sounds and some vowel sounds. He just cannot seem to use this knowledge when confronted with the printed word. When reading orally, he substitutes words, loses his place, and confuses letters. Often he'll stop and ask what particular letter is in a word. He dislikes going to remedial reading and says the other children make fun of him.

Classroom behavior is erratic. He has problems sitting still. Sometimes he is capable of moving his chair far away from his desk while he is still sitting on it. He cries easily, loses his temper, and is always in the center of a struggle. He is disorganized, and his handwriting seems to be getting sloppier. Assignments are mislaid, notes are not brought home, and homework, when it does get returned to class, is wrinkled and unreadable.

Mrs. Jones is further worried because Johnny's parents have difficulty managing him at home. Mrs. Jones rereads Johnny's records. She sees that he has normal intelligence on group standardized tests, yet his reading scores are still on a first-grade level. These scores place him 50 percent below his grade level. Feeling that Johnny is not making progress and fearful that problems will get more serious unless he gets help, Mrs. Jones refers Johnny's case to the school principal.

The First Meeting

The principal convenes the CST. All the team members are present including Mrs. Jones, the classroom teacher. The referring teacher is always asked to participate in "Operation Child Find." When a meeting is scheduled, those members who might have worked with Johnny, such as the reading teacher, bring any information or test results. This meeting only addresses results of testing previously given to Johnny. No new testing will be done for the first meeting because it has not been determined if Johnny will need a full CST evaluation. Once this determination is decided upon, the parents must give written approval before new testing can proceed.

Mrs. Jones is the first to present to the team. She discusses Johnny's behavior, both academically and socially. She informs the members of previous standardized test scores, past classroom teachers' comments on report cards, and so on. She answers questions from the team members. The resource room teacher, who has never met Johnny, is now getting a picture of the child he will soon be meeting. He asks Mrs. Jones questions and takes notes, not just for scores, but for things he might want to evaluate based on Mrs. Jones' report. He might write down such things as to check if Johnny knows the alphabet, time concepts, months of the year, days of the week, handedness, and pencil grip.

The principal might want to intervene. She has had Johnny in her office on a few occasions, especially after lunchtime. She remembers an incident where Johnny tried to jump over a grating and missed, scraping his forehead on the concrete. She also recalls the time that Johnny tried to catch a ball and got hit in the eye.

The school nurse concurs with the principal's assessment of Johnny. The child appears to be "accident prone." The nurse discusses Johnny's health record. Johnny does not wear glasses, and his hearing is within normal limits. His health record reveals only typical childhood illnesses, such as chicken pox. He is in the nurse's office, often as a result of playground mishaps, but he is physically healthy.

The LSH teacher is next to report. He has met Johnny when he routinely evaluated the school population for articulation problems. Johnny appears to have no difficulty in this area. The LSH teacher has not assessed Johnny's language ability, as this evaluation is his function as a member of the CST.

The reading teacher knows Johnny. She has screened him, evaluated him, and is currently servicing him in remedial reading. Johnny is easily distracted, loses his place while reading, and has difficulty functioning within the reading group. The remedial students do not have his particular problems and are progressing more quickly than Johnny. In addition, the children in the remedial group can sit still for a longer period of time and are able to work independently if necessary. Johnny seems to require too much individual attention for a group that is apparently too advanced for him.

The resource room teacher does not report. He has neither done any testing nor has he formally met Johnny. Because he is a special education teacher, he must wait for the CST's decision to evaluate Johnny and for parental consent before he begins his assessment. Sometimes it is to the advantage of the resource room teacher that he has not made any assessment of Johnny or formed any opinion as to the nature of his problem. He can listen to all those involved in Johnny's education up to this point and remain objective. Although he is taking notes and asks questions of the various specialists, he has not formed any preconceived assessment of Johnny. Gathering his information and reviewing his notes, the resource room teacher is being presented with a child who has the following characteristics: (a) achievement levels approximately 50 percent below his grade; (b) average intelligence on group tests; (c) highly distractible with a short attention span; (d) difficulty relating to peers; (e) impulsive; and (f) at times accident prone.

Parent Authorization

The CST decides to evaluate Johnny formally. The principal's responsibility is to contact Johnny's parents and invite them to a personal conference. At this conference the parents will be told about Johnny's learning difficulties and the need for a formal testing evaluation. Such a personal conference is felt to be less anxiety-producing for the parents. At many of these conferences, the psychologist will also be present. After the parents are informed of the team's decision, they will be asked to sign permission forms. Although the parents will no doubt be anxious and concerned about the evaluation proceedings, in most cases these parents are already anxious and concerned about their child's academic and social behavior in school and at home. Many parents look at the evaluation as a way to understand finally why their child is having so much difficulty.

Testing and Evaluation by Team Members

Upon receipt of parental authorization, the CST will proceed with its testing of Johnny. The team will have 30 school days to complete its evaluation from the time written permission is received. The COH will also be given the parental authorization letter and the evaluation due date.

The evaluation forms are then distributed to the members of the CST. The evaluation packet consists of the following forms: (a) a learning disabilities report (filled out by the resource room teacher); (b) a reading assessment; (c) an LSH evaluation; (d) a classroom observation sheet; (e) a social history form; (f) a medical evaluation; (g) a physician's report; and (h) a psychological assessment.

Each report is color-coded to aid the individual members of the COH when they are assessing a completed packet. The cover sheet of the evaluation packet is a request for service from the COH. It is a checklist to be filled out by both the principal and the psychologist after the CST has evaluated Johnny and reached its conclusions. There is a section for a classification in which the committee recommends a specific handicapping condition of the child being evaluated. Another checklist includes the data in the packet and the type of service recommended (resource room, self-contained class, and so on), and is signed by both the psychologist and the principal.

The reason that the CST merely makes a recommendation for a specific service to the COH is that only the COH has the authority to make a classification. The COH is composed of the following members: the special education chairperson; the school physician; a school psychologist; two parent advocates; and the school social worker. The parent advocates represent the rights of the children and their families, who are being presented before the committee.

The members of the CST are now ready to proceed with their evaluation of Johnny. Each member will assess Johnny through the instruments of his or her specific discipline; however, the overall goal of each member will be to deliver as a team a clear, concise, and cohesive evaluation.

The psychologist will give tests to determine an intellectual and emotional profile of Johnny. He will want to know Johnny's cognitive ability, his current levels of achievement, and his behavioral characteristics. He will be concerned with assessing Johnny's intelligence and any emotional factors that might impede academic or social growth. One of the intelligence tests used by many school psychologists is the Wechsler Intelligence Scale for Children—Revised (WISC-R). It is a standardized test that gives a verbal intelligence score, a performance intelligence score, and a total intelligence score. The subtest breakdowns help the psychologist and later the resource room teacher conclude whether a child has a potential learning disability.

An achievement test such as the Wide Range Achievement Test (WRAT) is used by the psychologist as a quick tool for assessing how much Johnny has actually learned. It is also standardized. This test does not go into the depth that other specific achievement tests do and, therefore, is only used as a quick indicator of achievement levels. Many times the WRAT scores will be compared to more in-depth achievement tests given by other team specialists.

In order to assess Johnny's emotional functioning, projective testing is also done. These tests of imagination and fantasy allow the psychologist to pinpoint areas of concern for the child that might interfere with academic functioning. One such test is the Thematic Apperception Test (TAT).

When organicity or neurological impairment is suspected, the psychologist might also give the Bender Gestalt Test. Thus, Johnny might be given the WISC-R, the WRAT, the Bender Gestalt, and several projective tests.

The psychologist is also responsible for meeting with Johnny's parents and filling out a developmental social history of the child. The parents will be asked whether the pregnancy was full-term, if the birth was normal, and the ages at which Johnny walked, talked, and so on. This developmental history will trace Johnny from his mother's pregnancy through his current year at school. The social history is included in the CST packet because it provides data that cannot be obtained from the members' evaluations and is pertinent in giving the COH a total picture of Johnny.

The LSH teacher will evaluate Johnny. He will assess Johnny's use of language, his sentence structure, grammatical usage, pronunciation, and his auditory memory. The LSH teacher is interested in Johnny's ability to communicate. How does he respond to specific questions, not just on tests, but in general conversation? He will compare Johnny's ability to use language with other children of his age. He will assess the way Johnny reasons and draws conclusions, whether he is a concrete thinker or able to use abstractions.

One of the tests the LSH teacher may give is the Peabody Picture Vocabulary Test (PPVT), which assesses the child's receptive language. Another test that may be given is the Wepman Test of Auditory Discrimination, which measures Johnny's ability to discriminate between same or similar sounding words. The Test of Language Development (TOLD) will measure Johnny's receptive vocabulary, expressive vocabulary, auditory memory, grammatical understanding, and so on.

The LSH teacher wants to know if Johnny can use nouns with verbs to form meaningful sentences and if his language development is appropriate to his developmental background. Can Johnny follow directions? How many directions can he follow?

When the LSH teacher is through evaluating Johnny, he should have a clear and concise idea of Johnny's language strengths and weaknesses. He will then determine how Johnny's language will affect his ability to absorb what is spoken in the classroom, and whether or not his ability to communicate both verbally and nonverbally (pantomime, gesture language) is appropriate for his age.

The reading teacher knows Johnny. She has worked with him in remedial classes and has past reading reports, tests, and information on Johnny in his reading file. She will now give a current reading test for the CST and has the advantage of comparing these tests to past performances. The reading tests given for a child like Johnny would include the following kind of assessment:

- How are Johnny's word attack skills?
- Does he use a consistent method to decode unknown words?
- Does he use phonics?
- Has he been able to amass a reasonable sight vocabulary?

- Is oral reading fluent, or are words skipped and substituted?
- When reading silently, does the child comprehend, and can he answer questions about what he has read?

The reading teacher will also compare Johnny's reading scores with other children in his class and in his remedial group. She knows the extent of his remedial reading program and will be able to assess Johnny's progress. Some of the tests and techniques used in her reading evaluation could be the Stanford Diagnostic Reading tests, the Woodcock Reading Mastery Tests, and an informal reading inventory. All reading evaluations will assess both oral and silent reading, as well as word attack, vocabulary, and comprehension skills.

The resource room teacher is essentially concerned with the way Johnny can process information. His primary goal is to determine the channel through which Johnny can best learn. Like the LSH teacher, the resource room teacher is interested in the child's ability to communicate. Communication, however, also involves his ability to receive, interpret, and express academic information as well. If Johnny is not learning to read, the resource room teacher will be seeking out the processing problem that might be impeding success. He is interested in what breakdown (if any) is occurring that is preventing the visual or auditory channel from perceiving the letters, sounds, and words, and preventing them from being "read."

The resource room teacher will look at academic areas and beyond, for answers to the following questions about processing problems:

- Is inability to read only one aspect of a more global problem?
- How are Johnny's social skills?
- How long can he attend?
- Does he have a sense of orientation about himself, in time and space?
- How much of a role does memory play in his academic difficulties?
- What channel causes him the most frustration?
- How are his motor skills?

The resource room teacher's first meeting with Johnny is important. He will start assessing Johnny's behavior and reactions immediately upon meeting him. Does Johnny go willingly with him? Is he able to converse? Are his responses to questions one word, phrases, or sentences? It is equally important that the examiner be able to put Johnny at ease so he will feel comfortable responding. It must be emphasized that Johnny has never worked with the resource room teacher and in some cases may never have even seen him. For his evaluation to be valid, this teacher must be able to make Johnny comfortable about being with him.

Johnny's tests results should tell the resource room teacher whether or not Johnny is performing according to his ability. If Johnny's intelligence score is at least average, Johnny should be able to produce academically. If he doesn't, the resource room teacher will be looking for tests that tell why not.

A test like the Woodcock-Johnson Psycho-Educational Test Battery can be given to Johnny by the resource room teacher. Its scores are standardized, and the examiner will get an aptitude cluster score predicting achievement levels. After giving Johnny the achievement tests, the resource room teacher has an excellent source of comparison. For example, part one of this test, which measures aptitudes, may anticipate Johnny's reading level to be on grade, while part two (achievement) may show that Johnny is reading two years below his anticipated score.

Another test that may be given to Johnny by the resource room teacher is the Detroit Test of Learning Aptitudes. This test will help the teacher measure Johnny's mental processing, including his ability to attend auditorily and visually, to reason, to follow directions, to interpret language, and to use fine motor skills. Since this test is standardized, the score can be computed into an age level and a ranking.

There will be occasions when the resource room teacher will evaluate Johnny's performance and not have a standardized score. The teacher might ask him to read from a specific book, recite the alphabet, tie his shoe, or tell a joke. This informal evaluation is usually done in addition to formal testing. A test that might be given to Johnny that is not standardized is the Slingerland Screening Tests for Identifying Children with Specific Language Disability. As a screening test, it can be helpful to the resource room teacher in analyzing the way Johnny processes information. It allows the resource room teacher to appraise Johnny's near and far point copying techniques and his use of auditory and visual channels, with or without a written response in language-related subjects.

The rest of the CST evaluation packet includes a classroom observation sheet that is filled out by the classroom teacher and a medical evaluation that is filled out by the child's physician. (See Exhibit 3–1 for a list of the evaluative tests cited in this chapter.)

Final Evaluation and Recommendations

When the members of the team have concluded their testing, the principal once more convenes a CST meeting. The members assemble, prepared to discuss their individual findings. Each member's assessment is eventually incorporated into one final evaluation. It is therefore important to understand that not every specialist needs to give a multitude of tests,

Exhibit 3-1 Tests Cited in This Chapter

1. *Bender-Gestalt Test.* Psychological Corp., New York, New York, 1962.
2. *Detroit Tests of Learning Aptitude.* Bobbs-Merrill Company Inc., Indianapolis, Indiana, 1958.
3. *Peabody Picture Vocabulary Test.* American Guidance Services, Inc., Circle Pines, Minnesota, 1959.
4. *Screening Tests for Identifying Children with Specific Language Disability.* Educator's Publishing Service, Cambridge, Massachusetts, 1970.
5. *Stanford Diagnostic Reading Test.* Harcourt, Brace, Jovanovich, Inc., New York, New York, 1976.
6. *Test of Language Development.* Empire Press, Austin, Texas, 1977.
7. *Thematic Apperception Test.* Harvard University Press, Cambridge, Massachusetts, 1943.
8. *Wepman Test of Auditory Discrimination.* Language Research Associates, Chicago, Illinois, 1958.
9. *Wechsler Intelligence Scale for Children—Revised* (WISC-R). Psychological Corp., New York, New York, 1974.
10. *Wide Range Achievement Test, Revised Edition.* Guidance Associates, Wilmington, Delaware, 1965.
11. *Woodcock Reading Mastery Tests.* American Guidance Service, Inc., Circle Pines, Minnesota, 1973.
12. *Woodcock-Johnson Psycho-Educational Test Battery.* Teaching Resources, Boston, Massachusetts, 1977.

since all the protocols, data, and test results are freely discussed and reviewed by all the members. This interchange of information is extremely important for the resource room teacher, who may ultimately be servicing the child and needs to begin to plan a remedial program. Thus, when the team once more convenes, each specialist will have given approximately three tests, and, together as a team, these tests will provide a clear and cohesive view of the child's functioning.

The psychologist is the first to report results to the team. The information the psychologist provides is of the utmost importance to the resource room teacher, who wants to know whether Johnny has average or above average intelligence. The resource room teacher also is interested in Johnny's emotional condition. Do the results of the WISC-R confirm the resource room teacher's assessment? If Johnny appears to be having visual discrimination difficulties on the resource room teacher's examinations, are the performance scores on the WISC-R also lower? The resource room teacher is also interested in subtest scatter on the WISC-R. This may confirm his diagnosis and help with future planning. If, for example, Johnny scores poorly on picture arrangement and block designs on the WISC-R, did he also have a problem with incomplete pictures and memory for designs on the Detroit?

Projective test results are also important to the resource room teacher, who needs to know if there is an emotional component to the child's learning problem. The resource room teacher also needs to know whether the emotional component (if it exists) is the primary cause of the child's inability to learn or if the learning problem is not the primary cause of emotional difficulties. Knowing the primary reason for the learning difficulty is of utmost importance in planning an academic program. For example, a child who is learning disabled is taught differently than a child who is emotionally distressed or a slow learner. The definition of the handicapping condition will also influence the type of supportive services the child will receive.

The psychologist will report on the way Johnny views his world. Does Johnny have a positive self-image? Is he aware of his problems in school? How does he explain the reasons for his problems? Is Johnny angry or resigned? This kind of information will help the resource room teacher in initial sessions with Johnny and with placing him in a small group setting.

The psychologist reports that Johnny's aptitude and intelligence scores indicate he has an average intelligence and should be able to function on an academic par with his classmates. However, he is easily distracted, impulsive, and is having difficulty with visual processing. Johnny's social skills are extremely unsophisticated, and Johnny lacks the self-control to relate to his peers appropriately. Johnny is often disoriented and confused, as if he does not know what he is expected to do or how he should respond. When overwhelmed, he gets frustrated, cries, and eventually gives up. Unless Johnny establishes a new learning pattern, both his academic and social performances will become more frustrating and more difficult to manage.

The results of the psychologist's achievement test scores may be compared with the resource room teacher's scores on the Woodcock-Johnson Psycho-Educational Test Battery Part 2.

The LSH teacher is next to report. He discusses his test protocols and Johnny's performance. Johnny's auditory memory is good. The resource room teacher concurs and makes note to use this obvious source of strength in the program for Johnny. His speech pattern is good, and articulation is adequate. Johnny had the most difficulty following oral directions with a written response. This difficulty to incorporate what is heard into what is written was further evident when the resource room teacher gave his tests. The resource room teacher writes in his notes to introduce new material through the auditory channel. He is trying to avoid frustrating Johnny, especially in the initial stages of the new program.

The reading teacher discusses Johnny's current reading scores and compares them to past evaluations. He has made little progress. His ability to discriminate auditorially isolated sounds in words is excellent. He can recognize initial, medial, and final sounds, and letters in words presented to him orally. His confusion occurs on the printed page. He is erratic in reading, missing words one day that he knew the day before. Sometimes he will try to decode a word and focus on the middle or ending sound. Many times during the testing session, he asked the reading teacher to identify a letter, such as a b/d or p/q. She sees a reading problem due mainly to visual confusion. This information coincides with the other specialists' findings, including the resource room teacher's.

The resource room teacher is next to report. He agrees with many of the findings. Johnny's weakest channel is the visual, which is most seriously hampered when he is asked to write. He has been able to compensate to an extent by his adequate auditory skills, but even then his impulsiveness and distractibility cause him to function at an extremely low level in class. If overwhelmed by visual stimuli, Johnny will become anxious, frustrated, and incapable of performing.

His visual channel deficits, including sequencing and directional confusion, are preventing Johnny from reading. He has fine motor problems and an insecure feeling about the way letters look and are written. He takes a long time to write because he has difficulty remembering how some letters look, what sequence to put the letters in, and how the word is spelled. The resource room teacher further explains that the words on a page appear to "move" for Johnny. He doesn't know where to focus his attention.

Achievement test scores in math are lowest in written computation. Johnny can do calculations "in his head," but not on paper. Numbers appear out of sequence, and directional confusion prevents him from having success in subtraction.

It is at this point that the dual role of the resource room teacher is most apparent. He is evaluating and assessing Johnny, while organizing and recommending an educational plan for him. He must assess Johnny in his classroom, as in the resource room, and make sure that the program for Johnny be accomplished in both settings.

The members of the CST are now ready to fill out their individual evaluation forms. The team has decided to send its evaluation to the COH. The learning disability form is filled out by the resource room teacher. (See Exhibit 3–2.) Needless to say, this form is extremely important to the COH and must be filled out carefully.

The learning disabilities form is divided into different sections. The first section asks for identifying information such as the child's name, address, telephone number, and school. Another section asks for the reason for

Exhibit 3-2 Sample Learning Disabilities Report

Name _____ School _____

Address _____ Grade_____

Telephone No. _____ Date of Birth_____

Parent's Name _____ Date of Evaluation _____

Reason for referral:

Previous services provided:

General observations:

Tests administered:

Analysis of test results:

Diagnostic impressions:

Recommendations:

_____

Signature

Source: Reprinted with permission of the Office of Special Education, Baldwin Public Schools, Baldwin, New York.

referral. Included in this section is the original referral source, such as the classroom teacher or parent.

Under the section entitled, *Previous services provided,* the resource room teacher notes any inhouse service the child has been receiving, such as remedial reading or speech therapy. Under *General observations,* he describes Johnny's physical characteristics, such as size, weight, and hair coloring. Also included in this section is handedness, coordination, and speed of responses. The resource room teacher may also include Johnny's ability to attend, his test behavior, and his attitude.

The resource room teacher lists those tests he gave in the section entitled *Tests administered.* Test scores are listed and discussed in the section entitled *Analysis of test results.* He is explicit in his discussion, avoiding learning disability jargon that may not be readily understood by some COH members. Johnny's performance scores are discussed in terms of his ability to process information. Included in this discussion are whether the scores are aged or graded. If the resource room teacher gives reading scores, he will explain if the scores are on the independent, instructional, or frustration level.

Under *Diagnostic impressions,* the resource room teacher explains how Johnny's difficulty with visual processing will affect his academic performance. It is important to explain how Johnny's specific deficits prevent him from having success in reading, math, and spelling.

The final section of the learning disability form is entitled *Recommendations.* In this section, the resource room teacher briefly describes the program he recommends for Johnny. These recommendations can include the appropriateness of the resource room setting, the use of a specific approach to reading, suggestions of ways to decrease visual confusion, and so on.

COH Review

When the evaluation forms are completed, they are collected by the psychologist, who completes the cover sheet and sends the packet to the COH. Johnny's parents are invited to meet with the principal to discuss the CST recommendations and to be notified that Johnny's case will be reviewed by the COH within 30 school days.

The classroom teacher is given recommendations by the CST to help her best manage Johnny. Hopefully, these recommendations will alleviate some of Johnny's anger and frustration, and make the classroom a more positive environment. These suggestions might include ways of preventing visual overstimulation by focusing on Johnny's auditory strengths, appointing a classmate as scribe, and using a tape recorder. Also discussed will be ways to rechannel Johnny's energy toward more acceptable goals, such as running errands or washing the blackboard.

When the COH approves Johnny for resource room service, then both the resource room teacher and the classroom teacher will coordinate a program based on his individual needs.

RESULTS OF THE CST

Johnny's parents agree with the COH that he is in need of resource room service. Johnny is scheduled to begin service on a daily basis. He will be mainstreamed. He will be placed in the least restrictive environment for a child with a learning disability. He will spend the bulk of his school day in his classroom and one session in the resource room.

Since Johnny is now acquainted with the resource room teacher, he will be more comfortable coming for service. This is one reason why being a member of the CST is so important to the resource room teacher. He knows Johnny, and Johnny knows him. If the resource room teacher had not evaluated him, he might lose valuable remedial time getting to know Johnny and making him feel comfortable. It is also to Johnny's benefit that he did not have to meet a teacher who tested him, and then another one who services him. For a child like Johnny, the resource room can be an anxiety-provoking situation. He may question why he is there. Did he do something wrong? Is this the place for "stupid" or "bad" children? If he recognizes the teacher in the room as one who was kind and supportive, he will feel more comfortable.

Having been a member of the CST will also help in other ways. The resource room teacher knows Johnny's levels of instruction. He knows how Johnny best learns and how he reacts when frustrated. The teacher may program all new instruction through the auditory channel. Johnny will use cassettes.

The input from the other specialists on the team is also important. The resource room teacher has gained insight into the way Johnny views himself from the psychologist. He knows that Johnny angers easily, cries when frustrated, is distractible, and has a poor self-image. Johnny may benefit from short, varied activities that provide him with opportunities for success.

The LSH teacher has reported that Johnny's language ability is normal. This information will help the resource room teacher program Johnny for oral reports and tape presentations in the resource room as well as the classroom.

Johnny's remedial program will be based on his test performance, behavioral characteristics, and team recommendations. Johnny will be made aware of his learning difficulties and how certain modifications in his program will make him more successful. He will be seen either individually or in a small group, depending on his program. Those school activities that Johnny has success with (art, gym, music, and so on) will not be missed.

Each year Johnny will be reevaluated by the CST, and a recommendation will be made to the COH whether service should be continued. A yearly IEP will be presented to Johnny's parents by the resource room teacher.

Johnny may remain in the resource room for several years until he graduates or is dismissed from service. He will establish a unique relationship with the resource room teacher. The teacher will become his advocate, making him more aware of his environment and himself.

At Issue

THE USE OF STANDARDIZED TESTS TO DETERMINE EDUCATIONAL PLACEMENTS: THE DEBATE CONTINUES

The validity of standardized tests has been hotly debated for the past two decades. Today, however, this debate is exacerbated by the primacy of standardized tests in the process of identifying and placing children with handicapping conditions. If standardized tests are invalid for some or many segments of the population, then the process of diagnosis may become invalid as well.

When a referral is made to a CST, a decision must be made as to whether or not further assessment is warranted. The psychoeducational evaluation that is then conducted by a team is done to provide comprehensive information about a student's intellectual skills, level of achievement, and learning processes. While the methods for collecting this data may vary from district to district, a fairly consistent battery of standardized tests is relied upon to provide the necessary information. Simon describes the process of identification and the ensuing use of standardized tests that her district uses. Obviously, these instruments are felt to be valid and reliable by those who have chosen the test battery, but others are not in consent.

Criticisms about the use of standardized tests revolve either around the general practice of using this type of assessment or the validity of an individual diagnostic tool. Of all standardized tests, the intelligence test has aroused the greatest controversy. In some cases the scrutiny of intellectual assessment has resulted in the total elimination of intelligence appraisal as a routine form of group testing. Some feel that the lack of validity in using these tests, particularly with culturally divergent groups, and the resulting abuses far outweigh their educational merit.

Historically, when group intelligence tests were used to screen for mental retardation, the proportion of black and other minority group children identified was disproportionately too high and thus seen as invalid. The use of these measures is still debated both in periodicals for the general public and within professional organizations.

Vitro, in his recent article in defense of intelligence tests, succinctly summarizes the major criticisms:

- Tests are unfair to many cultures and minority groups.
- Tests tend to result in stigmatization of children with categorical labels such as "retarded," "slow learner," and "genius."
- Tests tend to favor the glib individual while penalizing the thoughtful or creative person.

- Tests tend to invade individual privacy.
- Tests are often misused and misinterpreted.[1]

Vitro's defense of intelligence tests revolves around a plea for the appropriate and discerning use of instruments that are admittedly less than perfect. Teachers, counselors, and other professionals must be trained to use the information gathered from intelligence tests more effectively by realistically viewing the information gathered from the tests as indicators of student potential that may be contaminated by such factors as socioeconomic status, language ability, motivation, emotionality, immaturity, and school achievement. The judicious use of information drawn from students' performances on intellectual assessments can substantially add to clinical judgment in the process of educational placement. While these tests are far from perfect, they seem to be the only objective means available of appraising intelligence.

In evaluating the validity of specific tests commonly used in a diagnostic battery, Coles has reviewed the research on several of the most frequently used standardized tests for learning disabilities: Illinois Test of Psycholinguistic Abilities, Bender Visual-Motor Gestalt Test, Frostig Developmental Test of Visual Perception, Wepman Auditory Discrimination Test, Lincoln-Oseretsky Motor Development Scale, Graham-Kendall Memory for Designs Test, Purdue Perceptual-Motor Survey, and the Wechsler Intelligence Scale for Children.[2] His review of these tests is based on a thorough examination of the research literature. He concludes that there is little empirical evidence that these tests have construct validity, particularly as they are used to test for learning disabilities. He feels that there is little objective evidence for the continuation of using these instruments, and many do not truly test the traits that they were designed to evaluate. Specialists who continue to base diagnoses on evidence gathered from such standardized instruments may find that, while there may be consistency between the various tests, in the end the etiology of test performance cannot be ascertained. In effect, Coles says, that while how students perform on these tests can be described, there is no basis for concluding whether their achievement is the result of neurological, emotional, pedagogical, developmental, or other factors. This thereby invalidates the concept of differential diagnosis based on standardized test scores. It is interesting to note that the trend in special education placement today seems to be away from labeling by etiology, that is, mentally retarded, emotionally disturbed, and so on, and toward needs assessment in learning.

Coles feels that learning disability specialists have been too quick to apply assessments whose validity is questionable, are too presumptive in concluding causative factors, and act "as if they had in their hands diagnostic instruments that would lay bare the cognitive processes of a child's mind."[3] Ascribing motivation to those who use these instruments, Coles says that the field of special education is attempting to provide rational answers to the inexplicable reasons why children fail to learn. Continuing his argument, Coles explains that use of such test batteries places the responsibility for failing to learn on a biological-deficit model existing within the child, rather than having schools take the responsibility for failing to educate those labelled as learning disabled. In fact, by using the medical model, the resulting educational jargon associated with special education may create illegitimate prestige. As a case in point, Coles says:

> How mundane to tell someone you teach remedial reading. How awesome to announce that you do clinical work with minimally brain dysfunctional children, more dyslexic than dyscalculic, who are benefitting from methylphenidate.[4]

Coles concludes that eventually the standardized tests he has reviewed will be eliminated as the profession continues to scrutinize them closely. However, whether they will be replaced by other questionable instruments remains open, as it seems that the sophistication of the measurements does not correspond with the need of educators for valid information. It may well be that those who acknowledge the inherent weaknesses in testing instruments but who continue to use them do so because of the unavailability of better measurement devices.

The Education for All Handicapped Children Act of 1975 contains language that specifically refers to the process of evaluation and practices for fair testing. Swanson and Willis summarize the legislation that attempts to ensure fair evaluation practices:

- Testing and evaluation must be conducted so as not to be racially or culturally biased.
- Tests and other evaluative materials must be conducted in the child's native language.
- Tests and other evaluative materials must be proven valid.
- Testing must be conducted by trained personnel.
- Tests should include various areas of educational need and not provide just a general intelligence appraisal.
- No one test should be used for placement.
- A multidisciplinary team should conduct the evaluation.
- The child should be assessed in all areas affecting the disability, such as health, language skills, and so on.[5]

It is obvious that the need for unbiased, valid measures of children's performance is not as yet commensurate with the ability of standardized tests to provide the information. The concern for cultural bias will continue, as it seems unlikely that a test can be produced that will not discriminate against some geographic, ethnic, or racial segment of the population. The ability to evaluate children in their own native language presupposes a sufficient number of instruments translated to many different languages and a sufficient number of experienced, multilingual evaluators. This, of course, does not presently exist.

We are left using a set of less-than-perfect testing instruments that, coupled with experienced, clinical insights, can help make educational decisions for handicapped children. The placement of children into programs based on their learning needs rather than disability category is an encouraging trend. Resource room teachers must have extensive training in the use and interpretation of the commonly used test batteries, and should be encouraged to use review literature and such basic resources as Buros' *Mental Measurements Yearbook* to evaluate the utility of tests.[6]

Testing is only one means of evaluation, and the larger task of assessment is an ongoing process. Salvia and Ysseldyke provide a good summary statement about the multidimensional task of assessment:

> Assessment in educational settings is a multifaceted process that involves far more than the administration of a test. When we assess students, we consider the way they perform a variety of tasks in a variety of settings or contexts, the meaning of their performances in terms of the total functioning of the individual, and likely explanations for those performances. Good assessment procedures take into consideration the fact that anyone's performance on any task is influenced not only by the demands of the task itself but also by the history and characteristics the individual brings to the task itself and by factors inherent in the setting in which assessment is carried out.[7]

NOTES

1. F. Vitro, "In Defense of Intelligent Intelligence Testing," *Academic Therapy* 14, no. 2 (Nov. 1978): 223.

2. G. Coles, "The Learning Disabilities Test Battery: Empirical and Social Issues," *Harvard Education Review* 48, no. 3 (Aug. 1978): 313–40.

3. Ibid., p. 329.

4. Ibid., p. 334.

5. B. Swanson and D. Willis, *Understanding Exceptional Children and Youth* (Chicago, Ill.: Rand McNally, 1979), p. 25.

6. O.K. Buros, ed., *Eighth Mental Measurements Yearbook* (Highland Park, N.J.: Gryphon Press, 1978).

7. J. Salvia and J. Ysseldyke, *Assessment in Special and Remedial Education* (Boston, Mass.: Houghton Mifflin, 1978), pp. 3–4.

Chapter 4

Instructional Strategies: Translating the IEP into Instructional Goals and Approaches

Gail Reiter

The goal of educators has been to provide every child with the fullest educational opportunities for physical and intellectual development. The enactment of PL 94-142 has helped this goal become a reality. The Act assures each handicapped child the right to a free and appropriate education.

PL 94-142 sets forth procedures for the implementation of educational programs to meet the unique needs of individual children and, therefore, has had a profound influence on the roles of teachers. The Act makes teachers responsible and accountable for assuring that each child receives the required special education and related services set forth in the IEP.

Alan Abeson and Frederick Weintraub define the concept implied by the term *individualized education program* as the following:

> *Individualized* means that the program must be addressed to the educational needs of a single child rather than a class or group of children. *Education* means that the program is limited to those elements of the child's education that are specifically special education and related services as defined by the Act. *Program* means that the individualized education program is a statement of what will actually be provided to the child, as distinct from a plan that provides guidelines from which a program must subsequently be developed.[1]

The IEP is the essence of PL 94-142. Its development serves as the cornerstone of the law as well as the central management tool for the attainment of its intent.

A standardized form for writing IEPs, however, is not prescribed. As a result, there are many different formats and procedures used by the various school districts.

The Act stipulates that the written statement for each handicapped student be the result of a consensus among (1) a representative of the local educational agency or an intermediate educational unit who shall be qualified to provide or supervise the provision of instruction tailored to meet the unique needs of handicapped children; (2) the parents or guardians; (3) the teacher; and (4) whenever appropriate, the child. A sample IEP form including relevant data regarding student, persons present at the conference, and parents' signatures is presented in Exhibit 4–1.

Since parents have the right to participate in the planning, they can make an important contribution to the education of their child. Their presence at the IEP conference provides an opportunity for them to contribute information about the development, medical and educational history, and needs of their child.

During this planning session topics such as curriculum, behavior performance, placement, special services, and future contacts may be discussed. Public policy entitles parents to be involved in all aspects of their child's placement and in the decision-making process.

The teacher is another partner in the child's program development. Because teachers have the major responsibility for program delivery, they

---

Exhibit 4–1 Sample Form Including Relevant Data Regarding Student, Persons Present at Conference, and Parent's Signature

---

Individualized Education Program

Student Chris Parker   DOB 11/13/69   Age 10 years 10 mos.
School Elm Elementary
Teacher Ms. Lawrence

Parents
Name   Mr. and Mrs. Wm. Parker
Address 21 Dell Drive
Phone   Home 225-5252   Office 421-6700

Committee Members   Relationship to child

Dr. Reilly   Psychologist
Mr. Parker   Father
Mrs. Parker   Mother
Ms. Lawrence   Resource room teacher
Mr. Cohen   Classroom teacher
Dr. Santoro   Special education coordinator

Signature _____ Date_____
         (Parent/guardian or student if 18 yrs. or older)

are an important link between program planning and placement decisions for handicapped students.

Difficulty for teacher participation in the development of IEPs frequently occurs at the secondary level. For example, a student may have four or five regular teachers as well as at least one special educator. The logistics to provide released time during school hours present a complex problem. Federal law does not require that all the child's teachers develop the IEP.

Since teachers have direct communication with parents, this helps to establish a common basis for mutual understanding. This reduces the misunderstandings and confusion that frequently result when administrators and psychologists are the exclusive communicators with parents throughout the assessment and placement process.

Although the parent-professional alliance is in an early stage of development, their collaboration enhances the development of relevant and appropriate educational programs.

THE FRAMEWORK OF THE IEP

PL 94-142, section 121a-225, Content of the Individualized Education Program, sets forth the framework of the IEP. The components must include *a statement of present levels of educational performance*. This information is obtained as a result of diagnostic assessment procedures determined by individual districts. The assessments help to determine both the abilities and disabilities of children, and should describe strengths, weaknesses, and deficits in learning. This part of the written program documents the student's skills and competencies at the time of entry into the special education program. Such information might include the level of functioning in reading and math skills, as well as language, social, and motor development.

A suggested form for the development of this component of the individualized education program is presented in Exhibit 4-2.

The components of an IEP must also include *a statement of annual goals, including short-term instructional objectives*. A significant part of the student's IEP is the section that lists the annual goals and short-term objectives.

Much anxiety arises as teachers frequently perceive the IEP as an accountability measure that can be used against them if the student does not attain the specified annual goals or short-term objectives. PL 94-142, however, does not require that any teacher, agency, or other person be held accountable if a child does not achieve the growth projected in the IEP.[2]

Exhibit 4-2 Sample Statement Containing Present Levels of
Performance

Present Level of Performance

Test Name	Date Adminis- tered	Interpretation
Slingerland D	9/80	Total—35 errors. Poor spatial relations, inability to recall geometric shapes and number sequences, fine motor difficulty
Wide Range Achieve- ment Test (WRAT)	9/80	Spelling—4.2 Math computation—3.9
Peabody Individual- ized Achievement Test (PIAT)	9/80	Reading recognition—5.0 Comprehension—5.2 Mathematics—3.8
Key math	9/80	Addition—3.9; Subtraction—3.8; Multiplication— 3.4; Division—3.4; Geometry—2.9; Money—4.1; Measurement—3.2; Time—4.2

*Modifications in Testing Procedures**

Student Behaviors

Academic Strengths	Academic Weaknesses
Reading	Math computation and concepts, organization skills, handwriting

Personal/social strengths	Personal/social weaknesses
Highly motivated, cooperative, good peer relations	Poor self-image, incomplete assign- ments

Other relevant strengths	Other relevant weaknesses
Good school attendance	

*Modifications could include waiving time limit, test administered in special loca-
tion, questions read to student, permission to use calculator, copy provided in Braille
and large type, answers recorded in any manner, and so on.

The writing of goals and objectives helps make teaching more relevant
and effective. By definition, a goal is a statement of long-range directions
and is usually presented in general terms.[3] In order to determine a goal,
the teacher must know specific present levels of a child's performance.
Such information can be derived from tests given by psychologists, educational diagnosticians, and teachers, as well as from teacher observations.

By examining the levels of functioning, the teacher can tell the critical areas of development that need attention. Goals should be written for each area in which the student is deficient. Suggested curricular areas are: (1) reading skills; (2) language arts skills; (3) perceptual-motor skills; (4) gross motor skills; (5) social skills; and (6) prevocational and vocational skills.

The annual goal should be an estimate of what the child will be able to accomplish within the year. It should be based on the child's present level of functioning as determined by the assessment procedure. If the goals are accomplished sooner than anticipated, additional objectives should be written.

The following are examples of annual goals:

- Student will recognize and articulate letters of the alphabet.
- Student will write upper-case letters of the alphabet.
- Student will regroup in addition.
- Student will complete work on time.

Once the annual goals have been determined, the next step is to identify the short-term objectives for each goal.

An objective is a much more specific statement, may be derived from a general goal, and includes three essential characteristics: a statement of a pupil response, a description of the conditions under which the response is to occur, and a statement of the criteria for acceptable performance.[4]

An example of a short-term objective would be: Given addition examples with two-digit addends requiring regrouping, the student will write the sums with 80 percent accuracy.

The short-term objectives reveal the specific behavior that the student is expected to acquire as a result of receiving special education services. The objective should permit measurement of its attainment, and therefore determines the content for lesson plans.

Teachers have considerable freedom in specifying and formulating objectives. They should be familiar with the hierarchies of skills on which certain behaviors depend.

A variety of published sources are available to assist in writing short-term objectives. Texts, such as *Teaching Children Basic Skills,* offer teachers reading, spelling, handwriting, arithmetic, and social skills objectives.[5] The information is arranged by subject matter and is sequenced by the level of difficulty. Criterion-referenced tests, curriculum guides, and teacher manuals in the content areas are also useful.

When using such references to write short-term objectives, the teacher should locate the child's present level of functioning as determined by the assessments and the anticipated annual goal. The skills to be mastered in order to reach the goal are the short-term objectives.

Three or four objectives should be written on the IEP. The teacher should document the student's attainment of the objectives. The documentation of achievement provides the necessary data for annual review, as well as a systematic procedure for evaluating each skill.

To illustrate this technique, consider the IEP form for student Chris Parker. Chris' assessment profile indicates that mathematics is a deficit area of development. Testing procedures pinpointed the areas for which remedial instruction is necessary.

An item analysis of test performance revealed that Chris' skills in addition and subtraction requiring regrouping were adequate. Computational errors on the Wide Range Achievement Test (WRAT) indicated sign confusions.

Chris presently knows all the multiplication combinations except for the six, seven, and eight tables. Chris can multiply a two-digit number by a one-digit number, but cannot regroup. Chris' ability to recall division facts is poor.

By the end of sixth grade, Chris' teacher thought that Chris should be able to multiply and regroup as well as compute division examples.

A specific goal in the area of mathematics could be: Chris will demonstrate the ability to improve computational skills in multiplication and division. The skills needed to reach this goal are the short-term objectives. Suggested objectives are listed in Table 4–1.

For Chris to attain the objective of multiplying a three-digit number by a two-digit number, Chris will have to master specific prerequisite skills. The sequential steps necessary for mastery of the objective become the content of the teacher's weekly plans and the student's assignments.

After the diagnostic assessment is made and the goals and objectives determined, it is necessary to formulate a program of instruction to meet the student's unique needs. The determination of an instructional strategy is based on the student's strengths and weaknesses, learning style, and level of performance. The use of appropriate methods and materials is strictly within the teacher's domain and is contingent upon experiential knowledge and availability of materials.

The IEP should include *a statement of the specific educational services to be provided*. Resources within the school district that are outside the realm of special education can add to the district's ability to meet the child's needs. Such services might include speech and language therapies, remedial reading or math instruction, psychological services, counseling

Table 4–1 Annual Goals, Short-Term Objectives, Materials, and Evaluation Criteria

Student's name Chris Parker   Subject area Mathematics

Goal: Chris will demonstrate the ability to improve computational skills in multiplication and division.

Instructional Objectives*	Methods or Materials	Evaluation	Annual Review**	Date Instruction Began	Date Objective Achieved	Date of Review
Given multiplication and/or division facts, the student will write the answer with 90% accuracy.	Stern Structural Math, Sullivan Multiplication, Sullivan Division, Lennes Book 4, Teacher-made games and materials, flash cards	Informal assessment	Exceeded criteria___ Met criteria.___ Did not meet criteria___	9/25/80		
Given a three-digit number multiplied by a two-digit number requiring regrouping, the student will write the product with 80% accuracy.	SRA Math, Lennes Book 4, Sullivan Multiplication, Developmental Learning Materials (DLM), Moving up in Numbers, teacher-made materials		Exceeded criteria___ Met criteria___ Did not meet criteria___			
Given a three-digit number divided by a one-digit number, the student will write the quotient with 80% accuracy.	SRA Math, Lennes Book 4, Sullivan Division, DLM, Moving up in Numbers, teacher-made materials		Exceeded criteria___ Met criteria.___ Did not meet criteria.___			

*Additional forms would be used for the development of goals and objectives in other deficit areas.
**PL 94-142 mandates an annual review. Frequency is determined by individual districts.

services, social work services, library or media center supplies, equipment, media, and other resources.

The IEP should outline *the extent to which the child will be able to participate in regular education programs*, and *the projected date for initiation and anticipated duration of such services*. The IEP must document when special services began and how long they will be offered. A sample form detailing services and schedules, a summary and recommendations is provided in Table 4–2.

Finally, the IEP should provide *appropriate objective criteria, evaluation procedures, and schedules for determining, on at least an annual basis, whether instructional objectives are being achieved*. PL 94–142 mandates an annual review of each IEP. The documented information should include whether the student has achieved the annual goals and any necessary program modifications.

The evaluation of pupil progress is a continuous task. Assessment is an essential element of individualized instruction. Systematic, routine checking of pupil performance helps to determine progress, appropriate placement, and relevancy of goals, and assists teacher planning.

Student progress should be reported at regular intervals throughout the school year. A logical time for furnishing progress reports for special education students would be during the regular reporting period.

The student's year-end achievement of goals becomes the present level statement for the following school year. It is therefore important to indicate the student's exact progress at the year's end.[6]

IMPLEMENTING AN IEP

An objective of the educational system has been to develop instructional programming to accommodate individual differences in children. PL 94-142 recognizes this objective and has accelerated the need for providing effective programs of instruction for handicapped children.

The trend in special education today is toward the establishment of noncategorical resource rooms. Teachers have to work with a disparate group of children who present a challenging variety of educational disabilities. Most children bring different entry skills, progress at different rates, and finish with different amounts of knowledge and levels of proficiency.

Resources in the field of special education present a myriad of specific teaching strategies that have been developed to be effective within a specific category of disability. Resource room teachers should familiarize themselves with theories and techniques that have merit. Teachers should have a repertoire of alternatives for specific instructional tactics.

Table 4–2 Table of Services and Schedules, Summary, and Recommendations

Type of Service	RE	SE	Time	Frequency	Personnel	Curriculum	Date Began	Date Ended
Resource Room		X	1 hr.	daily	Ms. Lawrence	Math	10/80	
Psychologist		X	½ hr.	1x wk.	Dr. Reilly	Counseling	10/80	
Reg. Ed.	X		½ hr.	2x wk.	Mr. Owens	Gym	9/80	
Reg. Ed.	X		40 min.	1x wk.	Ms. Smith	Art	9/80	
Reg. Ed.	X		40 min.	1x wk.	Mr. White	Music	9/80	
Media Center	X		30 min.	2x wk.	Ms. James	Math	10/80	
Reg. Ed.	X		45 min.	daily	Mr. Cohen	L. Arts, S.S., Science	9/80	
Reg. Ed.	X		1 hr.	daily		Lunch	9/80	
Reg. Ed.	X		40 min.	1x wk.	Ms. Tyler	Library	9/80	

End of year summary:

Recommendations for next year:

Perhaps, given a clinical profile, a particular technique might appear to be the most logical approach. If the resource room teacher does not see positive results forthcoming after a period of time, an analysis of causes is suggested. The teacher should examine the strategy being used for instruction. Perhaps a change in methodology or technique would produce the desired result. If the strategy is appropriate, then an examination should be made of the materials and resources used for the delivery of instruction. Sometimes nonmastery can be the result of an objective not being realistic for a particular pupil.

The essence of a successful program is its flexibility and adaptability. The teacher should be alert to the needs of individual pupils and resourceful in finding ways to meet these needs.

A specific method can work well in one situation but not in another. Children learn to read through various approaches: linguistic, phonetic, sight word, or a language experience. It is important to determine which method of instruction matches the child's learning style, needs, and pattern of skills and abilities.

Literature on the education of exceptional children describes several characteristics that appear to be common to most instructional approaches developed for handicapped children.

Following are some principles for effective instruction across traditional disability categories and instructional situations.

Motivation

Children with learning deficits have experienced many failure situations. Because they are easily discouraged, it is necessary to put special effort into motivating them to continue. Some suggestions are to provide high interest lessons and materials; alternate low probability tasks with high probability tasks; or use social reinforcements, such as teacher praise, attention and approval, or the use of material rewards.

Teach Sequentially

When planning instruction, teachers must have a sequence in mind. A systematic approach to instruction is based on careful assessment of the student's performance, followed by goals and short-term objectives. The tasks to be learned by the student should be in an ordered fashion, progressing from easy to difficult. Achievement should be rewarded, regardless of how slight it may be.

Models and Cues

The technique of modeling is frequently used by teachers for reading and math instruction. Many handicapped children benefit from instruction in which a visual model is provided. Teachers often demonstrate how to solve a math example on the board while the students observe. The students are then asked to imitate the teacher by completing the same problem at their desks. They then solve similar examples using the model that has been provided. Sometimes a model can be provided on the pupil's worksheet for reference.

In addition, it is sometimes necessary to provide cues. The use of color cues, dashes, and so on for teaching reading, spelling, and math skills is also recommended. Students with memory or sequencing problems benefit from this technique.

Drill and Practice

In order for pupils to acquire a skill, they must have ample practice in applying it until it becomes an automatic process. After the initial presentation, a variety of multisensory learning experiences should be provided in order to reinforce the task. Many opportunities should be provided for the student to see it, hear it, say it, and do it.

In order to maintain the response, practice and frequent reviews must be provided. These techniques help to ensure maintenance of an acquired skill.

Recommended materials are worksheets (commercial or teacher-made); flash cards; manipulative materials, such as letter tiles and beads; and media materials.

Response Generalization

Performance of a skill within the resource room is no guarantee that the child will be able to apply the skill in another situation. Children with learning deficits have difficulty generalizing from one set of responses to another. For example, a child who has learned to apply a phonic rule to recognize a word may not be able to use the rule to spell a word.

A variety of experiences, which include modeling, prompting, and curriculum sequencing, should be provided so that students can transfer a learned behavior or task to a new situation.

Individualized, personalized instruction is desirable in many instances. Usually it is not possible because the number of referrals often exceeds the capacity for one-to-one instruction.

Grouping of children for instructional purposes can be done in a variety of ways and may depend on other factors. Grouping of students according to achievement and analysis of performance is suggested. It is desirable, whenever possible, to group those students with common needs. Although it is preferable to group pupils with their peers, interage grouping can also be effective.

Sometimes poor social interaction of students necessitates a group change. Some handicapped children also require the services of other specialists in the building, that is, speech teacher, psychologist, and so on, and a scheduling conflict will occur. The resource room teacher will have to arrange alternatives to accommodate the needs of the students.

Within a specific group, the needs of the children are continually changing, resulting in the formation of subgroups. The use of student contracts is a technique the resource room teacher can employ in order to meet the students' wide ranges of abilities and learning styles. Contracts enable the teacher to tailor a program of instruction relevant to each student's needs, abilities, interests, learning style, and degree of self-discipline.

The contract for each pupil is based on the instructional objectives of the IEP. It provides the student an opportunity to learn independently. It includes a variety of learning experiences through which the student may master the necessary skills and information. Contracts enable students to progress at a comfortable rate. Contracts allow the teacher to work independently with other students in the group.

Learning Materials

The materials selected for use should have the following characteristics:

- The material should break a learning task into small sequential steps.
- There should be a logical sequence to the material presented.
- The material should provide easy, immediate correction and feedback.
- The material should be appropriate to the student's level of functioning and allow for progress to higher task levels.
- The material should be interesting to the student.

Review to Evaluate Progress

The Education for All Handicapped Children Act stipulates an annual review of each IEP. Evaluation of pupil progress is an important component of individualized instruction. The development of accurate and systematic recordkeeping procedures facilitates this aspect of the program.

Students' folders should contain psychological and diagnostic information, and copies of the IEP. Samples of work, data related to the attainment of skills and objectives, anecdotal reports describing student behavior and discipline problems, and reports of conferences with school personnel and parents should be documented.

* * * * * *

The resource room teacher provides both direct and indirect services for children with learning problems. The nature and severity of the problem determines whether the student will receive direct services from the resource room teacher or indirect services through consultation with the classroom teacher.

A need exists to help the regular teacher become effective in delivering instruction to special children within their classrooms. Sometimes children who exhibit inappropriate social behaviors or minor academic problems can be helped through consultation.

Classroom observations, and informal and formal testing enable the resource room and classroom teachers jointly to pinpoint tasks and behaviors that need intervention. The identification of current performance levels allows the teachers to develop and implement intervention programs.

Consultation with the classroom teacher is necessary in order to maintain a full continuum of services for the handicapped student who receives direct instruction in the resource center.

Specific recommendations for instructional strategies and materials, techniques for managing unwanted behavior, peer tutors, and the establishment of reinforcement contingencies to influence performance are often helpful.

The consultant role of the resource room teacher does not have parity with the teacher's other activities. Continuing communication is important between the specialist and the classroom teacher. The use of forms is a practical technique to ensure communication between them. Checklists or daily progress sheets that describe the student's behavior, classwork, and other assignments are also suggested to monitor pupil progress.

The implementation of PL 94-142 gives all concerned the long-awaited opportunity to plan a better and more fruitful educational life for handicapped children.

NOTES

1. Alan Abeson and Frederick Weintraub, "Understanding the Individualized Education Program," *A Primer on Individualized Education Programs For Handicapped Children,* ed. S. Torres (Reston: The Foundation For Exceptional Children, 1979), p. 5.

2. Josephine Hayes, Joseph Higgins, Scottie Torres, "Issues Regarding the IEP: Teachers On the Front Line," *Exceptional Children,* January 1978, pp. 267–73.

3. N.G. Haring, *Teaching Special Children* (New York, N.Y.: McGraw-Hill, 1976), p. 90.

4. Ibid.

5. Thomas Stevens, Carol Hartman, and Virginia Lucas, *Teaching Children Basic Skills* (Columbus, Ohio: Merrill, 1978).

6. Scottie Torres, ed., *A Primer*, p. 42.

BIBLIOGRAPHY

Anderson, Lee; Barner, Sandra; and Larson, Harry. "Evaluation of Written Individualized Education Programs." *Exceptional Children* 45: 207–8.

Becker, Laurence. "Learning Characteristics of Educationally Handicapped and Retarded Children." *Exceptional Children* 44: 502–11.

Brown, Louis F.; Kiraly, Jr., John; and McKinnon, Archie. "Resource Rooms: Some Aspects for Special Educators to Ponder." *Journal of Learning Disabilities* 12: 480–82.

Dunn, Rita; and Dunn, Kenneth. *Educator's Self-Teaching Guide to Individualizing Instructional Programs.* West Nyack, N.Y.: Parker Publishing Company, Inc., 1975.

Dunn, Rita; and Dunn, Kenneth. *Practical Approaches to Individualizing Instruction: Contracts and Other Effective Teaching Strategies.* West Nyack, N.Y.: Parker Publishing Company, Inc., 1972.

Evans, Susan. "The Consultant Role of the Resource Teacher." *Exceptional Children* 46: 402–4.

Goldstein, Sue; Strickland, Bonnie; Turnbull, Ann; and Curry, Lynn. "An Observational Analysis of the I.E.P. Conferences." *Exceptional Children* 46: 278–85.

Haring, N.G. *Teaching Special Children.* New York, N.Y.: McGraw-Hill, 1976.

Hayes, Josephine; Higgins, Joseph; and Torres, Scottie. "Issues Regarding the I.E.P.: Teachers on the Front Line." *Exceptional Children* 44: 267–73.

Jenkins; Joseph, and Mayhall, William F. "Development and Evaluation of a Resource Teacher Program." *Exceptional Children* 43: 21–29.

McLeskey, James; Rieth, Herbert J.; and Polsgrove, Lewis. "The Implications of Response Generalization for Improving the Effectiveness of Programs for Learning Disabled Children." *Journal of Learning Disabilities* 13: 287–90.

New York State Education Department, Office for Education of Children with Handicapping Conditions. *Regulations of the Commissioner of Education Subchapter P.* Albany, New York, 1979.

Oliphant, Genevieve. "Program Planning for Dyslexic Children in General Education." *Bulletin of the Orton Society* 29: 225–37.

Siegel, Ernest, and Siegel, Rita. "Ten Guidelines for Writing Instructional Sequences." *Journal of Learning Disabilities* 8: 203–9.

Smith, Robert M., and Neisworth, J.T. *The Exceptional Child: A Functional Approach.* New York, N.Y.: McGraw-Hill, 1963.

Stephens, Thomas M.; Hartman, A. Carol; and Lucas, Virginia H. *Teaching Children Basic Skills.* Columbus, Oh.: Charles E. Merrill Publishing Company, 1978.

Torres, Scottie, ed. *A Primer on Individualized Education Programs for Handicapped Children.* Reston, Va.: The Foundation for Exceptional Children, 1979.

At Issue

THE USE AND VALIDITY OF PEER TUTORING

The mandate of PL 94-142 is clear with respect to the quality of instruction that a handicapped child should receive. Teachers of these children are required to provide intense, individualized instruction based on a comprehensive needs assessment. Reiter describes the complicated process of going from the diagnosis to the formation of an IEP, and then delivering instruction to meet each child's individual needs. The resulting problem is to find an instructional system that will deliver quality education to each child on an individual basis. Teachers are limited in their capacity to work individually with students by the size of their caseload and the idiosyncratic nature of scheduling. How much individual time is each child likely to receive in the resource room program? Is this time sufficient for academic improvement to take place?

The use of aides and adult volunteers is one method of providing instructional assistance for the resource program that will be discussed more fully later in the text. The number of student teachers is dwindling because of limited opportunities for young teachers in a difficult job market. When student teachers are assigned, they need close supervision by the master teacher and may not be ready to provide as much assistance as is needed. There is a current trend toward the extension of an undergraduate's teacher training program to a fifth year of internship within a school district. These internships will provide greater field-based training for new teachers and will provide supplementary teaching staff in areas of special need. In New York state new legislation has been recently approved that will require all new teachers to complete an internship program before becoming certified. This legislation, which is referred to as "Teaching as a Profession," will become effective in 1983.

Another method of assistance for the resource teacher is the use of peer tutoring. This instructional system has been discussed in the special education literature for the last ten years. Reviewing the major studies that have been done to evaluate the effectiveness of this approach, Chiang, Thorpe, and Darch have found "cross-age tutoring experience to be mutually beneficial for both tutors and tutees."[1] Gains that were accomplished appeared to be both academic and affective, as both partners in the tutoring team profited from the social interaction while skill improvement took place.

To validate further the technique of peer tutoring for students with learning problems, Chiang, Thorpe, and Darch conducted a carefully controlled research study to eliminate such confounding factors as the "Pygmalion effect" (students improving simply because they are given extra attention and are expected by all to improve) and other variables such as experimental designs of short duration.

Eight subjects who had been identified as learning disabled were chosen for the study. The four tutors were from fifth-grade classes, and the four tutees were in the second and third grades. All subjects had a history of poor reading achievement. The subjects were paired by the resource teacher, who oversaw their 15- to 20-minute daily tutoring sessions, which were conducted at separate stations in the resource room. The instructional material for the sessions was composed of 60 flashcards, each with a morpheme typed on it. Another list of 50 polysyllabic and compound words, containing the target morphemes, was used to evaluate the tutors' knowledge of the morphemes and their ability to apply this knowledge in complex situations.

The tutors were told to use the following method to instruct their partners:

- The tutor modeled the correct pronunciation of a morpheme, and the tutee repeated it.
- The tutor required the tutee to pronounce each morpheme independently.
- Steps one and two were repeated for the instructional session using the flashcards.
- Tutors were told to reinforce the tutees' accurate responses with praise.

Employing an experimental design in which baseline data on word recognition ability across subjects were obtained before and after tutoring intervention, the researchers found that all subjects improved "appreciably" during the experimental treatment. There is strong evidence that employing this simple instructional design proved beneficial in improving word recognition skills at the two levels of difficulty. In addition, classroom behavior and attitudes toward reading were positive.

The effectiveness of this study is based on its strong teaching techniques, which can be easily replicated in other situations where peer tutoring is to be employed. Specifically, the following factors should be considered:

- Instruction should be individualized.
- The instructional time period should be short and highly structured to provide an intense experience.

- Immediate feedback for correct and incorrect responses is essential with a great deal of positive reinforcement applied for correct responses.
- Tutors should be well-rehearsed and practiced before engaging in work with peers.
- Target learning skills should be clear and specific.

If teachers feel that valuable instructional time may be lost when tutors are employed, this did not seem to be the case. If teachers pair students who have complementary learning deficits at differing levels of complexity, both the tutor and tutee can show improvement. In most situations, the tutors should be chosen from students who have mastered a basic skill, but who are in need of application and reinforcement. The researchers suggested the case of a student who knows alphabetization skills, but who is unmotivated to practice. This student could be asked to tutor a student who lacks the skill, and then together they can apply the skill to locating entries in a dictionary, index, or directory.

The appropriate pairing of students is essential for the tutoring sessions to be effective. Students must be matched on their compatibility, and the researchers suggest that pairing students who have had previous contact in the same class or group will enhance the likelihood of their getting along and will pose fewer scheduling problems. Both academic skills and attitude about learning seem enhanced with the peer tutoring technique. The tutors' self-concepts were enhanced when they served as instructional models, and the tutees benefited from the highly personal, individual interaction. There is evidence that subjects working with their peers appear to be more relaxed than when working under intense teacher direction. In order to teach a skill, a person needs a thorough mastery of it.

Peer tutoring does provide instructional assistance for the resource teacher while helping to improve the academic and social skills of students with learning problems. Teachers should be encouraged to employ the technique after carefully selecting subjects, pairing them appropriately, training tutors adequately, and choosing instructional tasks that are clear and specific and are of benefit to both tutor and tutee. The instructional demands of creating an effective resource program require creativity and versatility on the part of the resource teacher.

NOTE

1. B. Chiang, H. Thorpe, and C. Darch, "Effects of Cross-Age Tutoring on Word-Recognition Performance of Learning Disabled Students," *Learning Disability Quarterly* 3, no. 4 (Fall 1980): 11–19.

Chapter 5

Equipping the
Resource Room

Gloria Wilson

Being granted a resource room position, handed a pile of requisition forms and catalogs, advised of the amount of money allocated, and told to have the completed purchase orders in as soon as possible is often the manner in which equipping a resource room begins. Although many teachers have been working in the field of special education for a number of years, they have often been severely restricted in the amount and type of commercial materials that could be ordered. Faced with a new found freedom, it is easy to fall prey to colorful catalogs, publishers' promises, and what seems to be an endless budget. However, the results of an ordering binge might be a room filled with new materials and a year spent in countless hours trying to fit materials with students, and then desperately creating more materials that will be constantly used. Materials purchased without careful deliberation can turn out to be square pegs that do not fit round holes.

Therefore, an initial warning: Do not underestimate the importance of equipping the resource room. It takes time, thought, knowledge, and organization. The selection of materials, equipment, and furniture has an ultimate effect on the management, efficiency, and success of the resource room program. It also has an effect on the teacher's sanity.

The materials that are initially selected form a foundation from which the resource teacher can create and adapt more appropriate materials. However, from the outset teachers should beware of confusing dedication and commitment with the amount of hours spent preparing materials. Too often, special education teachers both pride themselves and at the same time complain about the amount of time required to create programs. Much of this time is the result of the frustration of a poorly or inappropriately equipped room. With the proper selection of materials, the productive use of preparation time can be possible.

There is a wide diversity in the quality of available materials. The best items are often those that are created to custom fit each student. However, it is virtually impossible to design materials personally for 20 or more students who differ in age, interest, ability, and who are seen daily for the 180 days of the school year.

Consequently, special educators must rely heavily on a good base from which adaptations and innovations can be made. Before any selections can be judged appropriate, certain detailed information should be known. The words "equip" and "order" should be taken in a broad sense, and teachers should be "equipped" with facts and "order" priorities.

The resource room teacher will need to assess expectations, identify needs, investigate resources, analyze the room, and determine teaching styles before any ordering is done.

ASSESSING EXPECTATIONS

The resource room teacher's job is complex. Frustration and possible failure will result unless personal expectations and those of others are understood. This knowledge should neither be limiting nor does it necessitate agreement. The resource teacher must know the particular characteristics that are to be dealt with in a setting and rethink, reaffirm, monitor, or change accordingly. The focus and views for the setting will affect the type and range of materials needed. Federal and state guidelines, district policy, and principals', psychologists', guidance counselors', social workers', mainstream teachers', parents', and children's expectations must be known. What do these people foresee as the necessary goals and accomplishments of the resource room? Do they want the children to pass mainstream classes, pass competency tests, improve basic skills, prepare for the world of work, become more socialized, or become more comfortable with themselves? Do they view the resource room as merely complying with regulations, a place for the children to escape, or a place to send the children when they're disruptive? What do they view as the resource room teacher's role? Do they want the resource teacher to help mainstream teachers or act as parent, psychologist, social worker, truant officer, tutor, and miracle worker? Resource teachers may ultimately need only a few of the answers, but they should know all the expectations that exist. Working successfully with students is not all that a resource teacher must know how to do.

IDENTIFYING STUDENT NEEDS

Although each child's disability has its own nuances, the general areas in which a child might have difficulty should be used as a guideline when ordering materials and equipment. The ages, grades, functioning levels in various areas, and interests of students should be known. The mainstream curriculum demands, tracking system, and supplemental services offered are important considerations. The resource teacher should also be able to approximate the number of students to be serviced, their resource room time allocation, and how the grouping and scheduling are decided.

Included here is a cursory listing of areas in which children often encounter difficulty. Its sole intent is to act as a *guide* while ordering so that important curriculum areas and learning skills are not inadvertently overlooked. This happens quite often when random ordering is done and money runs out before the pile of catalogs is studied. The levels of the materials needed in each category will depend on the range of functioning and expected levels of performance in the children to be serviced.

Reading

- sight recognition
- structural analysis
- phonics, other decoding techniques
- vocabulary
- literal comprehension
- abstract comprehension
- interpretive comprehension
- textbook and personal reading

Written Expression

- handwriting (manuscript/cursive)
- spelling
- form and structure
- grammar
- creativity, motivational techniques

Mathematics

- concepts
- computation
- application
- word problems

Auditory Skills

- discrimination
- attention
- memory
- comprehension

Visual Skills

- discrimination
- attention
- memory
- comprehension

School Survival Skills

- note taking
- homework
- study skills
- test-taking skills
- organizational skills

Curriculum (Mainstream)

- English
- Math
- Social Studies
- Science
- other

Verbal Expression

- articulation
- structure
- effectiveness of communication

Personal Development

- awareness
- interaction/behavior
- insight

BUDGET AND RESOURCES

It is important to know not only what the present money allocation is for the resource room, but also the projected budgets for the years to come. Usually, the fullest budget is for the initial establishment of the room, with subsequent years declining in the amount of money allowances. Unfortunately, no matter how well a teacher plans, expertise in choosing materials is left to on-the-job experience in a particular setting, and when the funds are needed most, they are often least available.

It is important to find out if there are separate budgets for hardware (furniture, audiovisual equipment) and software (kits, workbooks, supplies), and what is available to the resource program without new purchasing. Will the school supply desks, chairs, tables, metal closets, typewriters, file cabinets, and bookshelves? Will the audiovisual (AV) department lend cassette recorders, record players, overhead projectors, timed readers, filmstrip projectors, movie projectors, and opaque projectors? How far in advance must these items be ordered? How long can they be kept? Admittedly, it is more convenient to have this equipment in the resource room to be used at a moment's notice or at the hint of a crisis. However, if funds are low it might be wise to spend the money elsewhere and adapt to the rules of the AV department. An occasional coffee and an honest kind word to an already schedule-strained AV coordinator goes a long way toward cooperation.

What types of materials are available from the library and curriculum offices? How willing is the main office to supply erasers, chalk, pencils, pens, ditto masters, magic markers, composition paper and books, looseleaf binders, file folders, index cards, and graph paper? How much of these materials will it supply? In one school the resource teacher consumed much of the school's supply of pencils and file folders. Subsequently, this resource teacher ordered those items from the resource room's budget to ensure that the entire stock was not depleted by one person.

What materials are available from the remedial reading department, math lab, and any other existing supplementary programs? What materials are available from community and public sources, such as libraries, colleges, teacher centers, and education clearinghouses? What materials are free from agencies and industry? Some colleges offer a course in "Begging and Scavenging for Teachers." Graduates from these classes can always be identified by the multicolored sample carpet squares lining the floors and travel posters lining the walls.

TEACHING STYLES, RECORDKEEPING, AND ROOM ARRANGEMENT

Although similarities do exist among resource rooms, each situation is unique. The most important factor in this specialness is the teacher. What is known about the many different techniques and methods for educating children with learning problems will hopefully be integrated with the particular teacher's personality to form a style of teaching. This style and perspective will influence the manner in which the children will learn and the types of materials and equipment that will be used. The preference for group or individual instruction, teacher-corrected or student-corrected assignments, contract systems, and multisensory, remedial, perceptual-motor, compensatory, and/or learning strategies is among the many choices for consideration. Application of any method and strategy will depend on the students' needs. Yet, teaching strategies and materials, custom or commercial, are only as beneficial as the interchange between student and teacher.

Teaching style, along with specific factors of room size, number of children taught, and types and needs of students, will determine how the room is arranged. The resource teacher must spend time thinking about how the room should run and how the teacher envisions working with the students. The teacher should spend time daydreaming in the empty room and visualize the room with children, materials, and furniture. The teacher should also think about situations that might be encountered, such as what the various needs are and how these needs will be met. Since the room usually must accommodate a wide diversity of uses, it is useful to section the room. This is done not only for instructional purposes but also to facilitate children's needs for privacy and to accommodate their behavior and moods at any particular time.

Figure 5-1 presents an example of a possible room arrangement and is given only as a guide in demonstrating a rational approach for furniture placement. There are sections for group and individual work, use of AV equipment, storage of personal belongings, and resource room work and assignments. The location of particular areas is based on the entryway, availability of board space and electrical outlets, lighting from windows, and convenience. The teacher's desk is placed in the corner of the room

Figure 5–1 Sample Resource Room Arrangement

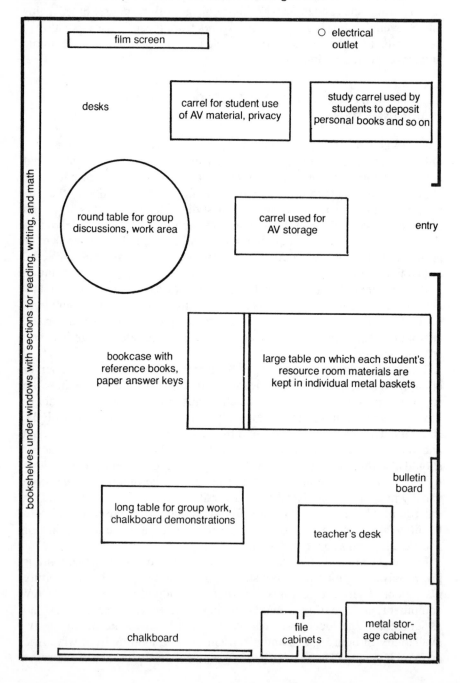

so that, if the teacher were at the desk, all of the students could be viewed. However, in a functioning resource room the most underused piece of furniture is the teacher's chair.

The type of recordkeeping will again be determined by the following factors: teaching style, student needs, room size, number of students, and administrative priorities. There are multiple possibilities for recordkeeping systems. Each variation in a method of keeping records results from a need that a previous system does not meet. Forms used can range from an accounting of what the students do to a system that incorporates assignments, accomplishments, difficulties, and newly assessed needs.

Exhibit 5-1 gives an example of a recordkeeping tool for organization and monitoring. It provides a workable instrument for lesson planning, as well as for feedback between student and teacher. This particular system allows each child the freedom to choose when he or she would like to work on particular areas, with the stipulation that all the assignments be com-

---

Exhibit 5-1 Sample Recordkeeping Form

Name: _____	Week of: _____

Resource room skill activities

Date	Skill Area	Material	What was this lesson about? What did you learn? Do you need more practice?	Teacher comments

What are you learning this week in:	What are your questions about what you are being taught?	Next test date	Grade
Math teacher _____			
Social studies teacher _____			
Science teacher _____			
English teacher _____			

pleted by the end of the week. It also provides space for monitoring work that is being done in mainstreamed classes. The children have to be taught to use this system, and, depending on the age and abilities of the particular students, they will complete the forms independently or need some teacher assistance. At the very least, this system will keep track of what assignments have been given and how well the child is following mainstream classes. Handicapped students frequently have difficulty summarizing the work they are doing both in the resource program and their mainstream classes. It has not been unusual for children to be unable to state what areas they are working on in the resource room or what section of the world they are studying in social studies. The continual use of this form will train students to focus on and recall what is being taught in school. The space for test dates and grades is an important aspect in this record-keeping system. A disabled student typically forgets or ignores a repeatedly announced test and then calls it a surprise quiz. Some handicapped students also have difficulty with realistic self-appraisal. They are often unaware of how well or how poorly they are doing in particular classes, and then they are shocked with a failure on a report card.

TEACHER-MADE MATERIALS

When resource teachers realize that particular materials need to be adapted or created to best suit a particular child and undertake the task of making something, the most important facet to this procedure is most often overlooked. This is "ego." When teachers spend time thinking about and constructing materials, they are making a choice. The preparation time is spent at the expense of something in the teacher's personal life, whether it be reading, writing a letter, visiting a friend, watching television, going out on the town, or sleeping. When the choice is made to spend time developing materials and when presenting these creations to students, there is much more at stake personally than if published materials are presented. Spending hours preparing task cards only to have them chewed up, written on, or found on the floor can be frustrating. Spending days preparing lessons that students complete, to their satisfaction, in only minutes can seem like wasted time. Not all teacher-made materials fail, and when they work well it is exciting and thrilling. Yet, when the material that has an investment of time and energy is tossed aside or completed but does not result in as much learning as was intended, it is difficult not to get exasperated with the student and personally frustrated for having "failed."

Teachers should be particular in what they make, but it is a fallacy to believe that everything must be custom-made in order to be a good teacher. Teachers are instilled with a belief that if they are good teachers and the materials are right, children will automatically learn. Therefore, if children are not learning to teachers' satisfaction, they must change, make, and remake materials and strive for perfection. When children continue not to learn, teachers again castigate themselves, take more courses, and make and remake materials. There is often such a divergence between expectations, desire to accomplish, and reality that there is no wonder teaching is a profession that is often plagued by frustration and a high burnout rate.

Teachers should conserve energy and time in order to become more effective. This is *not* to suggest that teachers become lazy or apathetic. Materials have degrees of adequacy. Weigh this against what improvements can be made, and then judge how much more appropriate it will become with revisions. A piece of material can almost always be made better, but will the improvement make a difference? If the answer is yes, then do it; if not, don't feel compelled to change it any way.

Teachers should set priorities for needs. For example, if it is important to tape social studies and science textbooks, reconstruct English curriculums using special education methods, and design more sequential and organized math problems and word problems for all the tracks in the seventh, eighth, and ninth grades, then teachers should set aside time for intense work in these vital areas. Everything cannot be accomplished at once. First, teachers should see if any of the needed changes have already been done by other teachers, curriculum departments, or services for students with learning problems. They should then decide what can reasonably be accomplished and which areas should receive attention. Student and teacher aides can be valuable in the instructional program. If all areas seem to be imperative, then teachers should pick one out of a hat and concentrate on it. Self-pacing is important, and realistic goals should be set. By the end of the first year, all of the seventh-grade intermediate tract, social studies text can be taped. With luck, next year they will be using the same text, and the teacher can move on to another area for modification.

GUIDELINES FOR ORDERING

- A list of publishers can be found in Appendix A of this book. To receive a catalog, simply send a postcard to the company or organization.
- Familiarity with particular merchandise can be obtained by attending professional conferences that offer displays of materials. Professional journals often critique new materials. Talk to other special education teachers.

- When ordering, keep in mind the interest and needs of the students (See Exhibit 5-2), because a variety of the same type and level of materials will probably be needed to accommodate children seen for consecutive years.
- Initially, it would probably be beneficial to order comprehensive kits, programs developed for a wide range of skills and levels. More specific materials can be ordered when the teacher knows the specific needs of the students in the program.
- Look for materials that have an organized, developmental system with goals specifically stated.
- When looking through materials, look for well-organized tasks that give clear directions for task completion. If the teacher cannot figure out what the child has to do without looking it up in the teacher's manual, chances are the child will be confused when attempting the task.
- Keep in mind the various aspects presented in this chapter that are outlined in Table 5-1.
- Question publishers' promises. There is no doubt that each program will have some degree of usefulness, but no program will always work with every child.

Exhibit 5–2 Sources of Free Materials for Special Educators

National Institute of Mental Health
5600 Fishers Lane
Rockville, Maryland 20857

Educators Guide to Free Materials ($12.95 + postage costs)
Educators Progress Service, Inc.
214 Center Street
Randolph, Wisconsin 53956

Handicapped Learner Materials Distribution Center
Indiana University
Audio-Visual Center
Bloomington, Indiana 47405

Table 5-1 Outline for Equipping a Resource Room

ASSESS EXPECTATIONS

Federal
State
District
Principal
Psychologist
Guidance counselor
Social worker
Teachers
Parents
Students

IDENTIFY STUDENT NEEDS

Age
Sex
Interests
Mainstream classes
Number of students
Supplemental services
Grade placement
Strengths
Weaknesses
Attitudes
Motivation
Curriculum
Scheduling
Level of classes

INVESTIGATE RESOURCES

Budget allocations:

Hardware
Desks
Chairs
Tables
File cabinets
Bookshelves
Study carrels

Software
Erasers
Chalk
Pencils
Pens

Ditto masters
Magic markers
Composition paper
Index cards
Graph paper
Stapler
File folders
Looseleaf binders
Paper clips

Equipment
Calculators
Cassette recorders
Record players
Overhead projectors

Table 5–1 continued

Room analysis	*Teaching styles/methods*
Size	Individual contracts
Shape	Group contracts
Color	Stations
Placement of windows	Teacher-centered
Chalkboard space	Child-centered
Bulletin board space	Remedial
Lighting	Compensatory
Electrical outlets	Tutorial
Film screen	Daily, weekly, monthly, yearly goals
Maps	Task cards
Flooring	Workbooks
Soundproofing	Activity pacts
Storage area	Self-directive
AV materials	Learning strategy
Films	
Tapes	
Filmstrips	*Community sources*
Records	Special education departments
	Universities
Free materials	Teacher centers
Government	Curriculum libraries
Community	
Family	

At Issue

A MANAGEMENT APPROACH FOR UTILIZATION OF INSTRUCTIONAL MATERIALS

Wilson has described the plight of many teachers who are given a budget for materials, asked to order the materials without knowledge of the student population and their needs, and consequently find a wealth of materials that remain unused or are not adequate. How then can teachers develop greater expertise in fitting instructional materials to the students' needs?

Instructional Materials for Exceptional Children by Stowitschek, Gable, and Hendrickson provides a systems approach to the task of selecting, managing, and adapting learning materials for exceptional children.[1] The authors of this text make a true statement about teacher preparation with respect to instructional technology. Teachers are not well trained in the skills of evaluating instructional materials, matching the materials to instructional goals, adapting instructional materials, and evaluating progress. Referring to a study about the perceived needs of teachers, the authors report that teachers of handicapped children say that "increased knowledge in the area of curriculum programming and materials resources" ranks high among information needed to become more effective teachers.[2] Preservice and inservice teachers frequently are required to take a curriculum course in special education. Such a course focuses on the diversity of materials available for the education of handicapped children with emphasis on topics in the students' curriculums and special techniques of instruction. Unfortunately, the assumption is too often made that teachers will be able to choose, match, and use instructional materials appropriately without additional study.

The mandate imposed by the implementation of the IEP is such that teachers must develop greater expertise in the management of materials and resources. The technique proposed by Stowitschek, Gable, and Hendrickson involves the use of a "management system" in the classroom. This technology fits well with the instructional approach that teachers adhere to when the program focuses on the development and use of each student's IEP. Criterion-referenced diagnostic tests and the specification of discrete learning objectives make such a technology possible in every special education class.

The authors of the text are correct when they say:

Teachers are in the process of assuming a different role. Instead of acting as direct interveners, they are rapidly becoming managers of instruction. The need to individualize instruction, particularly with handicapped learners, has made it necessary for teachers to seek ways other than direct minute-by-minute teacher contact to provide adequate instruction. Materials are increasingly relied upon to assist teachers. Consequently, the demands upon teachers to improve their organization and management skills has also increased.[3]

While the sophistication of this management approach is such that teachers are encouraged to study it in detail, this system is a common-sense way of specifying what many teachers may already be doing in haphazard fashion. While functioning without much deliberation can succeed in a crisis intervention program, it can no longer succeed in a complicated and demanding resource room program.

The following 11-step outline is a management system proposed by Stowitschek, Gable, and Hendrickson for the selection of materials in a special education program:

1. Examine (or develop) a scope and sequence of subjects taught in the class.
2. Inventory classroom materials.
3. Review and critique materials presently in the classroom.
4. Pinpoint material needs.
5. Complete preliminary selection: (a) study catalogs and brochures; (b) use available information retrieval system summaries; and (c) examine textual resources.
6. Determine if a purchase can be made at this point. (If yes, go to "8"; if no, go to "7.")
7. Obtain and critique actual materials: (a) through local materials centers; (b) through other teachers; (c) through loan by publisher representatives; and (d) through trial approval from the publisher.
8. Match selection information with budget information.
9. Set priorities and decide whether to purchase now or store for later reference.
10. Purchase material.
11. Store information.[4]

Ample explanation is given for each step in the system. In addition, there are sample inventory sheets and forms for materials review that make the system efficient.

When a teacher initially develops a resource program, there are four categories of materials that can be purchased:

1. instructional or core materials;
2. drill and practice materials;
3. test materials;
4. free-time activities materials.[5]

Obviously, the instructional or core materials will form the basic component of the ongoing instructional program, and this is the category that should be given highest priority when ordering. By reviewing the IEPs of the group of students to be serviced in the program, the resource teacher can set instructional priorities both in terms of curriculum areas to be taught and in terms of the students' learning styles. Once these priorities are established, the teacher can then use a variety of evaluation procedures to help choose the best instructional materials. Stowitschek, Gable, and Hendrickson suggest five types of evaluation procedures to use when examining materials. Each procedure has advantages and disadvantages, but the resource teacher should learn to develop objective criteria for materials selection. Without such criteria, choosing and purchasing materials can often be based on cursory appraisal when time is at a premium. The use of expert appraisal, marketing research, learner verification, comparative-materials research, and validation research can form the basis for a critical appraisal system.[6]

Another significant component in this materials management approach is the concept of adapting instructional materials to meet the idiosyncratic needs of the individual learner. Exceptional children may differ widely in their learning characteristics, or they may share many learning needs and styles. With the current trend toward specifying instruction based on the student's instructional needs rather than by the label of exceptionality, more commonalities among exceptional learners may become apparent. By recognizing the individuality of each learner, by specifying instructional objectives to improve areas of deficit, and by adapting existing instructional materials for each learner, a resource teacher can provide individualized instruction with a central core of similar materials.

The core of commercial materials can be adapted in a variety of ways to meet the needs of each learner. The sequence and content of instruction can be changed. Visual displays, such as are found on recordkeeping charts, can be changed for easier use. Mastery level criteria can be raised or lowered appropriately based on the learner's ability. Additional practice can be incorporated when repetition is essential. The modification of directions is often appropriate when students have difficulty understanding written directions. Adding a "warmup period" gives opportunity for learning a new instructional program. Frequently, supplementing a commercial program with appropriate teacher-made materials makes the commercial program usable and effective.

A section of the text entitled "Tapping All Resources" gives practical suggestions for avoiding waste in the purchase of instructional materials.[7] Teachers might consider these suggestions:

- collaboration with colleagues when ordering materials;
- spending the full budget each fiscal year instead of trying to carry over budgets from one year to the next;
- choosing a uniform time period each year in which to make choices about ordering materials;
- ordering materials in bulk amounts to save money;
- not buying representational materials (play housekeeping tools) when the real items are more durable and practical;
- volunteers, such as local craftspeople, to construct materials, such as counting frames;
- use of samples for a try-out period;
- attendance at conventions and conferences where materials can be sampled and then field-tested;
- soliciting public service groups, citizen groups, or local charities for contributions and aid.

In times of fiscal austerity and the consequential limiting of material budgets, teachers must make wise choices when purchasing materials. As Wilson has said in the preceding chapter, "It is much more important to know how to assess the types of merchandise needed than to be told what specific materials to order." However, "the most expensive materials . . . are those that do not work."[8] Establishing a resource program and purchasing the appropriate instructional materials are expensive. Lerner suggests that original estimates for a resource budget suggested in 1973 "should probably be doubled to take inflation into account. Thus, a minimum of $4,000 should be available, and in addition, an annual budget of $2,000 is needed to maintain the program."[9] Therefore, a management system for the selection, use, and evaluation of instructional materials is a vital addition to teacher education that too often has been ignored.

NOTES

1. Joseph Stowitschek, Robert Gable, and Jo Mary Hendrickson, *Instructional Materials for Exceptional Children* (Germantown, Md.: Aspen Systems Corp., 1980).

2. Ibid., p. 248.

3. Ibid., p. 122.

4. Ibid., p. 26.

5. Ibid., p. 96.

6. Ibid., pp. 236-38.
7. Ibid., pp. 110-14.
8. Ibid., p. 95.
9. Janet Lerner, *Learning Disabilities* (Boston, Mass.: Houghton, Mifflin, 1981), p. 424.

Chapter 6

Using Aides and Volunteers in the Resource Program

Rita Gordon

A decade ago, the responsibilities given to aides and volunteers were limited to the school halls, the lunchroom, the playground, the library, and the school health office. Today, aides and volunteers assist in all areas of the school building. They are involved in functional and diversified clerical and instructional jobs. They take part in procedural tasks that deal directly with the child's daily program and with the organization and implementation of a school day. Aides assist youngsters in every academic task.

AIDES

With aide assistance, clerical tasks can be completed in a shorter time, and the emotional, social, and academic needs of youngsters are satisfied more quickly. By fulfilling their job description, aides have freed the teacher to teach, the supervisor to supervise, and the administrator to plan, organize, and implement the school program.

Definition of an Aide

A school aide is an adult who assists in the general performance of a youngster and in the daily tasks required for the maintenance and functioning of the curriculum. The responsibilities of aides may be clerical or instructional. An aide receives a salary, works a specified number of hours in a designated time slot, receives fringe benefits, and is required to follow rules and regulations of the school district. An aide may be pretrained or learn on the job, and is responsible to a member of the school staff. Attendance at general school staff meetings may be required.

Recruiting Aides

In order to find a qualified person to assume an aide's responsibilities, recruiting must extend into a broad cross-section of the community. The following efforts have been used and have been successful:

- Posters can be placed in neighborhood stores and on appropriate bulletin boards. The information on these posters should include a job description, prerequisites for the job, number of work hours required, place of employment, name of the person to phone for an appointment, phone number, and the hours to phone.
- A publicity release can be placed in local newspapers.
- A release can be sent to local radio stations to be read periodically throughout the day as a public service.
- A release can be sent to community, fraternal, charitable, and religious organizations to be included in their bulletins.
- A staff member can attend community, religious, fraternal, and charitable group meetings. The staff member can describe the need for adult assistance in the school and seek candidates.
- Residents in the neighborhood can be recruited. Many fine aides have been brought to the school from the supermarket and the tennis court.

How to Interview

The interview should take place in a quiet area of the school building where the candidate can receive the undivided attention of the interviewer. Establishing an immediate rapport with the candidate sets the tone for the remainder of the interview. Smiles and positive remarks from the interviewer are recommended in order to encourage candidates to speak about themselves. Typical opening questions might include: "Have you worked with children before? Tell us about it." "How did you find out about our school?" "Do you have hobbies that you would like to share with the children?"

After some moments of casual exchange, direct questions related to the candidate's job should be introduced. An administrator usually interviews the candidate. Occasionally, the teacher to whom the aide will be assigned is present. The interviewers should be alert to the candidate's particular talents, skills, and especially, personality traits that reveal a devotion to children, consistency, self-confidence, patience, a sense of humor, and an ability to articulate.

All the details of the job must be discussed during the interview. A candidate should be made aware of job responsibilities, hours of work, rules and regulations, and salary and fringe benefits. The candidate should be encouraged to ask questions. It should be clearly understood at the time of the interview that inservice training will be required for school aides and that these training sessions may take place before, during, or after school hours.

Orientation and Inservice Training

On the first day of work, a school staff member should escort the aides around the school building. Special areas in the school, as well as the aides' own work areas should be identified, and they should meet other staff members. If the aide is to assume clerical duties, then the special details of the job should be worked out by another clerical aide or by the administrator. If the aide is to be involved with the instructional program, there will be materials to read and demonstrations to observe. The staff member who supervises should provide daily guidance and training.

Inservice training can be minimal or continual, but in all placements, the aide is directly responsible to an administrator, a teacher, or a clerical worker who oversees the workload.

Accountability

In a clerical position, the satisfactory completion of typing, filing, and maintaining school records should indicate whether the aide is performing the job competently.

An instructional aide assists the teacher with preparation, and works with individual children and small groups. The instructional aide should be required to keep written records of work with the children. These may be in the form of a tally sheet, a checkoff list, a log, or a descriptive anecdotal record. Instructional aides should meet regularly with their supervising teacher for guidance, direction, and support.

Clerical Aides

In most schools, specific titles, which usually identify responsibilities of the job, are given to aides. A clerical aide might assist with office duties, answer telephones, make appointments for conferences, distribute supplies, order and schedule films, duplicate materials, arrange field trips, keep attendance records, record test scores, process library materials, and maintain health records.

When details in certain areas require longer periods of time, an aide's work can be limited to just one area, for example, a media aide, an office aide, or a library aide.

Instructional Aides

These aides work as general classroom assistants, or with one child or a small group under the supervision, direction, and guidance of a teacher. Instructional aides can work in a regular classroom, a kindergarten, a special education classroom, a learning disabilities program, or a subsidized program. They may assume the responsibilities of a reading aide, science aide, kindergarten aide, resource room aid, special education aide, bilingual aide, or Teaching English as a Second Language (TESL) aide.

In each area, training and preparation is required. Through daily communication between teacher and aide, appropriate exposure to the particular needs of the children, and by observing demonstrations by skilled personnel, aides are able to produce lessons that are meaningful and significant.

VOLUNTEERS

What Is a Volunteer?

A volunteer is a person of any age who assists and facilitates in the functioning of a school program. A volunteer receives no salary, can select a convenient work schedule, receives no fringe benefits, and is required to follow rules and regulations of the school district. A volunteer may receive instruction, depending on the assignment. Although not required to attend school staff meetings, inservice training sessions are required.

Recruiting Volunteers

Recruiting people to volunteer their time in a school program requires the same efforts recommended in the section on recruiting aides, with the following additions:

- A staff member can be sent to senior citizen organization meetings to show slides of the program, discuss the need for assistance, and explain how the senior citizen is able to help.
- Community services offices who place volunteers in appropriate positions can be contacted.

- A request for assistance can be distributed to scouting groups, 4H clubs, and so on. Youngsters can perform many volunteer tasks in a school.
- A release can be sent to the local high school and college to be posted on their bulletin board.
- Ethnic clubs can be contacted within the community for bilingual assistants to work in bilingual and TESL programs.

Interviewing Volunteers

All volunteers must be interviewed by the school staff member who directs a particular program. During the interview, the staff member should look for qualities and general characteristics in the volunteer's personality that will complement the specific program. Most important are a willingness to attend inservice meetings and a commitment to maintain consistency in attendance.

It has often been asked, "How can you reject a volunteer?" Sometimes it must be done. An inappropriate person may require so much guidance and supervision that it takes time from the needs of the child. Although the volunteer may have positive personality traits or talents, particular skills may not be effective for a specific program. It is best to reject a person as soon as possible before any problems can develop. A volunteer can be overqualified as well as underqualified. Both traits can destroy a program.

Orientation and Inservice Training

Several types of orientation procedures may be effective:

- immediate participation in a placement with training on the job
- pretraining sessions where goals, objectives, and procedures are explained, and step-by-step strategies are worked out
- observations of lessons that are demonstrated by a supervisor and then a gradual involvement in a program

Volunteer Placements

Volunteers can perform clerical, instructional, and supportive roles. All volunteer assignments should utilize the skills and talents of the individual.

A weekly time schedule should be posted so that volunteers can easily identify daily assignments and independently go to that area to start working. The success of any volunteer program is nourished by its organization, direction, and consistency.

The presence of volunteers in a school provides extra hands to satisfy the immediate needs of children, extra eyes to identify children who are too shy to ask for assistance, and extra pairs of ears to listen to children express their needs.

Accountability

A volunteer can be trained to keep appropriate data in the form of tally sheets, logs, anecdotal records, or checklists. When a volunteer is able to keep these records, a teacher has more time to devote to the children's needs.

Maintaining Volunteers

A volunteer must be given the courtesy and respect that is demonstrated to all members of the school staff. Since volunteers perform important adjunct tasks in the school program, they require a place to hang their coats and a comfortable place to work. All lessons and materials must be outlined for them. When volunteers are sufficiently skilled, they can proceed with tasks unassisted.

If a request is made to secure a particular piece of material or if the volunteer mentions a lack of progress or the need for additional material, the supervisor should provide support and assistance.

If volunteers ask permission to bring in certain gift materials or cookies, they should be allowed to extend these feelings of giving. The children thrive on being remembered. Consideration should always be given to a volunteer's efforts for its positive results on the children. Supervising personnel must be available to meet volunteers' needs at all times and to provide their direction and support.

Parent Volunteers

Parent volunteers are the parents of a child within the school district. These parents want to volunteer their time during the school day for the hours their child is present in school. Parent assistance can ease clerical and classroom tasks. They may prepare and gather materials for a specific lesson, type dittos, inform other parents about classroom happenings or special classroom needs, assist on a field trip, assist in the health office, assist with lunchroom supervision, assist in the library, play a game with a child, tutor or drill a specific skill, or assist with the decoration of hall bulletin boards.

When assigning parent volunteers to a responsibility within the school, the influence that the parent's presence may have on his or her child or on other children must be considered. Children whose parents are assigned to their own room may withdraw, overreact, or resent the invasion of their domain. Other children within the classroom may not respond to someone they know who may report their behavior.

Also, there are parents within the community who would prefer that their children's behavior and academic progress remain a private matter between school and home. Therefore, when placing parents in a workable school situation, teachers must ensure that the parent volunteer's efforts will have the most value and place the least restrictions on a child's school life.

Student Volunteers

A student volunteer is a student of any age who wishes to volunteer time in a school. The student may be a member of the school or from another school, high school, or college in the area. Student volunteers may assist teachers during gym, art, and music class; listen to a child read a story; read a story to a child; help a youngster with a project; drill a particular skill; collect milk and snack money; write lessons on the chalkboard; duplicate materials; clean up areas outside of the school; tend a school garden; act as usher during a special night at school; decorate bulletin boards; operate audiovisual equipment; collect resource material from different areas in the school; or give a spelling test to another child.

The age of student volunteers, and their skills and talents, are important considerations in placing them. A third grader would be more effective in assisting a kindergarten child than in assisting a fourth-grade child. A child who tends to be bossy would achieve more positive results functioning in an independent task than in working with another child.

AIDES AND VOLUNTEERS IN THE RESOURCE ROOM

For a portion of each day, the resource room teacher provides the assessment and remedial services to learning disabled children who are in regular classes. The programs are planned to remediate disabilities. The teacher may work with one child or with a group of children from different classes. Scheduling is complex because children are removed from their classrooms in order to receive this remedial training. In planning the schedule, every attempt is made to prevent the child from missing important subject matter.

The resource room teacher is responsible for developing appropriate programs for the children assigned. When these are planned carefully, with materials identified and daily assignments placed in individual folders, a trained aide or volunteer can follow through.

An aide or volunteer assigned to this program will require prejob training, on-the-job supervision, and participation in evaluation sessions. If well trained, they are often able to move from one task to another with a minimum of supervision.

Resource Room Tasks That Aides and Volunteers Can Perform

- prepare and gather together specific materials
- process classroom equipment
- distribute materials for a particular lesson
- tutor an individual child
- help teacher maintain daily progress reports
- maintain cumulative files
- type reports
- decorate bulletin boards

The guidelines in Exhibit 6-1 and Exhibit 6-2 can be given directly to aides to assist with their job orientation.

Exhibit 6-1 Working Suggestions for the Aide/Volunteer

1. Equip yourself with the prerequisites for your assignment.
2. Be prompt for your assignment.
3. Become the children's friend by supporting their needs and developing their trust.
4. Develop some relaxation activities to keep the children motivated and involved, such as a game, a song, or taking a walk.
5. Remember the children on special days with an appropriate reference or token.
6. Help the children to keep their belongings in order and encourage them to put away any supplies they may have used.
7. Have on hand a list of alternative activities available for the times when the youngsters cannot function and will require additional support.
8. Give youngsters space and time when they need it.
9. Check with your supervisor regarding any need for change, material, or alternate program.
10. Avoid discussing a child or revealing confidential information to anyone in or out of the school.
11. Do not pry into a child's private thoughts or home life.
12. Do not give first aid or medication to a child unless assigned to do so.
13. Avoid conversations within the hearing range of children.
14. Refer parents to teachers for information regarding their youngster.
15. Follow the rules and regulations of the school and school district.

Exhibit 6–2 Activities for the Aide/Volunteer

1. Read a story to a child.
2. Listen to a child read a story.
3. Supervise a group in a subject area.
4. Prepare dittos.
5. Duplicate dittos.
6. Type reports.
7. File reports.
8. Prepare and/or organize materials for a particular subject.
9. Distribute materials.
10. Arrange field trips.
11. Accompany classes on field trips.
12. Play a game with a child.
13. Assist a child with a project.
14. Assist a child with a report.
15. Process library materials.
16. Assist a child with a research report in the library.
17. Decorate bulletin boards.
18. Write a story that is dictated by a child.
19. Write an experience chart for a reading group.
20. Role play.
21. Assist children in creating a puppet show.
22. Proctor tests.
23. Order and schedule films.
24. Show a film.
25. Supervise audiovisual squad.
26. Gather together material for a special project.
27. Dictate spelling test.
28. Flash and drill.
29. Supervise science experiments.
30. Make a specific tape.
31. Collate reading and math supplementary materials.
32. Assist music teacher by supervising chorus.
33. Assist in the health office, playground, cafeteria, office, bus duty, or halls.
34. Supervise play rehearsals.
35. Write daily progress reports.
36. Take inventories.
37. Assist kindergarten teacher.
38. Supervise the painting of a mural.
39. Organize and schedule assembly programs.
40. Construct charts, posters, and simple equipment for classroom use.
41. Maintain attendance records.
42. Record test scores.
43. Answer telephone.
44. Schedule use of media equipment.
45. Accompany child to a special program.
46. Maintain cumulative file.
47. Write lessons on chalkboard.
48. Assist with kindergarten registration.
49. Assist the art teacher in preparation of materials.
50. Work with an individual child in a specially designed remedial program.

A SPECIAL EDUCATION PROGRAM THAT IS STAFFED WITH VOLUNTEERS

In 1965, the school district in which the author is employed implemented a new and different kind of special education program for the emotionally handicapped within the district. A committee of administrators and teachers followed a research path that included visits to other school districts to observe special education programs and a study of written material on the subject of the emotionally handicapped child. Many visits later, and from the accumulation of printed matter, the committee chose the "teacher-mom" program as the format for the new class.

The volunteers are called teacher-moms or dads, and, as the name implies, they perform their responsibilities through parenting that is coupled with assisting youngsters in their school work.

Originally, the teacher-mom program was developed and used in the Elmont, New York, school district. Nictern and Donahue describe their experiences in developing and using the program in their book, *Teaching the Troubled Child.*[1] The basic philosophy of the book is still in effect in this school district.

Philosophy of Program

An individual approach to the emotionally handicapped child's needs is achieved through a relationship with an adult who is especially selected and trained to work with a particular youngster. The adult will set an appropriate role model and will provide the attention and guidance to assist the child toward an ultimate goal of stabilized behavior and mainstreaming.

Recruiting

The prerequisites to qualify a person for the volunteer position are patience, reliability, empathy, and a love for children. No prior training or education is required.

The recruiting style for these volunteers is the same as mentioned in the earlier sections of this chapter for recruiting. In addition, current volunteers often bring in members of their own families and personal friends to assist. Again, it is important to remember the goals and objectives of the program when interviewing candidates. The overqualified as well as the underqualified can jeopardize progress for these special education children.

Orientation and Training

When a candidate has been accepted for the position of volunteer in this program, the person is requested to appear in the classroom as soon as possible in order to observe the youngsters, the procedures, and the performance of the other teacher-moms. In addition, some reading matter that defines and describes the program's goals and strategies is provided. The volunteer is asked to read the given materials and to feel free to discuss them with the teacher and the consulting psychologist before or after school hours.

A candidate who has observed the program for a period of time and feels comfortable with the youngsters makes the next move by communicating with a child in conversation or by initiating a game or crafts activity. Considering these impromptu activities, the teacher gradually increases the amount of time the volunteer spends with a child.

The new teacher-mom/dad might work with a child for an hour, as a substitute for the session or as an assistant to the teacher. No definite assignment is made until the volunteer has been indoctrinated into a variety of activities and has had some direct relationships with the children.

They are required to attend training sessions. These range from full staff meetings where volunteers learn about methods and strategies, to small informal groups and individual sessions where applications are developed for the particular child.

Implementing the Program

Each child in this special education class has an IEP that is designed and written for him or her by the teacher and his or her parents. This plan is required by law. It contains academic, emotional, and social goals and objectives, and provides the structure for the child's school day. The implementation of the plan and the coordination of the child's entire program are the responsibility of the special education teacher. The volunteer assists by working with one child in a program that is derived from the IEP and the behavioral strategies that were developed at the inservice sessions.

Throughout the morning, the volunteer and the child work together in an atmosphere of support. The volunteer guides and assists the child with academic tasks, helps the child develop a feeling of responsibility, a sense of security, and finally the skills needed to function independently.

Teacher-moms and dads participate in this program either one, two, or three mornings a week from 9:30-12:30. They arrive by car, car pool, bus, bicycle, or on foot. During inclement weather the volunteer's attendance is always perfect.

Relationships

There are important considerations in selecting volunteers to work with a particular child. Just as important are the child's needs, which must be evaluated carefully in order to achieve a compatible and productive relationship. Does the child need total supervision? Can this child function independently without total supervision? Does this child require a minimum kind of direction and support?

In designing the volunteer-child union, many variables arise. The total result of each relationship depends on the appropriate volunteer assignment. At times, the relationship between the adult and child does not work well. When this happens, the supervising teacher must be alert to the signs of friction and step in quickly to make appropriate adjustments.

The teacher-mom program is a total effort that involves the entire school. Its success depends on the contribution of the volunteers, the administration, the special subject teachers, the special personnel assigned to the building, the regular classroom teachers, and the children outside this program who will be meeting the special education youngsters during lunch hour and in mainstreaming.

Since the program began, many children have profited from relationships with these special people; subsequently, they have been able to return to the regular mainstream of school.

CONCLUSION

Aides and volunteers have demonstrated their effectiveness in all areas of the school situation. They have proven to be a valuable adjunct to the classroom teacher on all levels and to the supervisory staff in every department. They have brought a new dimension into the schools.

Aides and volunteers are an available resource, willing, understanding, responsible, and devoted. Educators, aides, and volunteers together can build a school environment that will be of maximum benefit to children.

NOTE

1. George Donahue and Sol Nichtern, *Teaching the Troubled Child* (London: The Free Press, Collier-MacMillan, 1968), out of print.

At Issue

ONE TO ONE INSTRUCTION—EDUCATIONAL ASSET OR LIABILITY?

The key factor in the teacher-mom program described by Gordon is the one-to-one instruction that takes place between the student and the teacher-mom. Certainly, individualized instruction in all of its various forms has become an important and highly respected part of education at all levels of instruction. Whether it be conducted through contract teaching, team teaching, nongraded classes, open classrooms, or IEPs, the essential ingredient in individualized instruction is the development of an instructional program tailor-made for the individual child. However, individual instruction, the sustained one-to-one interaction between student and teacher, is less common. Budgetary restrictions and limited staffing have made the possibility of sustained individual instruction quite rare. The exception to this would be programs supported through special funding or the education of children through home instruction when they are unable to attend school.

Most people look at the ratio between students and teachers found in regular classes and laud the concept of one teacher and one child. The teacher-mom program builds upon this concept, and many might find this type of individualized instruction so beneficial that they may attempt other applications. However, are there unforeseen problems with one-to-one instruction that must carefully be considered before volunteers are incorporated into other special education contexts?

When the contemporary thrust in special education is toward mainstreaming handicapped children into the regular school program, could the dependent relationship, potentially developed by the use of one teacher for one child, impede the exceptional child's growth? Does this type of instructional system provide therapy rather than instruction? Is it likely that a child receiving one-to-one instruction can survive in the mainstream environment?

Gordon has described the evolution of the teacher-mom program. Some students in special education were too disabled and disruptive to function within the usual special education context. However, there was a realization that much could be derived from the social and physical contact of disabled children working in a social context. Rather than put these children on home instruction, another approach was tried. Obviously, differentiated staffing was mandatory if the plan was to work. The use of the highly trained volunteers under the direction of an astute special educator made the plan viable. The full support and commitment of the administration was necessary for the plan to become functional. Since its inception in 1965, the teacher-mom program has expanded and changed. With the recent mandate to mainstream handicapped children, much has had to be done to accelerate each child's potential date of return to the regular school setting to the greatest extent possible.

What benefits are to be derived from one-to-one instruction? Ernest Siegel, in his book *Teaching One Child: A Strategy For Developing Teaching Excellence*, summarizes the assets of one-to-one instruction:

- Lessons can be developed for individual needs.
- Teachers become intimately familiar with the child.
- Ongoing, "instant" evaluation is facilitated.
- Changes in the child's style of learning can be accommodated more easily.
- Distractibility is decreased.
- Flexibility is enhanced.
- Continuity of instruction is ensured.
- The teacher becomes more involved with the "whole" child as well as with the child's family.
- Some children function better without peer interaction.
- One-to-one instruction can enhance a child's self-concept by providing a close, personal interaction.
- Tutoring becomes therapeutic when success is achieved.[1]

However, Siegel cautions that:

It should be made abundantly clear that as each of these advantages is presented, a case is not being developed for all teachers to teach only individually; this would not be feasible, nor even desirable from any standpoint—financially, administratively, educationally.[2]

There are disadvantages that could occur under the one-to-one instructional plan. A dependent or symbiotic relationship between the teacher-mom and the student can easily develop, particularly when employing volunteer teachers who are, by role, supposed to function in some respects as surrogate parents. It is easy for these surrogates to pity the disabled youngsters with whom they are paired. This must be avoided. Preservice training and careful monitoring by the trained professional can be used to avoid this emotional trap. When feelings between the child and teacher-mom become too intense, independence is not fostered.

Gordon has established a series of strategies that facilitate a child's movement into the mainstream of the school program. Walks through the building, visits to the librarian, and sitting in on a reading class are all ways of getting past the reliance upon the teacher-mom. At times, the teacher-mom is asked to accompany the child into a mainstream class and then stay in the class to assist other children with learning activities.

In addition, some handicapped children may find that the intensity of the relationship in the teacher-mom program makes them feel uncomfortable. Such children may feel as if they are always on display or have a negative emotional reaction to working with adults. Every child is not suited for this type of one-to-one instruction.

When a child graduates from the teacher-mom program, postelementary placement can create tension. Finding such individual support for the handicapped youngster outside the elementary program is unlikely. Upon graduation from the teacher-mom program, a new placement has to be made into a self-contained special education class or into an alternative secondary program. With this in mind, all children who are part of the program need to be carefully monitored to assist their growing independence.

This program, originally designed for emotionally handicapped children, can be incorporated into other programs for atypical learners. Even minimally handicapped children enrolled in resource programs can benefit from the continuity of individual attention supplementing the work of the special educator. Implementing the program on a parttime basis, so that each child is paired with a well-trained volunteer, can create differentiated staffing in the resource program. Children encountering behavioral adjustment problems can be helped by the intensity of the personal relationship in such a program. Using trained volunteers from groups of preservice teaching candidates, eager high school students, and community residents can both facilitate the education of handicapped children, as well as break barriers created by stereotyped thinking about disabled children.

Before beginning such a program, the special educator should put ample time into the recruitment of volunteers for the program and into their preservice training. Ongoing supervision will be necessary to ensure that the program participants are conducting instruction in an appropriate manner.

While all children can benefit from sustained individualized instruction, many children may not benefit from sustained, individualized emotional involvement. However, the dictum "Each one, teach one" can be a viable approach in many special education settings.

NOTES

1. Ernest Siegel, *Teaching One Child: A Strategy for Developing Teaching Excellence* (Freeport, N.Y.: Educational Activities, 1972.), pp. 12-13.

2. Ibid., pp. 11-12.

Chapter 7

Developing an Elementary School Resource Program

Beverly Zimmerman

Resource teachers must seek out the causes of a youngster's academic failures and design a program that is commensurate with the child's particular needs. Astute classroom teachers quickly recognize symptoms in youngsters that will require further appraisal and investigation in order to determine causative factors. The teacher will take note of the youngster whose academic achievement is below the standards appropriate for the grade level. A quick examination of the permanent record card can often disclose whether or not the child has the intellectual capacity to deal with the prescribed curriculum. Other data, such as standardized tests, health records, family background, experiential opportunities, and a child's daily performance, are all helpful in assessing the child's potential for learning.

REFERRAL

When the classroom teacher has become convinced that further investigation is appropriate, there are several courses that can be taken. At a general faculty meeting, the principal and the resource room teacher may wish to discuss the program and the procedures to be followed in referring a child. These referral forms and procedures often vary from school to school or from state to state. However, they should be consistent within the school building and the school district.

An appropriate referral form that is as direct as possible is preferable. The information contained within the form should include what is legally required and is useful for program analysis and planning. A sample of one that may prove useful is shown in Exhibit 7-1.

After the child has been referred to the resource room teacher, it is a good policy to notify the parents that a referral has been made and that with a parent's consent the youngster will be undergoing a battery of tests.

Exhibit 7-1 Sample Referral Form—Resource Room Program—
Interventional Services

Referring teacher _____   Date _____
Child's name _____   Grade level _____

Check those academic areas in which the child is not functioning adequately.

1. Reading
   a) Decoding _____
   b) Comprehension _____

2. Math
   a) Concepts _____
   b) Computation _____

3. Spelling
   a) Daily written work _____
   b) Weekly tests _____

4. Spoken language _____

5. Written language
   a) Handwriting _____
   b) Expression and content _____

Check those areas in which the child appears to demonstrate inappropriate
classroom behavior.

1. Socialization with adults _____
2. Socialization with peers _____
3. Attention _____
4. Self Control _____
Additional comments _____

This eliminates the possibility of any misunderstanding on the part of the parent when the child goes home and explains that he or she was taken out of the classroom to see an adult and "play games."

A note before the testing usually reduces the anxiety level of the parents and reassures them that the school is doing everything possible to help their youngster make academic gains. Since all parents want their children to do well in school and are concerned when they do not, most of them will appreciate that their child will be given whatever additional services are needed. In addition, explaining to the parents that a meeting will be arranged as soon as the testing has been concluded to review all of the pertinent information with them and to plan an appropriate educational program for their child is advised. The posttesting meeting will provide the opportunity to gain additional knowledge about the child from the parent as well.

DIAGNOSIS AND THE CHILD

In the anxiety to do a thorough diagnosis of a child's educational needs, educators sometimes overlook one of the most important aspects of the process: that is, establishing a rapport with the youngster before any formal testing begins.

To begin, resource room teachers should not ask that the child be sent to their room, but they should call for the child personally. By doing so, the classroom teacher, with whom the child feels comfortable, can introduce the resource room teacher and make the necessary positive comments.

The short walk from the classroom to the resource room enables the diagnostician to talk to the child as one would to a new acquaintance and lessen the child's concerns. With young children, walking hand-in-hand down the hallways to the resource room provides the physical contact that helps a relationship develop. Of course, there are some children who are shy and would recoil from physical contact. The resource room teacher must be sensitive to that youngster's personal reaction and act accordingly. Much can be learned about children's abilities to verbalize and their trust in adults from a short stroll to the resource room.

When children come into the resource room for the first time with the diagnostician, it is equally important to allow them to look around the room, touch those things that "call out to be touched," explain where they will be working, and generally familiarize themselves with the physical surroundings.

Initial testing is best if it is one-to-one. This allows the diagnostician to observe the youngster's testing behavior closely, and it also enables the resource room teacher to continue to develop rapport with the child.

Children, like adults, respond best to an honest approach to a situation. Therefore, an explanation to children, regardless of their age, about why they are being tested and how a teacher hopes to help them is always appropriate. It is well worth the time spent in getting to know the youngster when the decisions for selecting materials and techniques have to be made. At the same time, the teacher is asking for the child's help. In other words, this becomes a sharing experience.

INFORMAL TESTING

With all children, but with primary children in particular, it might be best to begin with informal testing. Exhibit 7-2 gives examples of the types of questions that might be asked that would reveal a great deal of information about children and their interests that would be useful in developing a diagnosis.

The testing described in Exhibit 7-2, although simplistic in nature, is not standardized and will not result in a grade level score, a stanine, or a percentile rank, but it will provide many clues about the youngster's developmental maturity and readiness for academic tasks.

This information will either confirm or negate future test data, and will furnish a strong basis for determining the entry level of the child. In addition, most children are not threatened by these questions and seem to enjoy them because they are not pencil and paper tasks.

The tests suggested earlier can be adapted and used with children of all grade levels. Children, even in the intermediate grades, often exhibit difficulty with the days of the week, the months of the year, and spatial concepts such as "beneath," "above," and "near." A personal preference profile is certainly applicable for all children.

The informal tests suggested are by no means conclusive, but they do provide an additional way of getting to know the youngster in a nonthreatening manner. There are also many other questions that can be asked and many more tasks the youngster could be asked to perform. However, if the informal testing is too lengthy, its purpose as an initial diagnostic tool will be defeated.

FORMAL TESTING

There are a multitude of tests available for assessing a youngster's academic achievement. Some testing instruments are accepted for pre- and posttesting by certain states, and others are not. Many times the testing instruments to be used depend on their availability within the school district. Educators always appear to be looking for new and better tests, but the perfect testing instrument has never been achieved.

The tests referred to in this portion of the chapter are some that the author has found beneficial. This is *not* an attempt to describe all of the available instruments, but rather the ones that this author has found useable and informative.

The Slingerland Test of Specific Language Disability[1]

One of the purposes of this test is to ascertain the youngster's learning style. It is not a test of academic achievement, but a measure of the manner in which a particular youngster learns best. The analysis of the Slingerland Test can provide the diagnostician with the following information:

Exhibit 7–2 Informal Student Interview and Evaluation

A. A personality profile would be useful for initial motivation and would give clues to personal preferences and interests.

    1. Child's name _____

    2. Address _____

    3. Age _____ Birthday _____

    4. Brothers _____ Sisters _____(name and age)

(This will often develop into a discussion about their sibling relationships.)

    5. Favorite TV show _____

    6. The thing I like best to do on Saturday _____

    7. Favorite food _____

    8. Favorite subject in school _____

    9. Something I hate _____

B. A body awareness profile gives clues as to the child's body awareness, place in space, and ability to differentiate right from left.

    1. Can you point to:

        your elbow _____ your chin _____ your knee _____

        your waist _____ your shoulder _____

    2. Can you:

        raise your right hand _____

        raise your left foot _____

        touch your left leg with your right hand _____

        place your left hand on your head _____

        put your right hand under the table _____

                over the table _____

                beside the table _____

                near the table _____

C. A general knowledge profile gives the tester clues to the child's sequencing ability, language awareness, and auditory memory. It also suggests the reading readiness familiarization with terms such as "rhyme" and "opposite."

    1. Name the days of the week _____

    2. Name the months of the year _____

    3. Can you rhyme something with:

        cat _____ top _____ in _____ run _____

    4. Can you give an opposite for:

        hot _____ boy _____ tall _____ under _____

- The child learns best when the information is presented visually.
- The child learns best when the information is presented auditorially.
- The child is having difficulty integrating the visual stimulus with the motor output.
- The child has problems with sound/symbol associations.
- The child has not established left/right directionality.
- The child has difficulty with near or far point copying.
- The child has difficulty with visual or auditory memory.
- The child has difficulty with visual or auditory perception and/or discrimination.

Strengths

The extent of the child's difficulty can be measured. The problems can be severe, moderate, or mild depending on the combination or intensity of the errors.

The test itself is a group test and an advantage is that it can be administered without too much difficulty to a group of as many as ten youngsters. However, because observing the child's *test behavior* is extremely important, another teacher should be present to take written notes while the test is being administered. Another advantage is that the behavioral observations recorded at that time will aid in the accurate diagnosis of the child's needs. For example, observing youngsters mouthing the letters, numbers, or words they need to remember might indicate difficulty with visual memory. Chidren tracing in the air what they need to remember might need a kinesthetic approach to learning.

A third advantage of the Slingerland Test is that it has been tailor-made for children from prereading through eighth grade, as is shown in the following breakdown:

- Prereading is appropriate for kindergarten and early first grade.
- Test A is appropriate for grade one and beginning grade two.
- Test B is appropriate for grade two and beginning grade three.
- Test C is appropriate for grade three and grade four.
- Test D is appropriate for grade five and grade six.
- Malcomesius can be used for grades six, seven, and eight.

A fourth advantage to the Slingerland Test is that each booklet comes with an individual detailed analysis sheet, which helps the diagnostician to categorize the errors the youngster has made. The important thing to remember in grading the Slingerland Test is not only the number of errors the child has made, but the type of errors. An analysis of these errors will result in a much better idea of how the child learns best, and which method and materials would be most appropriate. Some children appear to be visual learners, while others learn better through their auditory channels. In some situations, the test analysis will disclose information that both visual and auditory channels appear to be impaired and another method of remediation would be more beneficial.

As a general rule of thumb, the theory for remediation is to use the child's strengths to remediate weaknesses. In other words, if the child appears to be a visual learner, new information should be presented in a visual way. That should be supplemented with auditory input. The converse is true, but for many youngsters, the multisensory approach is usually most effective.

Weaknesses of the Test

The only major disadvantage with the Slingerland Test is the marking of it. Since each error must be analyzed and categorized, it takes an inordinate amount of time to grade each test booklet. However, familiarity with the test manual and the test itself helps the experienced diagnostician to develop expertise in marking the tests, thereby cutting down the time needed for the analysis. The amount of information derived from the test is worth the management problem of marking it.

Other Formal Tests

Having established the youngster's learning style, it is crucial to learn what specific academic skills and information the child does not have. It has already been ascertained from an examination of standardized test scores and the teacher's observations that the youngster is functioning at a level that is not commensurate with his or her potential.

Since one of the most important jobs of the resource room teacher is to help the child function more successfully in the regular classroom, determining the specific skills that are lacking is essential. To do this, a battery of tests is necessary.

The Peabody Individualized Achievement Test [2]

The Peabody Individualized Achievement Test (PIAT) is an individualized achievement test administered on a one-to-one basis. It contains five subtests: (1) mathematics; (2) reading recognition; (3) reading comprehension; (4) spelling; and (5) general information.

Of these five subtests, three are the most helpful in that the tasks required relate most closely to the classroom curriculum. These three are mathematics, reading recognition, and reading comprehension.

Strengths of the PIAT. The PIAT is administered on a one-to-one basis. This allows diagnosticians to observe the children's testing behavior. They can note children's lack of confidence or impulsivity in answering questions, and can observe their thought processes with regard to their maturity.

No writing is required. This is particularly beneficial to those youngsters whose difficulty with motor output hinders their achievement on other standardized tests.

The PIAT is untimed. Children with learning disabilities often have great difficulty working under the pressure of a timed test. Often their achievement scores are depressed because they are not able to finish the test. Given added or unlimited time, many of them appear to do considerably better.

The most important advantage to the test may well be that it is nonthreatening to the children. Many of them enjoy it and consider it to be like a game.

Because the PIAT is administered on a one-to-one basis in a relaxed atmosphere with no time limit and no writing, it is a pleasant experience that the tester and the youngster share. This adds to the rapport that is so essential between the teacher and student.

Weaknesses of the PIAT. The PIAT has been criticized because it generally results in inflated test scores. Since that is an appropriate criticism, the diagnostician should not be concerned with the test scores, but with the specific skills that the child appears to be lacking.

Another disadvantage of the PIAT is that it is not realistic in terms of what a youngster can do on a group test or other standardized tests.

The third and perhaps the most valid criticism is that there is a great element of guessing in youngsters' responses. They must choose one answer from the four that are supplied. In actuality, they have a 25 percent chance of getting the answer right whether they know it or not.

Information Derived from the Test. Of the five subtests formerly mentioned, mathematics, reading recognition, and reading comprehension are of particular value. Since the time element is always a factor for the resource room teacher, it must be devoted to those aspects of diagnosis that appear to be the most essential.

The mathematics test deals primarily with math *concepts* and is especially informative. Although the manual does not indicate the need to do this, the resource room teacher should, as the test is administered, keep a record of the specific questions the youngster has missed. For example, scattered throughout the test are questions that deal with time, money and measurement. Children who exhibit difficulty with these questions often have problems in the area of spatial relations on the Slingerland Test as well. There are some questions that deal with the concept of *before* and *after*. Errors of this nature are often substantiated by difficulty on the Slingerland with directionality. In addition, by keeping an accurate record of the concepts that the child does not know, teachers can begin to teach those skills that are lacking. It is not necessary, beneficial, or expedient to devote time to teaching youngsters something they already know.

Youngsters often have a smattering of knowledge on different grade levels. Resource room teachers must be certain that they have those essential concepts and skills upon which new and more complex ideas are based. In this respect, the resource room teacher may be functioning much like the bricklayer who is called to "recement" those bricks at the foundation that are weak and wobbly, and may cause the eventual toppling of the building.

Many other testing instruments offer the reading recognition subtest, but the author prefers to use the PIAT. The format is not cluttered, as the print is large, and there is adequate space between the words presented. The words that were chosen appear to be a good sampling of words at the various grade levels. As a word of caution, youngsters who are able to identify the letters of the alphabet correctly but are unable to read any words at all are capable of achieving a reading recognition score of 1.3.

In the administration of this subtest, diagnosticians must note exactly what children say when they mispronounce the word. It is not enough to mark it wrong. The information gleaned from the mispronunciations will provide vital information about a child's process in reading words. It is also extremely important to encourage children to try to pronounce the word rather than to say simply, "I don't know it."

Children who say "father" for "feather" are indicating that they do not know the "ea" vowel combination, which may result in a short "e" sound. Children who read the word "fist" instead of "first" illustrate a lack of knowledge of the "r" modified vowels.

The third subtest of the PIAT that the author uses is the reading comprehension test. This is the least informative; however, there is some valuable information to be derived from it.

The test requires the child to read a sentence silently just once, and then select a picture, from four that are given, that illustrates the sentence best. The PIAT manual gives explicit instructions as to where to begin the testing and at what point to terminate it.

The reasons this test is somewhat inadequate are as follows:

- The child has a 25 percent chance of guessing the correct picture.

- Some children, particularly those with visual perception problems, have difficulty interpreting the pictures accurately.
- The comprehension tasks that the youngsters are required to do on a daily basis and on most other standardized tests are much more demanding. They invariably involve paragraph rather than sentence reading, and the comprehension skills they test usually pertain to literal, vocabulary, main idea, and inferential questions.
- This subtest does not help the diagnostician determine the specific comprehension skills the child has difficulty with.

The logical comments on the basis of these criticisms of the test would be "Why use it? What can be learned from the administration of this subtest?"

The reading comprehension test will confirm or negate the fact that the child is having comprehension difficulties. It will result in a comprehension grade level that can be compared with the reading recognition test score. A considerable disparity between these two test scores will provide the diagnostician with other key information.

If the tester is willing to take the time to go over the questions that the youngster missed with the child after the conclusion of the formal administration of the test, an understanding of the incorrect responses can be achieved. Also, this test is an easy one for the teacher to give and an enjoyable one for the child to take.

If there is a considerable disparity between the reading recognition subtest score and the reading comprehension test score (one year or more), one of many things may be indicated, including the following:

- Limited vocabulary—This is sometimes due to a bilingual environment or to a poor socioeconomic background where cultural experiences have been limited.
- Emotional interference—The child, as he or she reads silently, is not concentrating on the written material at all, but is preoccupied with his or her own thoughts, and consequently is unable to process the meaning of the written word.
- Distractibility—Although the child is able to decode words in isolation with some ease, he or she is unable to decode the important or key words in a sentence.
- Visual perception—The youngster has difficulty interpreting the pictures. This is sometimes due to figure/ground problems.
- Memory—The youngster has a poor short-term memory and has forgotten what was read by the time he or she is shown the pictures. With other standardized tests, the child can refer back to the printed matter.

Whatever the case may be, a poor score on the reading comprehension test and a great disparity between the two test scores should act as an alarm to the astute diagnostician, and further testing in this area should be considered.

Another test, the *Multiple Skill Series Placement Test,* will pinpoint specifically four different types of comprehension questions.[3] They are main idea (best title), literal comprehension, inferential comprehension, and vocabulary meaning. On the basis of the results of this test, the diagnostician is then able to select specific skill builders that deal with a particular skill for the child to work with. In addition, the resource teacher can place the youngster for instruction into one of the Multiple Skill Series booklets offered by the same publishing company.

Wide Range Achievement Test[4]

The WRAT includes spelling, mathematics, and reading recognition subtests. Although this test is not accepted for pre- and posttesting by New York state for its funding programs, it is a valuable diagnostic tool in the areas of spelling and mathematics computation.

The strengths of the WRAT include the following:

- This is a group test and is easy to administer.
- The testing time is short, and the grading is simple.
- The spelling portion of the test is particularly good because, when analyzed properly, it will often confirm the same difficulties that were apparent on the PIAT reading recognition test.
- Unlike the PIAT, the mathematics portion of the test deals with computation skills. It consists of a series of examples in graduated order of difficulty. The children are given ten minutes in which to complete the examples that they can, and it becomes quite evident where their computational skills "break down."

The weaknesses of the WRAT include the following:

- The reading recognition portion has a format that can be confusing to the child because of the physical closeness of the words.
- The spelling test, like many other spelling tests, requires youngsters to write the words in a list.
- The mathematics test is criticized because, although there are examples in graduated order of difficulty, there is usually only one of a particular type. Consequently, youngsters who may know how to do subtraction with exchanging may get that example wrong because of a careless error, for example, $17-9 = 9$.

If resource room teachers are dissatisfied with the information ascertained from the WRAT in mathematics, they may supplement that testing with the Key Math Diagnostic Arithmetic Test.[5]

The Key Math, like the PIAT, is an individualized test and will result in specific information about the child's needs in the following areas: numeration, fractions, geometry and symbols, addition, subtraction, multiplication, division, mental computation, numerical reasoning, word problems, missing elements, money, measurement, and time.

SUMMARY SHEET

The time available for testing and diagnosis, the tests available within the school, the individual needs of the child, the requirements of the state and local school district, and the mandates of funded programs are all factors in determining how extensive a battery of tests should be. Too much unnecessary time can be spent on testing and never really get to the remediation that is most important.

A thorough evaluation of all of the test data that have been accumulated on each child should result in a summary sheet, which the resource room teacher should file for repeated reference. The summary sheet can also be used when needed for parent and teacher consultations. A sample of a summary sheet which could be utilized in that manner is shown in Exhibit 7-3.

SCHEDULING

One of the most difficult tasks for a resource room teacher is scheduling the youngsters. There are many factors that must be taken into consideration.

Grouping

Some children benefit most from the remedial portion of the program if they are seen on a one-to-one basis only. Others function well in a small group (approximately five) made up of their own peer group. There are some youngsters who are able to function well in a large group (approximately seven to ten). Some children work well with interage groups where the older children act as models for the younger ones. The size of the group, the ages of the youngsters, and the emotional complexion of the group need to be considered when preparing schedules.

Exhibit 7-3 Sample Summary Sheet

Child's name _____ Age _____ Grade _____
Current teacher _____ I.Q. _____
Standardized achievement test scores   Reading _____
Date _____   Math _____
Slingerland Test   Date _____
  Number of errors _____
  Learning strengths   Auditory _____
    Visual _____
  Weaknesses _____
Peabody Individual Achievement Test   Date _____
  Reading recognition score _____
  Needs _____
  Reading comprehension score _____
  Needs _____
  Math concepts score _____
  Needs _____
Wide Range Achievement Test
  Math computation score _____
  Needs _____
  Spelling score _____
  Needs _____
Materials to be used
  Learning style _____
  Reading recognition _____
  Reading comprehension _____
  Math concepts _____
  Math computation _____
  Writing _____

Frequency of Contact

This is often determined by state or federal regulations if the resource room is being funded. It must also be based on the individual child's needs. Even if the individual school district is funding the program, rules governing frequency of contact may have to be adhered to. Resource room teachers, as they observe youngsters at work in the remedial setting, should have the benefit of flexibility, and should adjust and readjust the frequency of contact as the need arises.

Physical Facilities

The size of the groups and the possibility of having two small groups working simultaneously should be determined by the size of the resource room and the availability of appropriate furniture and materials.

Other Services

Many youngsters who participate in remedial sessions in the resource room are multideficited. They may require the help of a speech or hearing teacher in speech articulation or language development. Coordination of scheduling for services is essential so there is no conflict.

Special Supplementary Services

In many schools each youngster is scheduled for physical education, art, and music with his or her own class. Since many youngsters regard these periods as "treats" and feel punished if they miss them, scheduling the children into the resource room so that they do not miss their special classes is advised.

Lunch

The children should have their lunch period with their class and their peer group because it is a socialization time. Working around their class programs with this in mind is essential.

Religious Released Time

In some schools children are released for religious instruction once a week. They leave the school building one hour before the end of the school day. In deciding an appropriate schedule for a child, this also must be taken into consideration.

Classroom Teacher's Cooperation

The cooperation of the classroom teacher is the most essential aspect of the scheduling dilemma. Since children will be absent from their room for approximately 45 minutes to an hour, they will miss classroom instruction. Consequently, while children are in the resource room receiving the remediation they need in reading, math, or related language arts skills, they may be missing a lesson on explorers, state history, or the solar system.

If a child is not able to read, write, or do basic numbers, the social studies and science programs are secondary in importance. In other words, emphasis must be placed on the basic skills so that children will have the tools by which to study social studies and science, or whatever else they may choose. These are the survival skills.

Most classroom teachers agree and are willing to accommodate the child's loss of classroom instruction in other ways and at other times. Realistic goals for these special youngsters must be set to satisfy their priority needs.

In order to disrupt the classroom teacher's program as little as possible, children who are receiving special services should all be excused at the same time. For example, children going to the resource room for remediation, others going to the speech or hearing teacher, and others attending corrective programs should be scheduled simultaneously, if possible, so that there is not constant movement in and out of the classroom.

Once the preliminary schedule is prepared, it is a good idea to discuss it with the classroom teachers for their input. Revisions may then have to be made to accommodate classroom instruction time. For example, in some primary grade classrooms, large blocks of time are necessary for whole class instruction in reading or language arts.

With all of these considerations, it is no wonder that scheduling is perhaps the most difficult chore of the resource room teacher, regardless of the grade level of the youngsters being serviced.

A METHOD FOR SCHEDULING

Attempting to create a resource room schedule that considers all of the factors mentioned and many others that crop up, for example, a child's instrumental music instruction time, is like playing a game of checkers, but it can be done. The following six-step method may help:

1. Set up a chart of the days of the week that school is in session. It should resemble a game board.
2. Divide the days into time periods. The length of these periods will vary depending on individual schools and funding mandates.
3. Prepare small scraps of paper with the children's names as well as the names of the teachers.
4. Checking the times that a certain class is having physical education or music or art, place the scrap of paper in what would appear to be a good time slot. Do not attach it, as it may have to be moved around several times before an appropriate slot is found.

5. Using this same procedure, position each small group or individual child until the schedule appears to be workable.
6. Check the proposed schedule with the classroom teachers to verify its mutual convenience.

Scheduling changes are often made during the school year as circumstances warrant, and the needs of the individual youngsters also change. It is important to be consistent, however, for the sake of the children. Those with learning problems benefit from structure, and it is easier for them to remember their scheduled time and become responsible for keeping their resource room appointments if there is as little variation as possible.

In addition to notifying the teacher of the resource room schedule, the children should have a copy of the time they will be expected. The child's schedule written on a 3 × 5 card and taped to his or her desk becomes a visual reminder. For younger children in the earlier primary grades who are unable to tell time, a clock drawn on a card as a reminder serves the same purpose.

Without these visual reminders, much time is wasted waiting for children who forget to come or for teachers who are so busy with their daily class routines that they forget to send the children. The time arranged for remediation is too precious to be wasted having to call the classroom or go for the child.

At the beginning of the school year, until routines are established, a certain amount of reminding is expected, but as the year progresses, a well-run resource room program has children reporting for their remedial sessions as scheduled.

REMEDIATION

The subject of remediation is a lengthy one. Articles, chapters, and books have been written on this subject alone. There are a myriad of materials, methods, and techniques being used. However, none can guarantee success.

When dealing with human beings who have varying moods, emotions, intellectual potentials, levels of motivation, interests, states of health, home problems, peer pressures, and so on, all educators can hope to do is motivate them to want to learn and then make learning as pleasant and varied an experience as possible.

The atmosphere of the resource room is the key to its success. It should be a place in which the children feel comfortable and in which they can ask questions freely; touch the varying displays; do the kinds of projects that the classroom teacher cannot find the time for, lie on the floor if they feel so inclined when they are reading, sit in comfortable, living room chairs; play and create their own games; work with materials that are different than the ones they use in the classroom; use private listening stations; and have freedom of movement. All of this can be achieved with structure and routine.

The diagram in Figure 7–1 is based on having a full-sized classroom. However, many of the ideal criteria for a resource room layout will be dictated by the amount of physical space available.

The diagram in Figure 7–1, although hardly mandatory for a resource room, represents a workable model. A_1 and A_2 represent crescent-shaped tables for instruction of small groups. The advantage to this type of table is that the resource room teacher, who often sits in the center of the U (indicated by a T or an X) is within arm's-length of every child in the group. The teacher is able to reach over to the youngster to help or simply encourage or praise for the work the child is accomplishing. The work that each child is doing is easily seen by the resource room teacher from the center of the U. Should he or she choose to do so, the teacher can also be positioned outside the U and provide additional instruction, directions, or aid to any child.

The listening station (B) is reserved for those children who may be working with a tape recorder and a book, or a tape directing them to answer questions on a worksheet.

Youngsters should be given opportunities for "hands on" experiences. The project table (C) should contain displays, which are frequently changed, of things that interest children. Whether a shell collection, a rock collection, a group of puzzles or games, a collection of baseball cards and figurines, racing cars, or some Halloween masks are displayed, the project table should reflect the things that children like, and that are topical, are seasonal (like leaves), and are touchable. Many language arts lessons evolve from the project table displays.

The living room (D,E,F) is perhaps the most enjoyable section of the resource room. It consists of an area rug, three large overstuffed chairs, and a round table. Some children prefer to do their independent silent reading here. It is also the space used by some of the youngsters to engage in instructional games. It is not unusual to see two or three children sprawled on the rug reading a book. The living room is a comfortable place and most reminiscent of home.

Boxes of materials (G) provide the backbone of the instructional material. Specific skills in each subject area are categorized and alphabetized in these brightly colored boxes. As a needed skill is recognized, the resource room teacher goes to the appropriately marked box and finds

Figure 7–1 Sample Resource Room Layout

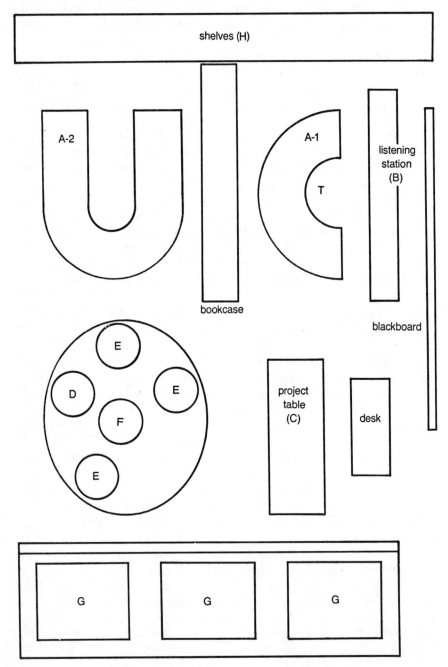

materials that will help to review those things that will be taught. For example, if a group of youngsters is having difficulty with long vowels, the resource room teacher can simply locate the duplicating materials that deal with that subject. The needed material is readily at hand and is continually being added to and improved upon.

The file folders in each box are color-coded in addition to being alphabetized and categorized. Consequently, all red folders deal with reading skills, yellow ones contain math worksheets, and the green folders hold materials concerned with the holidays, seasons, and so on.

Each youngster who works in the resource room has an individual work folder (H). Independent work materials are kept in these. In addition, a log is kept (stapled on to the folder cover), which is a record of the work the child has completed or is currently assigned. With a little more than a glance, the resource room teacher and the child each have a visual record of what has been accomplished and what remains to be mastered.

SUMMARY

This chapter has been devoted to the practical problems of developing an elementary resource room. Referral, testing, scheduling, and remediation have all been discussed at varying length. However, regardless of the materials available for testing and remediation and the physical composition of the resource room, the moving force, which will ensure success, is the resource room teacher. The resource room teacher must be compassionate, dedicated, aware of and sensitive to the needs of the children, and have the capacity to empathize with their struggle. These innate qualities are of paramount importance if the children are to have their self-esteem nurtured and restored, enabling them to grow not only academically but as human beings.

NOTES

1. Beth Slingerland, *The Slingerland Test of Specific Language Disability* (Cambridge, Mass.: Educators Publishing Service, Inc., 1967).

2. Lloyd M. Dunn and Frederick C. Markwardt, Jr., *The Peabody Individual Achievement Test* (Circle Pines, Minn.: American Guidance Service, Inc., 1970).

3. Richard A. Boning, *Multiple Skills Series Elementary Placement Test* (Baldwin, N.Y.: Lowel and Lynwood, Ltd., 1978).

4. J.F. Jastak, S.W. Bijou, and S.R. Jastak, *The Wide Range Achievement Test* (Wilmington, Del.: Guidance Assoc. of Delaware Inc., 1978).

5. Austin J. Connolly, William Nachtman, and E. Milo Pritchett, *Key Math Diagnostic Arithmetic Test* (Circle Pines, Minn.: American Guidance Service, Inc., 1976).

BIBLIOGRAPHY

Searls, Evelyn F. *How to Use WISC Scores in Reading Diagnosis.* Newark, Del.: International Reading Association, 1975.

Turnbull, Ann P., and Schulz, Jane B. *Mainstreaming Handicapped Students: A Guide for the Classroom Teacher.* Boston, Mass.: Allyn and Bacon, Inc., 1979.

Wiederholt, J. Lee; Hammill, Donald D.; and Brown, Virginia. *The Resource Teacher.* Boston, Mass.: Allyn and Bacon, Inc., 1978.

At Issue

THE PROCESS OF SCREENING, EVALUATING, AND DIAGNOSING STUDENTS WITH SPECIAL NEEDS

Simon (Chapter 3) and Zimmerman (Chapter 7) have both discussed processes of referral and assessment for individual children employed in two different school districts. An overview of a model of screening, evaluation, and diagnosis should prove helpful in formulating procedures for accepting children into resource programs.

Before decisions can be made about providing services for individual children in a resource program, it is necessary to ascertain which children are legally eligible for special education services if the resource program is to be maintained through special education funding. Determining eligibility is contingent upon rules and regulations that have been translated by the individual states based on principles of PL 94-142. Copies of this information can be obtained from the state education department or from a local education agency. Any policy on admission into a resource program must be consistent with policies developed at the state and local school district levels.

The first level of assessment within a student population is often referred to as screening. A New York state bulletin for administrators defines this level of assessment as "a preliminary method of distinguishing from the general population those pupils who may possibly have a handicapping condition or those who may possibly be gifted."[1] Screening programs should be developed to provide preliminary information about a child's development in the following areas:

- *Physical development*—Appraisal should include tests of a child's vision and hearing, as well as a review of the child's health history and immunizations. A physical examination conducted either by the family physician or a physician appointed by the school district may be required.

- *Cognitive development*—Appraisal should indicate whether or not the child is capable of functioning at an age-appropriate level in terms of verbal and nonverbal skills, such as reasoning, concept formation, problem-solving, and so on.

- *Language development*—Appraisal should include both receptive and expressive language skills to determine the child's ability to process spoken language.

- *Articulation skills*—Appraisal should determine the child's ability to reproduce sounds and words adequately, keeping in mind that articulation ability is affected by such factors as developmental readiness and sociodialect.
- *Motor development*—Appraisal should include an evaluation of both gross motor skills as well as fine motor skill development.
- *Achievement*—Appraisal should include an evaluation of achievement or readiness for learning in such key academic areas as language arts (particularly reading) and mathematics.

Screening instruments are decided upon at a district-wide level or may be mandated by the state education department. The contributions of an interdisciplinary team of specialists within the school district are necessary when the state allows the local school district to choose screening instruments. Screening programs are most often conducted at the child's first admission into the school system, and then periodically through the grades. In addition to other means of obtaining information, the completion of a detailed parent/guardian questionnaire is most helpful when the child is first registered for school.

The next level of assessment may be referred to as evaluation that involves "a comprehensive assessment of the pupil's abilities."[2] Students suspected of possessing handicapping conditions are referred to a central committee, which will decide about the need for further study of the individual case. To make this decision, a multidisciplinary team is convened at the district level, usually consisting of educators (administrators and teachers), medical specialists, psychologists, social workers, speech/language specialists, physical therapists, vocational therapists, and parents. Referral of children to this committee can come from a variety of sources. Those persons who review the gross data obtained from district-wide screening may make referrals along with parents, administrators, classroom teachers, or other interested agencies. Most districts find that conducting inservice education is necessary to inform classroom teachers of behavioral characteristics that may indicate handicapping conditions that are not overt. The committee decides if there is reason to assess an individual child further and then refers the child to a diagnostic team usually located in the school that the child is or will be attending. Priority is supposed to be given to those children with the most severe indication of exceptionality or to those children who have received no special services in the past.

The diagnostic team assigned to study the child further will be asked to describe in detail the child's individual pattern of aptitude, performance, and learning processes. Upon completion of this diagnosis, the information will be returned to the central committee, which is then charged with deciding if the child should be classified as needing special education. The decision about the appropriate educational placement and the formation of an IEP is the responsibility of the central committee. The writing of the IEP is most likely delegated to the professional or group of professionals most familiar with the child's learning strengths and weaknesses. Before diagnosis takes place, the parent or guardian is asked to consent to the process and is then consulted again when a decision has been made about educational placement alternatives and the formation of the IEP.

PL 94-142 enumerates the rights of due process for the parents or guardians of children undergoing the evaluation procedure. The due process that ensures the child's rights includes:

- written permission from the parent/guardian to consent to evaluation;
- parent/guardian right to give or withhold permission for placement in a school program;
- parent/guardian right to examine all school records pertinent to the child's evaluation;
- parent/guardian right to request an independent evaluation when there is no agreement with the district evaluation;
- parent-guardian right to request an impartial hearing with parent/ guardian representatives present;
- parent/guardian right of appeal to the state department of education and, ultimately, to the civil court system.

This elaborate model of screening, evaluation, and diagnosis is necessary to ensure that children in need of special education services can be appraised objectively with equal opportunity and protection under the law. Decisions regarding which children are to be admitted to a resource program are obviously much more complicated and elaborate than an individual teacher subjectively deciding which children warrant support services.

In 1976 the United States Office of Education projected that of the total population of handicapped children from ages 6-19 only 58 percent are served.[3] Diligent attention on the part of local school districts is mandatory if all children in need of special education are to receive appropriate services.

NOTES

1. *Screening in New York State* (Albany, N.Y.: State Education Department, Office for Education of Children with Handicapping Conditions, August 1980), p.1.
2. Ibid., p. 5.
3. B. Marian Swanson and D. Willis, *Understanding Exceptional Children and Youth* (Chicago, Ill.: Rand McNally, 1979), p. 11.

Chapter 8

Developing a Junior High School or Middle School Resource Program

Sheldon Horowitz

The adolescent population of handicapped students has only recently been brought to the attention of the public and professional communities. These students are perhaps the most diverse in characteristics and the most deficient in regard to immediate needs of all handicapped learners. Their poor performance in school might be attributed to any number of causes.

Numerous attempts to improve instruction for problem learners at the elementary school level have provided the teaching community with a plethora of literature regarding classroom management, implementation of instruction, and communication with parents, teachers, and students for optimal support in school. Today's adolescent with learning problems may have been yesterday's child in need of "special" attention, or simply one who could not adjust to a variety of teaching and management techniques over a period of five or six years. There are those who suggest that environmental and nutritional factors hamper certain types of learning, and that these factors, in combination with social, familial, and academic pressures, contribute significantly to the likelihood of failure in school. Still others attribute many of the difficulties evidenced by adolescent students to the nature of "communication" in society, namely, an often overwhelming dependence on spontaneous signals, spoken or depicted in dramatic sequence, as opposed to being represented in written form. This, in turn, presents barriers to students who are expected to master grammatical and syntactical writing, command expansive (and ever-growing) vocabularies, and demonstrate the ability to integrate these two skills with consistency, accuracy, and ease.

The incoming junior high school student is presented with an especially difficult challenge.[1] Adjusting to a departmentalized schedule of classes, establishing rapport with a variety of teachers and school related personnel, and exploring new peer relationships are compounded by an almost instinctive need to redefine parental and family ties and responsibilities. Young adolescents are also faced with the circumstance of a changing physiological status, which, aside from imposing new rules for social acceptability, necessitates a deepened awareness on the part of each individual regarding his or her own personal, social/emotional, and sexual self.

Concerned individuals might further their understanding and appreciation of a unique population of students, their special learning needs, and issues related to optimal and maximally effective service delivery options by reading this chapter. Familiarity with the resource room model, behavior-management techniques, writing educational and behavioral objectives, and planning and implementing instruction for adolescents would be beneficial if not essential for the reader to find this chapter useful and informative.

THE JUNIOR HIGH SCHOOL STUDENT

The student population at a junior high school often comprises children from a number of elementary placements. Students who completed part of their elementary school careers in programs outside their present school district or those who attended private and parochial schools converge to form a single body of learners who have different expectations of the upcoming semesters. Some students have always been high achievers and have been able to remain at the top of their class academically and perhaps socially. Others have been accepted by their teachers, parents, and peers as slow learners who have difficulty scoring well on standardized tests or in class measures of daily performance. Some are known as the best dressers, the best atheletes, the ones with the best senses of humor, or the ones who never speak out in class. Given all of these considerations, students who enter a new learning environment have the opportunity to redefine themselves as students and individuals, selecting new friends and exploring new avenues of expression. The student who was reputed to be the class "troublemaker" might now be identified as a potential candidate for referral to the school screening committee for the handicapped.

The incoming junior high school student is faced with a great many challenges at the onset of the school year. New administrative personnel and new procedures for school behavior and discipline can be sources of distress to the child who only a few months before had been a "big fish in a small pond"—a graduating sixth grader with a large body of envious younger students as onlookers. The new demands regarding the establishment of productive working relationships with guidance personnel, speech and language therapists, social workers, psychologists, and so on are compounded by the numbers of teachers with whom each student must maintain working rapport.

As each school district decides its own internal policies regarding curriculum and formal instruction, so too do individual teachers apply their own skills in the personalization and delivery of content area information. Students who previously have been exposed to any number of teaching situations (open classroom, team teaching, units/pods, departmentalized instruction, special/segregated classes, grouping) with emphasis on any number of instructional approaches designed for initial instruction are now faced with new classroom environments, unfamiliar instructional procedures, and supportive materials that may be vestiges of years past, not having been revised or replaced for a period of five or ten years. As classroom teachers are not often able to familiarize themselves with student records before the beginning of the school year, preparation of material for these incoming students (in anticipation of varying independent skill levels) is both time consuming and frustrating, especially in light of what appears to be a decline in basic skill performance (reading, writing, and simple arithmetic computation).

Students are faced with a vast and increasing body of knowledge during their early school years as a result of their exposure to television, radio, film, and the theater. They are better able today, in a society of advanced technology and rapid communication, to speak peripherally about any number of current events and personal interest issues, perhaps to a greater extent than students of past generations. Yet there is an undeniable trend toward automation and capsulization in the world today. This pervades education as well as the entire basis for oral and written expressive language.

Competency training in basic life skill areas (that is, reading advertisements, keeping and balancing a checkbook, and so on) has recently surfaced as a priority for students in secondary placements. Its importance is evidenced by legal precedents established at all levels of government for the construction and mandated administration of both regular and preliminary forms of Basic Competency Tests (BCT). Students are now being asked to demonstrate familiarity with and, in some cases, mastery of information that may or may not have been taught or practiced on the elementary level. As a result, a portion of incoming seventh graders must either be afforded direct supplementary instruction in areas of deficit or be subjected to the likelihood of academic failure early in their secondary school careers.

Familial concerns should also be considered when speaking about the junior high school learning disabled child. As is the case in many families, jealousy and competition among siblings can contribute to a student's behavior and academic performance in school and at home. In a family where an older brother or sister might have been an "A" student, the exceptional learner is confronted not only with the high expectations of parents and teachers but also with the frustration that accompanies knowing that he or she is being compared with others and not being evaluated for his or her own efforts and individual merit. This situation results in slow and often painful progress, as there are few if any models within the family structure from whom general conceptual and behavioral patterns and information may be learned.

Parent expectations about the nature and quantity of work presented in school can also lead to difficulties. Some parents advocate an "action-consequence" policy, whereby the efforts and quality of work submitted determine a student's final or cumulative grade. The ill effects of such a system for learning disabled and other handicapped students are obvious. Without some person or program to serve as intermediary, editor, proofreader, or simply overseer, work assignments might be completed improperly; spelling, syntactical, and organizational errors might appear with such frequency as to detract from the content of the work; and so on. Other parents might realize their child's frustrations and accept the responsibility of ensuring that assignments are completed properly. The consequence of this arrangement may very well be seen in the student who submits wonderful homework assignments and beautiful projects, maintains an impeccable notebook with pages numbered and dated, but cannot pass a test in class or answer questions when called upon by the teacher.

These examples are presented to clarify and illustrate rather than point an accusing finger at any one group of parents or teachers. Children who have experienced repeated academic failure may tend to be passive or assertive in their work or study habits. Parents of students with learning problems may also exhibit any number of responses in reaction to their child's need for help. Whatever the case, having parents, teachers, and the student meet to discuss the underlying reasons for difficulty is essential for setting the stage for remediation and the beginning of an independent and productive junior high school career.

The incidence of single parent homes is common within many communities, and a considerable number of children in these situations experience difficulties both in regard to their social and interpersonal relationships with teachers and peers, and in the completion and submission of work in school. These students most often remember the missing parent and may resent or at least show signs of detachment from a stepparent or substitute adult living with them at home. Students from broken homes may also have been forced to leave one or more schools before arriving at their present placement, each time being subjected to new teachers, new rules, a new neighborhood, and so on. Information about past school involvement may be difficult to obtain, and when available, it may be of little use in determining how best to help the student in need of support. It is especially difficult to accumulate accurate and comprehensive information on a student when, for example, one district acknowledges the need for support and meets that need by classifying the student as handicapped, while another district denies support services and provides a less appropriate tutorial service on a biweekly basis.

Sometime during the junior high school years, students begin to show a heightened awareness of their changing physical status. Physical maturation in boys may be somewhat slower than in girls, but there is little doubt that the combined effects on boys and girls causes distraction. Dating, concentrating on the latest fashions in clothing, keeping up with the rapid changes in the music world, a sometimes extensive introduction to and overindulgence in drugs, and the beginnings of what might be called exploratory sexual behavior become major factors in the assessment of students to determine why they are experiencing difficulty in school.

For the handicapped adolescent, a junior high school environment can be especially troubling. There are new social pressures that compound academic difficulties that already are a source of tension. Students often confess that they are concerned about "being cool" in the seventh grade when they know that the work is going to be harder than in elementary school. Students also begin to develop a certain amount of independence from their parents; this usually is accomplished by taking a job after school or on weekends. The effort expended delivering papers or playing ball with a community league can distract from both the student's incentive to complete school assignments and the attention with which the assignments should be completed. The junior high school student who experiences learning difficulties may also experience problems interacting with teachers and peers. Teachers are often blamed for picking on a student when all they have done is call on the student in class. The student who is not prepared to answer or who did not understand the question but is afraid to ask for it to be explained can easily be misrepresented as being disinterested or lazy. Some of these students are likely to blame teachers for their poor performance, while others are likely to blame themselves, wondering why they cannot think as quickly as their friends or generate correct work as efficiently as other students in their classes.

Repeated school failure may result in problems with social adjustment and social perception, self-concept, motivation, appropriate behavioral modeling, familial tension, and even delinquency. (Although attempts to correlate learning disabilities and delinquent behavior have been made, this premise has neither received notable attention nor been substantiated in the available literature current to the area of learning disabilities and adolescence.) These combined factors often persist over an extended period of time and create a confused and difficult-to-decipher performance profile to classroom teachers and educational-diagnostic personnel. Often, the student who initially experiences academic difficulties that are ignored or improperly identified, will show a type of masking effect that intensifies over time, making it increasingly difficult to plan intervention strategies. Patterns of noncompliant, uncooperative, and generally resistant behavior often result in students who are mislabeled as emotionally disturbed or behaviorally disordered. This maladaptive behavior may well be the outcome of a student's attempt to hide his or her problems or deny that there would be any benefit from added attention in a supportive setting. There is some question as to how the exceptional adolescent who demonstrates overtly inappropriate behavior in school should be helped. Should the emphasis in programming be more academic than behavioral, thereby suggesting that once a student can complete work assignments independently behavior will improve? Should programming assume a more behavior management perspective with emphasis directed toward improved behavioral controls and then later the remediation of deficit academic skills? Once this type of student is identified, behavioral programming usually takes precedence over remedial or supplemental academic instruction. This unavoidably detracts from the extent to which formal content area material can be emphasized, which slows student progress.

The decision to follow either of these approaches should be made only after the individual student, the learning environment (inclusive of staff, administration, scheduling), and the feasibility for consistency throughout the school day and extending into the student's home are carefully evaluated. An effective program of academic remediation will almost always lead to improved student behavior. The specification of behavioral objectives that would help these students identify and avoid potential conflicts, and assist classroom teachers in overseeing the fulfillment of behavioral goals over a period of time is strongly recommended.

POSTELEMENTARY SCHOOL ADJUSTMENTS

As mentioned earlier, perhaps the greatest change a student must face when moving from an elementary to a secondary school is the departmentalization of classes. Whereas the elementary school experience fostered a sense of group dependence and security, the junior high school integrates students from different elementary schools, with different skills, interests, and experiences, into classes that last for approximately 40 minutes. After these classes, students move independently to their next scheduled class with an entirely new selection of students and a different teacher. Given the child who cannot find the way back to a locker, cannot locate the gym, does not know how to read a schedule that includes alternate day classes, has difficulty changing focus from one subject to another (often in as little time as three minutes, the time allotted for passing from one class to another), or inevitably loses a pen or pencil en route to class and is reprimanded by the teacher for being late or unprepared, this new routine can be devastating.

In many elementary schools, students are programmed within a given class to work on different grade level materials. This means that in a class of sixth graders, one group of students might be working on grade-appropriate material, while other groups might be working on third- or seventh-grade levels. This situation is unlikely to be found at the junior high school.

Students functioning on a variety of independent skill levels with different expressive language abilities are scheduled for the same classes, often with little if any provision made for those who are known by past school performance to be accelerated or slow learners.

Another important difference between elementary and junior high schools can be seen by profiling the nature of skills, attitudes, and behaviors needed by a student to succeed in the secondary setting. Embodied in the notion of secondary education is an increased level of student independence. This can be exemplified in a number of ways. Students are now expected to seek help from teachers when they do not understand work presented in class rather than wait until the teacher asks to see them or arranges a meeting with their parents. Students are expected to confer with their guidance counselors about difficulties in classes and behavioral concerns rather than allow problems to become exaggerated and affect their overall school performance. Whereas teachers on the elementary level might be more prone to pass students in a marking period due to improved behavior and attitude, the teachers at the junior high school are often not allowed the same flexibility in grading and must adhere to more stringent guidelines. This would certainly apply to eighth- and ninth-grade students, where concerns such as preparation for advanced level courses and designated programs of study at the high school must be considered.

Grading might be viewed as an area of change and potential stress to the incoming junior high school student. Having previously been awarded only letter grades with accompanying comments, the student is now faced with a numerical grade and a brief coded comment at best, often excluding or misrepresenting the quality of work demonstrated in class. Should a student continue to demonstrate inadequate performance in class and achieve poor grades over a period of time, there is an increased possibility, in contrast to policy at the elementary levels, of failure and retention. This increases from grade seven upward. This is due, in part, to the more specialized curriculums in the junior high school and the decreased likelihood that students will be able to demonstrate improved ability simply as a result of maturation and developmental growth.

Throughout grades one through six, formal instruction in writing letters, words, phrases, sentences, paragraphs, stories, and compositions is ongoing. Similar instruction in reading is programmed as part of every student's educational plan. Despite this prolonged and seemingly thorough exposure to formal instruction in these areas, many students arrive at the junior high school with skills barely adequate for note taking, report writing, oral reading, and independent reading of texts and other assigned materials. Among these students can be found a group of handicapped youngsters who have any number of additional confounding variables that detract from the ease with which the students complete the transition from one school to another.

WHY A RESOURCE ROOM PROGRAM?

There are numbers of reasons why a resource room program would be the service delivery option of choice for exceptional junior high school students. Whereas prior instruction during a student's elementary school career was essentially offered in self-contained settings, the departmentalized nature of middle and secondary school instruction creates a new procedure to be followed. The movement of students from one classroom to another and the individualization of mainstreamed education in content areas is certainly complemented by a support program that students are able to attend on a parttime basis, thereby discouraging the unneccessary, but often inevitable, stigma associated with a program or class available to only a select number of students.

The roles and responsibilities of the resource room program on the junior high school level are a matter of considerable debate among theorists, administrators, and teachers. There are those who purport that the resource room should concentrate most heavily upon reteaching the student material that was presented in mainstream classes. There are others who suggest that helping the student to overcome skill and processing deficits should be the emphasis of a resource room program. These persons also believe that parents and tutors should be assigned the task of helping the child achieve passing grades, study for exams, complete homework assignments, and so on. There are still others who recommend that the resource room be used as a support base for general school concerns—both academic and behavioral—and that the nature of the work assigned in the room solely depends on the student's need for direct assistance in completing assignments or modeling a routine for staying out of trouble in a given class.

An effective resource room program should be able to encompass all of these concerns. It should support the information presented in content area classes and provide opportunities for students to learn or relearn material on a more individualized basis, or at least in such a way that they can experience independent success. This might be arranged by direct contact between the student and the resource room teacher or by helping the student make meaningful contact with classroom teachers and by scheduling meetings during or after school for supplementary instruction. The resource room program should ensure that each of its students is able to take adequate notes in class, thereby facilitating the review of material both in school and at home. Other management concerns, such as the maintenance of neat and complete notebooks, the recording of test and homework grades, and the timely completion of projects, are all matters that should be of concern to the resource room teacher.

THE RESOURCE ROOM TEACHER

The resource room teacher serves a variety of functions, both within the special education classroom and in the school and general communities. As a member of a school faculty, the learning specialist is required to fulfill such roles as bus monitor, cafeteria or office staff assistant, and attendance officer, as well as consultant, counselor, diagnostician, and teacher. Teachers of mainstream classes usually teach to groups of students in a given grade level, assigning work that is then graded and returned to students with numerical grades attached. Given each teacher's caseload of students and the different grades and levels of instruction being offered, there are often few opportunities for teachers to evaluate the work of each individual student critically, making annotated comments or meeting with the student to review errors and drill corrected responses. This role might be fulfilled by the resource room staff.

Teacher attitudes toward students have been a topic of considerable research and discussion in professional literature over the past two decades. Teacher expectations, considered in isolation, are neither good nor bad, and they are not easy to avoid, as most everyone readily forms a certain set of expected behaviors for individuals in a given circumstance. Studies have repeatedly demonstrated, however, that with time student behavior will conform more closely with teacher expectations, this holding true for students in a kindergarten setting, as well as for postgraduate students at the university level. Surprisingly, little information is available about the effects of teacher expectations on other teachers or school programs. It is not unlikely that regular class teachers would harbor feelings of jealousy or resentment toward special educators when they repeatedly see these coworkers receiving what might appear to be preferential consideration in terms of scheduling, the availability of conference time, phone usage, and so on. Classroom teachers might view the learning specialist as one who, by being credentialed in a specialized area, is unfairly afforded opportunities to work with fewer numbers of students in more individualized settings. These misconceptions and unspoken tensions are not easily clarified or alleviated. It is to everyone's best advantage that the entire school staff know who the resource teacher is, the person's educational background, responsibilities within the school, and the manner in which the program affects the education of students receiving resource support.

Parents, classroom teachers, administrators, and students have the most frequent and repeated contact with the resource room teacher. Guidance counselors, speech and language therapists, social workers, the school nurse, and the school psychologist are also key personnel with whom contact is ongoing. The latter group will be further discussed in the section of this chapter dealing with the processes of referral and evaluation.

When dealing with the parents of a disabled adolescent, the extent to which contact is maintained differs considerably with each encounter. Of primary importance is to establish an open line of communication between the school and the home, so that difficulties with work assignments and behavioral concerns can be the focus of prompt attention. Clarifying for parents when homework should be done (before dinner, after watching TV, and so on), how a child can ask for assistance without inducing an argument, and how to study for exams effectively are examples of issues that, although seemingly innocent, can be keys to success or failure. The resource room teacher is responsible for explaining the nature of the child's learning difficulties to parents in such a way that they are familiar with the measurable performance profiled during testing and assured that they can play a meaningful role in supporting their child's performance in school. It is not uncommon for parents to request that official school records and student transcripts be amended so that all indications of supportive services are deleted. Parents should be discouraged from hiding their child's special education involvement and be encouraged to oversee the relay of information from one program or individual to another. Parents should be guided by the resource room teacher and other personnel in establishing a productive routine that assures students the help they need when difficulties arise. The teacher should also serve as a liaison between parents and other school personnel when appropriate or refer parents to such persons or agencies as might be appropriate to their needs.

Classroom teachers and resource room teachers often share similar instructional responsibilities on the junior high school level. To a considerable extent in many schools, the resource room teacher serves as tutor and remedial instructor in support of information that a student might not have mastered during the limited time allotted in class. The resource room teacher can assist the regular classroom teacher in offering comprehensive and appropriate learning experiences to all students in the following four ways:

1. reading exams aloud to students who have poor decoding skills
2. preparing review materials that can be distributed to an entire class rather than a single resource room student
3. assisting in the design of homework assignments and projects that would allow for individuality and creativity while not penalizing learning disabled students whose independent research, study, and writing skills may not be comparable to those of their peers
4. assisting in the design and implementation of special behavioral plans for given students or an entire class.

The rapport between the resource room teacher and school administrators can often be a reliable predictor of whether a resource program will meet with resistance or experience success in a junior high school setting. Students who are known as school troublemakers are often either participants in or candidates for special support programs. The resource room teacher should clearly define the nature of the resource room program to school administrators and ask that they be included in discussions pertaining to inschool conflicts and parent concerns. The teachers' involvement in these matters would not interfere with the administrators' enforcement of school policy. It would simply be to assure both the parents and the school that energies and attention diverted in conflict were being redirected back into the classroom. This might be exemplified by a student who, aside from having difficulty with basic computational mathematics, is highly distractible and prone to calling out to other students in class. The student should be removed from the classroom for the remainder of the period, required to write a written apology, and reprimanded by having his or her parents called to school. After disciplinary measures are taken, the child might well be returned to the same classroom, assigned to the same seat during the same period, with little if any attention paid to the probability that the same incident will most likely reoccur or that work has been missed during the time spent out of class. The inclusion of the resource room teacher in these instances might serve to expedite the student's reentry and adjustment to the class without falling behind in the work. Working closely with administrators is also a way in which the resource room teacher can minimize conflicts or tension with mainstream faculty, especially in regard to behavioral concerns.

An administrator assigned to evaluating a resource room program would be faced with an exhausting, if not impossible, task unless the program was carefully explained beforehand. Once familiar with the workings of the program, an administrator can serve as an advocate (and at times defendant) of the resource room when confronted by curious (or angry) parents, teachers, and coworkers. The administrator can also be better able to evaluate the program and its effectiveness within the school. A further advantage of enlisting the cooperation of building administrators through exposure and familiarity is that they might be made more sensitive to the material, funding, and personnel needs of a resource room program.

ATTENTION, MEMORY, AND LANGUAGE CHARACTERISTICS OF LEARNING IMPAIRED STUDENTS

The areas of attention, memory, and language are perhaps the most frequently overlooked when considering both the developmental abilities of a student and experiential factors related to learning. Students are repeatedly taught to select a certain bit of information and use that information to complete a given number of steps in determining a correct response. Exceptional learners often have difficulty both in selecting information that is relevant to the task at hand and in retaining that information and accompanying data until the procedure is complete and a response is required. They may demonstrate an overly impulsive, short focus, leaving a task before it is fully understood, or a long compulsive focus, fixating on a task until it is no longer relevant or understood.

Broad and narrow field hypotheses concern themselves with the quality rather than the probability and duration of attention demonstrated by a student. The broad field hypothesis advocates that disabled students continuously process task-irrelevant information, whereas the narrow field hypothesis suggests that these students focus on only a small part of the relevant data presented. Other theorists propose an intermittent selection theory. This model suggests that the attending ability of learning disabled students is identical to that of their normal peers except in the probability of attention. A slight variation of this would be an intermittent intensity hypothesis, which suggests that the student does not switch from irrelevant to relevant processing/attending, or the student continues to attend to a given set of data after the relevant stimuli have been withdrawn. While these and similar learning difficulties have been noted across varying populations of students in both regular and special class settings, they are most often used to describe students who evidence specific learning disabilities. The need for the resource teacher, who most often services learning disabled students in public school settings to consider these characteristic areas of weakness, is self-evident.

If learning disabled and nondisabled students were compared for the purpose of identifying problem-solving and attention behaviors that contributed most significantly to their deficit performance in school, certain characteristics might be highlighted. The learning disabled students would probably demonstrate more frequent tendencies to perseverate incorrect responses or retain information that, although relevant to the total problem, would not contribute to the arrival at a final conclusion. They would be prone to remember the first bit of information presented without evaluating its usefulness in solving the problem, or they would fail to consider alternate answers before offering a final response. They might generalize this information, perhaps because they feel as though they must do something with it, and generalization is often an easy if not spontaneous process. This can be especially frustrating to the classroom teacher who, after having spent numbers of days teaching and reviewing a given topic or procedure, realizes that a number of students are far from mastery, but have learned bits and pieces of relevant data that may or may not reflect proper sequence, depth, or detail of instruction.

Verbal miscuing is a behavior common to many learning disabled students. It may be exemplified by a student who does not stop working and look toward the front of the room when the teacher suddenly begins to speak in a soft voice. Difficulty in understanding inflections and changes in intonation are also seen as problematic to these students, as is a sometimes unexpected tendency to misinterpret or simply not realize humorous statements. They are often annoyed by puns or punchlines to jokes that rely upon words with multiple meanings. These same students may have deficits in reauditorization, simple repetition of words, and the construction of phrases and sentences. One explanation for this might be that disabled students do not listen as carefully or do not remember what they hear as efficiently as others. A more likely explanation might be that these students have developed unique systems of dealing with language during their childhood and early school careers, and that the rules that apply to their personalized codes of communication differ in some way from those that are applied to standard English. The ninth grader who explains that the majority of native Indians living in Bombay speak "Buddahlism" may not realize the error, or be willing or able to learn the correct responses because the grammatical form and conceptual base for the answer are valid. Similarly, a student who asks whether all dinosaurs are "instinct" or who describes a psychologist as a "doctor with feelings" is employing revised and personalized morphological and syntactical rules, which are effective in conveying content, but confusing and improper to the average listener.

The student who has a great deal of difficulty repeating information orally might be quite adept at both remembering it and discriminating between its contextual equivalent and irrelevant information, as perhaps presented on a multiple choice exam. Another student might be able to repeat and retain information verbatim, but have little facility in evaluating this information for relevance and applicability to a selected situation. It should therefore be noted that attention deficits, although often overlapping, may not be equal in the extent to which they impair or inhibit learning.

THE REFERRAL AND EVALUATION PROCESS

One of the most time-consuming responsibilities of the resource room teacher is often to oversee the referral and assessment of students for eligibility in a learning disabilities program. While some school districts have teams of diagnostic personnel assigned to evaluate students using academic, social-behavioral, and cognitive measures, the resource teacher will probably be responsible for some part of the assessment process, even if the tasks presented are rated informally or on criteria, as opposed to standard population norms. Frequently, the resource teacher is solely responsible for student evaluation, which includes the accumulation of relevant teacher information, a review of past school records, the collection of medical and health data, and a parent intake procedure, not to mention the formal administration of instruments for the purpose of profiling a student's performance on selected tasks. Early identification of students with learning problems is recommended whenever possible. Resource teachers should be familiar with all of the services available within a school district that might expedite the referral process. They should also establish close rapport with support personnel and the teaching staff, formalizing a method through which data can be taken carefully and reliably. Teachers should be encouraged to submit a descriptive summary regarding each student presented for testing. A short answer format might be used for this purpose, with simple yes/no answers being strongly discouraged.

In some situations, the guidance office, office of the dean, vice-principal's office, or school psychologist can serve as intermediary between the resource room teacher and the referring agent. In these instances, students would be referred by means of a formal statement describing the reason for referral, the students' behaviors in the classroom, test scores and homework performance, and main concerns regarding student progress. These school personnel would then meet with students, teachers, and parents to discuss the difficulties specified on the referral form.

Often, an open confrontation in which these issues are discussed will suffice to alleviate or improve student behavior and performance. Many attempts, be they in the form of after school help, working with parents at home, or working with a tutor, should be made before a formal request for testing is made. Once parents submit a written statement requesting an evaluation, strict guidelines must be followed for the timely completion of testing and the presentation of data.

The types of information provided by referral forms will differ considerably from one school to another, as well as reflect the personal and professional biases of the referring agent. A student who is self-referred will most probably complain of poor test grades or not being able to complete homework assignments independently. Parents are likely to provide information regarding the extent to which they must work with their child at home to oversee the completion of even simple assignments, or they may complain that, although their child is doing little if any homework, no contact regarding grades and inschool performance has been initiated by the school. Social workers, speech and language therapists, psychologists, Title I reading and math teachers, and other school personnel will all provide information that reflects the behavioral and academic concerns of their respective disciplines. In addition, students who have received resource support during their elementary school years will be referred for continued services during their junior high school experience.

Classroom teachers should be encouraged to play an integral part in the evaluation process. Although not always the case, there is evidence to support the notion that students will frequently perform differently in an individual testing situation than they will in a regular classroom environment, thereby challenging the validity and usefulness of testing. Scores achieved on individually administered measures are little more than approximations of student performance on a sample of tasks from given areas. They are not true and stable measures of student ability, and are greatly affected by such variables as direct teaching, developmental correlates, and attention/distractibility. Classroom teachers should be asked to comment on these and other concerns, indicating behaviors that might contribute to the formulation of a comprehensive student profile. Difficulty concentrating while written work on a blackboard is being discussed, a tendency to answer a question with a generality or with information that reflects work that is dated and no longer applicable to class discussion, and a notable delay in the rate of writing or copying notes exemplify these additional concerns.

It is sometimes difficult to obtain health related information regarding students in school. Records of innoculations and general physical exams are not especially useful to the resource room teacher unless data pertaining to restrictions in gross or fine motor activity are indicated. What is of considerable value to the resource teacher are detailed reports profiling visual and auditory status, both in regard to acuity and perceptual functioning.

A number of other factors should be considered during the process of accumulating information for referral. Students should be questioned about their eating habits at home and in school, and the times during the school day when a student is scheduled for lunch and gym should be noted. The energy and activity levels of students can be greatly affected, as can attention and motivation, by these two required periods, and difficulties in school may result, at least in part, from poor scheduling. Sugar intake, generously provided by junk foods, can offset a student's ability to maintain an energy level that permits relaxed yet efficient attending in class. Allergies and their accompanying medication can also be contributing factors to decreased attention, motivation, and performance in school.

Once information from school personnel has been collected, parent statements have been made, sensory data have been updated, past school records have been reviewed, and behavioral comments have been accumulated, the process of formal student assessment can begin.

MANAGING A RESOURCE ROOM

The first few weeks of school are perhaps the most critical in determining the extent to which a resource room program will succeed in fulfilling its many roles within a junior high school. Opportunities for staff and administrative visitations should be arranged, and a review of building and district policies regarding the release of information to outside agencies and specified individuals should take place. Budgeting, the prioritization of teaching, testing, and teacher-consulting, and the roles of teacher assistants should be determined. A general schedule for parent conferencing should be set, and a notebook in which updated parent contact can be noted should be established. Forms for COH data and the recording of information to be added to student anecdotal folders must be prepared and duplicated. Work areas within the resource room must be organized, and materials, including paper, pencils, stencils, staples, paper clips, magazines, free-time games (chess, backgammon, scrabble), hand calculators, dictionaries, and samples of content area texts, must be sorted, stored, and displayed. Maps and charts must be positioned on walls, and storage areas for student work folders must be assigned.

The physical arrangement of the resource room should be established before the arrival of the students. Their adjustment to the junior high school is often cause enough for unrest without the added confusion of a supposedly supportive situation that changes every time they step foot in the door. Plants should also be situated in the room if possible. Students might bring in cuttings from plants at home, or the teacher might bring a plant to school and have the students start their own from cuttings done in the resource room.

A most important factor for every special educator to consider while working in a school setting is that of visibility. All too often classes for learning impaired students and those for the more severely disabled are tucked away at the end of a hallway, hidden behind the gymnasium, located in the basement, or situated near the custodian's office. Not only does this contribute to the students' feelings of discomfort and isolation, but it creates a physical as well as communicative barrier between instructional and support staff personnel. Mainstream teachers should be invited to visit the resource room regularly and, if possible, participate in the routine of helping students with their assigned work. Opportunities to speak, however briefly, at faculty meetings should be requested, and lists of students who are involved in resource room programs should be distributed to the faculty with occasional updates released as needed.

Programs for mentally retarded students are often envisioned as being housed in brightly lit rooms with attractively colored paint on the walls, mobiles hanging from the ceilings and in front of the windows, a large round table in the center of the main work area, and posters all about, either commercially prepared or drawn by the students. Rooms where learning disabled students work have been described as plain, uncolorful places where materials and books are hidden behind cabinet doors, and students are assigned to work carrels that are tucked away in the corners of the room or located behind bookcases.

Neither of these descriptions is applicable to the junior high school resource room. A resource room should allow for individual students to elect whether they would like to work at a table with other students nearby or in a more isolated spot where distractions would be minimized. Students should have ready access to resource books and reference materials, so that they might have opportunities to expand their general information and vocabulary skills while completing assignments. Whenever possible, they should be encouraged to interact with other students in such a way that opportunities for problem solving and appropriate social and behavioral modeling might occur. Posters, photographs, and charts should be carefully selected to reflect both the teacher's need to have visible and easily accessible records of student performance and student interests.

The departmentalized nature of junior high school instruction makes it extremely difficult if not impossible for the resource room teacher to keep abreast of classwork and assignments for all of the students enrolled in the program. Although they might share test grades or marks on individual projects or homework papers, students are not always the most reliable sources of information regarding assigned work presented in class. It is therefore recommended that a student worksheet form (SW) be distributed weekly to the teachers of learning disabled students. (See Exhibit 8–1.) This form will not only help the resource room teacher plan activities that would support content area instruction, but would facilitate a program of effective self-management, whereby students would be encouraged to assume greater responsibility for the neatness, completeness, and timely submission of assignments. Students would no longer be able to report that they did not learn anything new in class or that the teacher made no mention of upcoming notebook checks or exams, behaviors almost classic to the learning disabled adolescent.

Even though the majority of students enrolled in a resource room program may be eighth and ninth graders who are quite accustomed to moving between classes, lateness and truancy can become issues of concern to both the resource room teachers and building administrators. Some students may be stopped in the halls by friends or sidetracked by a visit to the bathroom, the result being that they arrive late to class. Others may pass the cafeteria and decide to buy a snack, or stop at their lockers to exchange books, which also result in their late arrival. Both lateness and truancy should be dealt with as serious offenses. Students should be apprised of their responsibility to be in class at a certain time, and parent involvement should be elicited as soon as problems arise. The student who sees repeated instances of lateness as unimportant and a matter for casual concern may be in need of some type of counseling. On the other hand, the student who has so much difficulty planning the route to and from classes that lateness is a repeated problem should be provided with structured opportunities to practice the routine of changing classes, with the teacher monitoring progress using behavioral objectives specified in an IEP.

As outlined by federal and state regulations, every student who receives special services must be provided with an IEP detailing the type of support; duration of involvement; nature of remediation, both general and specific; evaluation data; and a sampling of instructional methods and materials. These plans are a most valuable asset to a student receiving support over an extended period of time. They enable each teacher to understand what types of instruction have previously been offered to students; what materials have proven most effective; what behavioral concerns might be noted

Exhibit 8-1 Sample Student Worksheet

(Teacher) _____

(Subject) _____

(Date) _____

We are presently working with ___(names of students)___ in the resource room. We are in need of weekly plans, work assignments, dittos, units covered, or any other material, as well as notices of upcoming tests that will aid us in our efforts to support these students. We appreciate your cooperation in providing us with materials.

Please leave this form in our mailbox ___(names of res. rm. teachers)___ or bring it to the resource room ___(room #___). If we can be of help to you in planning for or evaluating students, please let us know.

Thank you,
Resource room staff

_____

Monday:

_____

Tuesday:

_____

Wednesday:

_____

Thursday:

_____

Friday:

_____

for improved scheduling and classroom management; and what procedures for general school staff, parents, and other support personnel have been employed to facilitate communication regarding the completion and submission of homework assignments, test grades, and inschool and after school activities.

If the IEP format used in a district does not enable the resource teacher to include descriptive or anecdotal information essential in profiling student needs and abilities, an accompanying form should be designed to supplement the required one. Parents, social workers, speech and language therapists, and a variety of other professionals find the additional information to be of great value. Such anecdotal records enable school personnel to coordinate comprehensive support services to special needs students, and they facilitate the maintenance of a productive rapport with regard to social, behavioral, and attitudinal considerations.

It is extremely important that parents understand the information presented on IEP and supplementary information forms. All too often a parent will reprimand a child for achieving a low score on an individually administered achievement test or express disappointment because of a low subtest score on measures of auditory or visual memory, or attention, discrimination, or a visual-motor performance. Parents should be helped to understand both the nature of the tasks presented on these instruments and the intent for which they were administered. The comparison of disabled students to a "normal" population is useful only to establish comparative baseline performance for possible inclusion into a supportive program, and the comparison often offers little information regarding a child's potential in given academic areas. The comprehensive profile, which includes scores and behavioral data on a variety of measures along with information available from diagnostic teaching trials, enables the teacher, parent, or clinician to understand the nature of the child's deficit performance and to design a program of support appropriate to the child's individual learning needs. Parents should be encouraged to play an integral role in overseeing the work and study patterns of students at home, as well as offering emotional support to improve an often fragile self-image. Their specific responsibilities might be outlined informally during school conferences or, if cooperation is inconsistent or difficult to sustain, detailed on the IEP form (evaluation section or an attached addendum). They should, however, be cautioned against serving as educational counselors, as this often results in arguing, tension at home, and general feelings of resentment toward both parents and the school support staff.

Grading in a resource room program is an area of great diversification as each teacher, school, and district has guidelines for student evaluation. Of primary importance is that grades assigned in content area classes not reflect work performed in the resource room, and vice versa. It may be that, due to the severity of a student's deficit in spelling, reading, and written expression, instruction in a mainstream class would be inappropriate. If this student is taught English in the resource room in lieu of a regular class, the marking period grades should be determined by the resource room teacher. If, however, the student remains in the mainstream placement and is given help on English assignments with cooperation between the regular and resource room teachers, grades should be determined by the classroom teacher, hopefully with the input of the resource room teacher and other support personnel.

Students, parents, administrators, and the general school faculty should understand that grades awarded in the resource room are not "gifts" that allow students to move from one grade level to another without demonstrating mastery in standard curriculum areas. Criteria for grading should be clearly defined, and scores awarded should not be contrasted with those reflecting work completed in regular classes. Resource room students are presented with assignments that are not easier; rather, they are more appropriate to the students' functional and instructional levels. The assignments are evaluated in relation to the students' functioning abilities and the progress they make.

Parents should be consulted when grades awarded might deter continued school performance. Students who succeed in earning high grades might falsely suppose that hard work and conscientious effort are no longer necessary. Other students might score poorly on report cards despite the supportive efforts of the resource room and resolve that there is little advantage in trying so hard when failure seems inevitable. Still other students may complain that, although their marks show improvement, they deserve higher grades as compensation for their rekindled efforts in school.

Whatever the situation, grading policies should be consistent for all students. This is especially important due to the close nature of interaction between students and teachers in a resource room setting. Differences in marks reflecting, for example, behavioral rather than academic performance could easily lead to tension and a break in trust and cooperation between the student and teacher. This might be exemplified as follows:

Todd is a loud and often disruptive student who, despite the adjusted level of work presented, requires constant one-to-one attention. Joan, working on similar skills, prefers to work independently, asking for help when necessary and calling the teacher when she has completed her assignments. Both Todd and Joan might perform similarly on tests, but improvement in Todd's overt behavior might sway the teacher to award him an inflated score on a report card.

An attitude or behavior grade should accompany each report card, and this should be supplemented by an annotated grade sheet or descriptive summary detailing not *that* a student received a grade but rather *how* the grade was achieved. It is with this information that decisions regarding continued instruction and support both inside and outside of the resource room can be made.

Resource room teachers may become so involved in supporting mainstream classroom content area work that they may overlook areas of weak processing and deficient cognitive and associative performance. Material presented in the resource room should be arranged in such a way that students are afforded opportunities to build skills while reviewing topic-specific material. Of primary importance is that students are made aware of what types of information or what kinds of in-class presentations will be most difficult to follow and absorb, so that note taking, outlining, and study strategies taught in the resource room are effectively employed. Resource room work should be graded for both content and completeness, and overall performance in regard to the student's behavior while working should be noted. This is most easily done in the student's work folder, where both the teacher and student can be reminded of performance and behavior on an ongoing basis.

The daily planning for resource room students is initially one of the most time-consuming responsibilities of the resource room teacher. As previously mentioned, students on different grade levels, who are assigned to different teachers who use a variety of texts and duplicated materials, converge upon the resource room five or more times each week, fully expecting that the resource room teacher will know what material they are responsible for, when tests will be given, when assignments are due, and so on. They also expect the resource room teacher to be able to offer them the support they need to pass their courses.

Once student worksheet (SW) forms are implemented and lines of communication with faculty members are formalized, an advantageous method for assigning and monitoring work in the resource room is through the use of individual student folders. These folders should contain a form similar to the SW sheet, where daily plans can be recorded, as well as comments made as to how much of the assigned work has been completed, and any other comments pertaining to behavior and ideas for future lessons. The SW sheet, with name and date affixed, should be replaced each week and stored at the end of each marking period with samples of student work and tests. This packet will serve as a comprehensive record of assigned work, work completed, attendance, and behavioral concerns for future reference.

CONCLUSION

Over the past decade, there has been a general awakening in the private and professional communities regarding educational opportunities for adolescent learners. Most recently, journals, including *Exceptional Education Quarterly* and *Learning Disability Quarterly,* have highlighted the current status of adolescent students on issues ranging from service delivery models, to methods for content area instruction, to motivational and behavioral factors that affect learning. These contributions to the literature are only a first step in the overall evaluation of present educational practices. The improved quality of managerial systems and the increased effectiveness of instructional programs are the responsibilities of every individual who comes into contact with students with special needs. Teachers, parents, administrators, and support personnel are all key agents in the recommendation, revision, and implementation of new and improved practices in schools.

The scope and intent to which careful research is indicated in regard to adolescent learning disabled students are boundless. Instruction in content and academic areas (math, English, spelling, social studies, science, and vocabulary), training in social and behavioral awareness (interpersonal relations, social roles, and sexuality), developing interests and competencies in vocational skill areas, revising curriculums, investigating communication skills in consideration of experiential and cognitive factors, and general program design options are only samples from the continuum of concerns still to be explored.

The resource room may be an opportune setting for the ongoing investigation of issues critical to the field of adolescent and learning disabilities. It may even be the link between mainstreamed and self-contained instruction that brings closer the realization of what is still an ideal: all education should be special education.

NOTE

1. The junior high school may be defined as an organizational structure that provides departmentalized instruction to students in grades seven, eight, and nine. The author recognizes, however, that a middle school structure (usually grades six, seven, and eight) is gaining popularity. In practice, the education of the young, handicapped adolescent described in this chapter is appropriate for either the junior high school or middle school structures.

BIBLIOGRAPHY

Adamson, William C., and Adamson, Katherine K., eds. *A Handbook for Specific Learning Disabilities*. New York, N.Y.: Garner Press Inc., 1979.

Alley, Gordon, and Deshler, Donald. *Teaching the Learning Disabled Adolescent: Strategies and Methods*. Denver, Col.: Love Publishing Co., 1979.

Bryan, Tanis H., and Bryan, James H. *Understanding Learning Disabilities*. 2d ed. Sherman Oaks, Cal.: Alfred Publishing Co. Inc., 1978.

Button, James E.; Lovitt, Thomas C.; and Rowland, Thomas D.; eds. *Communications Research in Learning Disabilities and Mental Retardation*. Baltimore, Md.: University Park Press, 1979.

Cullinan, Douglas, and Epstein, Michael H., eds. *Special Education for Adolescents*. Columbus, Ohio: Charles E. Merrill Publishing Co., 1979.

Kinsbourne, Marcel, and Caplan, Paula J. *Children's Learning and Attention Problems*. Boston, Mass.: Little, Brown and Co., 1979.

Mann, Lester; Goodman, Libby; and Wiederholt, J. Lee; eds. *Teaching the Learning Disabled Adolescent*. Boston, Mass.: Houghton Mifflin Co., 1978.

Marsh, George E.; Gearheart, Carol Kozisek; and Gearheart, Bill R.; eds. *The Learning Disabled Adolescent*. St. Louis, Mo.: The C.V. Mosby Co., 1978.

Reid, D. Kim, and Hresko, Wayne P. *A Cognitive Approach to Learning Disabilities*. New York, N.Y.: McGraw-Hill, 1981.

Salvia, John, and Ysseldyke, James E. *Assessment in Special and Remedial Education*. Boston, Mass.: Houghton Mifflin Co. 1978.

Wiederholt, J. Lee; Hammill, Donald D.; and Brown, Virginia. *The Resource Teacher: A Guide to Effective Practices*. Boston, Mass.: Allyn and Bacon, Inc., 1978.

Wiig, Elisabeth H., and Semel, Eleanor Messing. *Language Disabilities in Children and Adolescents*. Columbus, Ohio : Charles E. Merrill Publishing Co., 1976.

At Issue

THE RESOURCE TEACHER AND BEHAVIORAL MANAGEMENT

Junior high school teachers readily identify that behavioral management is a significant problem in the teaching of the young adolescent. Students at this level are faced with many psychosexual adjustments that create dynamic changes and can negatively affect their ability to learn. The general concern is that students who do not exhibit appropriate self-discipline do not learn effectively and can be perceived by mainstream teachers as impossible to teach.

In his recent work, *Motivating Classroom Discipline,* Gnagey enumerates the reasons why most children misbehave.[1] He cites ignorance of the rules and the trying out of various behaviors to determine which are enforced as a primary reason for misbehavior. Frequently, he feels, there is a distinction between what teachers say the rules of the classroom are and which rules they actually enforce. Conflicting rules between a child's home environment and the school environment are another cause of confusion that can result in deviant behavior in the classroom. Frustration created by the impingement of the teacher, classmates, or learning activities can create tensions that result in untoward behavior as well. Gnagey states that "Since academic achievement is the major goal of schooling, inability to learn is a major source of school frustration. . ."[2] and that "the relationship between achievement problems and misbehavior is well established."[3] Displacement of feelings from within the child externalized to the school environment can cause poor self-control. Hostilities created by the home environment are literally carried with the child to school, along with negative feelings from previous poor educational experiences. The last major cause of disruptive behavior is the result of anxiety. Such situations as test taking, performing in front of others, or being evaluated by the teacher can easily create anxiety for the student.

It is not difficult to see how each of these causes of disruptive behavior can be exaggerated in the case of the exceptional child who frequently suffers from poor school performance, nonacceptance by peers and teachers, confusion about rules and regulations, anxiety-provoking home life, and poor self-esteem. When the mildly handicapped child exhibits problems with self-control, whose responsibility is behavioral management?

Many resource teachers enumerate a wide range of services that they see as part of their work with special children. However, Leach and Quinby report that most resource room teachers list the following among the duties to be avoided: "The Resource Room teacher should not act as a disciplinarian and/or a crisis agent."[4] It is understandable that the resource teacher does not wish to contribute to the cycle of negative feedback that exceptional children may receive from their peers and other teachers; consequently, they do not wish to function as disciplinarians to children in the resource program. It has been documented that "learning disabled children (are) significantly less preferred by classroom teachers than their nonlearning disabled peers."[5] Classroom teachers of these mildly handicapped students label them as "hyperactive, less cooperative, less able to organize themselves, less accepting of responsibility and less tactful than other classmates."[6] Garrett and Crump have found a relationship between the teacher's perception of the exceptional child and the child's social status in the classroom. For example, if a teacher threatens to punish an entire class if inappropriate behavior occurs, the child causing the disruption will be rejected by his or her peers. The researchers conclude that "If the goals of mainstreaming are to be realized, social skills must be considered in the educational planning and programming for the learning disabled child."[7]

Therefore, an additional service that resource teachers should provide for their students is behavioral management approaches. In *Methods for Teaching the Mildly Handicapped Adolescent,* Marsh and Price specify several approaches to behavioral management.[8] These techniques are important for all special educators to use directly with students. In addition, they are also important in terms of resource teachers consulting with and advising mainstream teachers who have difficulty disciplining exceptional children.

Positive reinforcement is suggested as a prime behavioral management approach. Reinforcers are things that the students value or feel to be important and are used to reinforce appropriate behavior or responses. If reinforcers are to work, they must be valued by the children. Asking the students what they want placed in a reinforcement area and observing student behavior are suggested as means of choosing appropriate reinforcers. The authors list reinforcers that secondary students have self-selected:

- *Magazines: MAD, Popular Mechanics, Seventeen*
- *Games:* playing cards, poker chips, chess
- *Beauty aids:* nail polish, makeup
- *Musical equipment:* stereo, record player, earphones, tape recorder
- *Art Equipment:* oils, acrylics, sketch pads, clay
- *Books:* automotive repair, beauty/body care, fashions, jokes[9]

Token systems that allow the students to exchange tokens for tangible goods are other reinforcement systems. The tokens do not have intrinsic value, but they can be used to purchase items that are desirable to the students. Students may earn tokens through completing tasks appropriately, demonstrating desired behavior, inhibiting inappropriate behavior, or attaining a specified goal.

The use of contracts is most appropriate with adolescent students. Contracts are established so that the student and teacher agree to the attainment of a specific task or behavioral goal and the nature of the rewards for attainment. When contracts are established so that the student can assist in deciding goals and criteria for success, they take on the added psychological value of allowing the young adolescent to make choices and be responsible for his or her own learning.

Following is an example of a contracting system that was employed in a secondary resource room:

> The resource teacher designed a contracting program using verbal contracts, all of which adhered to established criteria agreed upon by the entire group of students served. The criteria for contracts were:
>
> 1. All aspects of task completed
> 2. Written tasks properly identified with name/date
> 3. Written tasks done on full-sized, lined notebook paper, double spaced or typed with double spacing
> 4. Product tasks (other than written) properly identified with name/date labels (example: science charts)
>
> Criteria were posted in the classroom and had been established by class members at the beginning of the program.
>
> The rewards consisted of amounts of free time in the "reinforcement area" of the classroom or appropriate areas outside the room, such as the gym, canteen, or open hallway. The time allotments were 5-, 10-, or 15-minute periods of earned free time.[10]

This contract approach consisted of seven distinct steps through which the student progressed toward completion:

1. choosing the contract from the "contract bin"
2. negotiating the contract with the teacher
3. recording the contract
4. performing the contract to meet the criteria
5. reviewing and grading the contract

6. clearing the contract
7. providing reinforcement[11]

When contracts do not work, the authors report that the causes may be the inappropriate difficulty level of the contract, unmotivating reinforcements for rewards, or unavailability of materials or equipment necessary to complete the contract.

Summarizing the use of token economy or contract systems, Marsh and Price caution that the tangible reinforcements are not sufficient to maintain appropriate behavior without additional social reinforcement.[12] These social reinforcers consist of praise, humor, positive physical contact, and other methods that work for an individual teacher. In addition, the process of change may be slow, and teachers should anticipate the need to maintain the reinforcement techniques over some length of time.

Leach and Quinby report on a technique of involving the middle school resource room program in changing students with discipline problems.[13] Students with obvious and severe behavioral problems are identified early in the school year. They are observed closely and counseled by the resource room teacher, who attempts to build a close, personal relationship with the students. Frequently, the student's behavior improves, the authors feel, because of the need to please the resource teacher, the availability of the resource room as a safe haven, and the resource teacher functioning for them as a student advocate.

When misbehavior results in the violation of a school rule or if the misbehavior requires punitive action, the resource teacher should not be solely involved. In many schools the assistant principal or dean of students is charged with the responsibility of disciplining students for more severe infractions, and this person should be involved. If ongoing monitoring of this student's behavior is called for, the resource teacher can be incorporated by designing an approach that would help the student develop appropriate behavior. The resource teacher can serve to facilitate the work of the classroom teacher or guidance counselor by providing techniques that are appropriate for behavioral management of students with learning or emotional problems.

The following sequence of events takes place in the model of behavioral management used in the middle school:

- The resource teacher, student, and other involved faculty meet to identify causes of misbehavior.
- The resource teacher meets with the student to collect information and identify appropriate behavioral management techniques.

- The resource teacher convenes a second conference. Specific behavioral goals are established by all involved. The IEP format is suggested as appropriate for the specification of the management of behavior as well as for learning objectives.
- The resource teacher monitors the process to ensure that all parties involved are complying with the behavioral management techniques that have been recommended. (The example is given in which a hyperactive student is allowed to move quietly in the classroom and not be required to sit silently for extended periods of time.)
- The student visits the resource room occasionally to prevent regression. The goal is to integrate the student into all school activities and classes, and to diminish the need for visits to the resource room.[14]

This model is both interactive and eclectic, as the resource teacher works with a team of concerned faculty and various behavioral management techniques can be employed. Leach and Quinby feel that the essential underlying element in any such plan is the relevancy and motivation inherent in the school's curriculum.[15]

During a period of time when many school systems are scrutinizing the junior high school design and may be opting for a middle school approach, there is an opportunity to revise curriculum and behavioral management approaches for the young adolescent. Educators of special children, both in the mainstream and in support services programs, should develop a team approach for preventing and dealing with students displaying disruptive behavior. The concern for discipline is of high priority to both the school and the community. Unless the exceptional child is assisted in developing appropriate behavioral patterns, he or she will remain unwelcomed and therefore uneducated in the mainstream environment.

NOTES

1. William Gnagey, *Motivating Classroom Discipline* (New York, N.Y.: MacMillan, 1981), pp. 38–44.

2. Ibid., p. 40.

3. Ibid.

4. D. Leach and S. Quinby, "The Resource Room's Role in School Discipline," *Forum 6,* no. 2 (Summer 1980): 6.

5. M. Garrett and W.D. Crump, "Peer Acceptance, Teacher Preference, and Self-Appraisal of Social Status Among Learning Disabled Students," *Learning Disability Quarterly 3* (Summer 1980): 46.

6. Ibid.

7. Ibid., p.47.

8. George Marsh and Barrie Price, *Methods for Teaching the Mildly Handicapped Adolescent* (St. Louis, Mo.: Mosby, 1980), pp. 225–30.

9. Ibid., p. 226.

10. Ibid., pp.226-27.

11. Ibid., p. 227.

12. Ibid., p. 229.

13. Leach and Quinby, "The Resource Room's Role," p. 6.

14. Ibid.

15. Ibid.

Chapter 9

Developing a Senior High School Resource Program

Joan Bossis

INTRODUCTION

There is growing evidence of the special needs of adolescents with learning and behavior problems. Many youngsters given services at a young age are still in need of support services during the senior high school years. A fundamental assumption in special education, as well as in education as a whole, has been that educational efforts are most productive if they are focused on the young child. Recent research, however, focuses on the long-lasting effects of early childhood intervention. For example, Alley and Deshler discuss a Stanford Research Institute report, "Compensatory Education in Early Adolescence," that focuses upon maturational deficiencies and the poor performance of some high school students. The report suggests that intensive educational efforts with certain adolescents may be as effective as early intervention, because in adolescence some students experience accelerated cognitive development.[1]

Another early assumption in special education was that handicapped children could be "cured." Research, however, has characterized handicapping conditions by their chronicity and changing manifestations as the student matures and school demands change. For example, Deshler has addressed the question of how manifestations of a disability vary as a function of chronological age:

> By adolescence there is a high probability that learning disabled students will experience the indirect effects of a learning handicap as manifested by poor self-perception, lowered self-concept, or reduced motivation. Disability in a basic learning process may be the root problem, but it must be considered not only by itself but also in relation to other problems that it may precipitate. . .
>
> Maturation and/or compensation tends to refine and integrate many psychological, perceptual, and motor functions. Conse-

quently, problems of incoordination, hyperactivity, distractabil-
ity, and poor attention may manifest themselves in more subtle
or controlled ways in older students.[2]

The adolescent with a learning problem is a student who cannot "make
it" in the mainstream of high school without special help. Typically, the
secondary school curriculum is content oriented rather than student
oriented, paying little attention to individual differences and needs. Therefore, energies must be directed toward effective programming that meets
the unique needs of the handicapped student in the secondary school.[3]

**The Failure-Frustration Cycle of the High School Handicapped
Student**

The exceptional learner in high school is usually an academic failure.
Failure breeds frustration, which lowers self-confidence, which results in
giving up, which guarantees failure, and on the cycle goes.[4] This cycle
begins when handicapped students become aware that they cannot learn
as their peers can. Often the emotional frustration and learning problems
are not completely remediated at the elementary level. Compounded with
affective developmental tasks of adolescence, these behavior problems
intensify significantly. Adolescents' emotional frustration is often chronic,
resulting in negative effects on self-confidence and self-concept. A self-
identity search is coupled with less willingness to accept and perform
nonrelevant academic exercises. Often, the results are acting out behavior,
dropping out of school, or psychological withdrawal. The handicapped
adolescent requires appropriate services to break the failure-frustration
cycle and succeed at the secondary level in terms of social adjustment
and career or academic preparation.[5] (See Figure 9–1.)

**Special Programming Needs for Handicapped High School
Adolescents**

The resource room at the secondary school differs from a junior high
school or middle school program. The two major components requiring
modification of the resource model are the high school organization and
structure, and the students themselves. High school programming is more
complex as tracked courses are scheduled for the college-bound and
vocational-bound student. Student-related differences necessitating a different approach in the high school result from the developmental growth
period of adolescence to young adulthood.[6]

Figure 9–1 A Diagrammatic Representation of the Failure-Frustration Cycle Experienced by the Handicapped High School Student and the Resulting Success-Motivation Cycle Provided by Appropriate Services

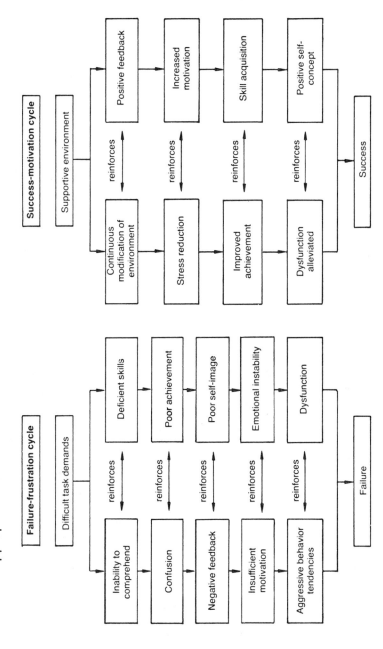

The high school handicapped learner is not only confronted with academic pressures upon entering high school, but also with the dilemma of independent decision making. The problems of drugs, alcohol, sex, delinquency, and peer pressure are unique to the senior high school adolescent. The confrontation of these problems is compounded by the daily pressures of family life, as well as by the necessity of making career decisions and life choices. The senior high school handicapped learner is almost always in limbo; the social systems of the high school (roles) and the overwhelming academic demands of the curriculum are at one end, and future planning and self-emergence, in terms of personality and sexual development, decision making, and awareness, are at the other end. Therefore, the handicapped adolescent begins to deal with reality at the senior high school. Without appropriate support systems and connections to help handicapped students cope with real world problems, the terms withdrawn, angry, aggressive, and defiant take on new meanings.

Alley and Deshler speak of the difference in demands of the secondary and the junior high school curriculums.[7] Since the senior high school curriculum is based totally on content acquisition, by the time students have reached this level, they should have mastered the skills emphasized at the elementary and junior high levels—reading, writing, spelling, mathematics, and spoken language—well enough to use as tools in acquiring further information. As Alley and Deshler indicate, many handicapped adolescents unfortunately have not mastered these skills well enough to compete with their peers in senior high school without supportive services. Secondary curriculums not only demand the basic skills of decoding and computation taught in the elementary and junior high school, but they also demand more extensive skills in listening, thinking, speaking, reading, writing, mathematics, and personal/social skills.

The senior high school handicapped learner needs to make the transition from junior high school demands to senior high school expectations. At the junior high school, the demands center upon introducing departmentalization of classes, physical movement within the building, scheduling and programming of classes, sharpening and refining of basic skill competencies, and the emergence of self-responsibility. At the senior high level, the handicapped learner faces the heavy emphasis upon content, as well as expectations of preparedness and demonstration of the acquisition of higher level cognitive skills. The senior high school handicapped learner needs to function on an individual basis in terms of programming of courses in the correct sequences, accumulation of necessary credits needed for graduation, career planning, and counseling services. The problems of specialization in subject areas, as well as curriculums that demand and do not adapt to student needs, create an environment that is quite different from the junior high school and one in which the student either sinks or swims.

THE UNIQUENESS OF THE SECONDARY SCHOOL AS A SERVICE DELIVERY ENVIRONMENT

The senior high school's unique service delivery environment encompasses both internal and external curriculum demands. These demands clearly distinguish the elementary and junior high school from the senior high school. The elementary school curriculum is developmental in its orientation and emphasizes instruction mastering basic skills in reading, math, and language arts. The junior high school's curriculum emphasizes the developmental process and a basic skills approach. The junior high school attempts to bridge the gap between the elementary school and the senior high school by offering departmentalized classes and beginning instruction in content areas. The senior high school curriculum demands can be divided into internal demands (specific classroom requirements) and external demands (that is, minimum competency testing, Scholastic Aptitude Tests (SATs), and so on).

Internal Curriculum Demands

Within the senior high school classroom, the student must learn the rules and requirements of each teacher. The high school student is expected to follow through on demands, such as notebooks, participation, and grading systems. The student must also be aware of attendance and tardiness requirements for each class. In addition to these requirements, the high school student's curriculum demands are compounded by various specific academic demands. Since the high school student must confront at least five or six content area teachers on a daily basis, the student is faced with high expectations for independent functioning and responsibility. Each teacher will offer the student varied methods of instruction, such as lecturing-notetaking, independent reading, group work, role playing, and audiovisual presentations. Students are also expected to perform on varied types of examinations, such as multiple choice, essay, fill-in, and open book. Students must also accommodate different frequencies of exams, that is, surprise, weekly, and unit tests. Assignments also vary from teacher to teacher, and the student is expected to complete long-term, short-term, and varied homework assignments.

The varied types of testing procedures as well as midterm and final exams, which place heavy emphasis on the entire term's material, present unique demands on high school students. Note taking, listening, organizational, and planning skills are prerequisites to success at the high school level. The high school student is confronted with feelings of alienation and isolation in that the teacher reacts to the class and not to the individual. All student problems must be dealt with during nonclassroom time and are not mandated, but have to be requested by the students.

The tracking of classes into honors, regents or nonregents, and basics is another curriculum demand placed on the high school student. The diversity of subject areas at the senior high school offers the student a greater variety of subject choices, such as theater, business, and college-bound courses. Compounding the demands of tracking and varied subject areas is the quantity of material required to be read by the student and the required written work when multiplied by five, six, or seven subject area teachers.

Boredom and the concern about irrelevant content are of great concern to the high school student. The curriculum is at times overwhelming and seems impractical to the older adolescent. The curriculum at the senior high school level can sometimes be an obstacle for the high school student. However, the diversity and quantity of courses offer the high school student a more fruitful and challenging environment than the junior high school. The internal demands of the senior high school curriculum are therefore flexible as well as restrictive; however, it is up to the student to contribute as well as to receive from this unique environment.

External Curriculum Demands

The external demands of the curriculum at the senior high school level include basic competency testing (including remediation), regents exams, SATs, post-high school concerns (vocational, career, college programs), and graduation requirements and diplomas. The external curriculum demands maintain the pressures that are unique to the senior high school. The individual processes of taking exams in cross-categorical content areas and the accountability for post-high school placement are part and parcel of the bridge from the senior high school into the real world.

The senior high school student must not only contend with the daily pressures of subject classes, but may also be prepared to take regents and SATs. In addition, the student must be aware of correct course sequences and precollege programs for admittance into specific college programs. The senior high school student needs to participate in the process of applying to college and choosing career options. Moreover, students must pass minimum competency tests in reading, writing, and math in order to graduate. The junior high school, on the other hand, introduces these tests as preliminary practice exercises, without the consequences of nongraduation.

Extracurricular activities assume a large role in the senior high school, unlike the junior high school. The senior high school student, in order to assimilate into the social system of the high school, can become involved in sports (interschool, intramural), clubs (social, academic, specific talents), and community affairs. Once again, participation in extracurricular activities is not a mandated part of the curriculum, but is left to the selection of the high school student. The diversity of external curriculum mandates and options, together with the specificity of the internal curriculum demands, creates a unique and challenging environment for the senior high school student.

THE COMPREHENSIVE RESOURCE ROOM PROGRAM: THE UNIQUE ALTERNATIVE FOR THE HANDICAPPED ADOLESCENT IN THE SENIOR HIGH SCHOOL

Effective programming to meet the needs of the handicapped high school adolescent evolves from the integration of educational instruction with the affective domain. This approach is especially critical to the handicapped adolescent. To achieve this, a comprehensive resource program for handicapped secondary students must be established. A comprehensive program should provide for both direct and indirect services.[8] This dual service-delivery approach encompasses remediation of deficit skills, compensatory or alternative approaches to content acquisition, personal/social coping skills, and the support and cooperation of mainstream teachers, guidance counselors, and parents.

A comprehensive resource room program for the mainstreamed secondary student with learning problems provides direct and indirect services in the least restrictive way possible. These services require two distinct roles for the resource room teacher. The first role is that of the traditional resource room teacher who deals with basic academic skill deficits and the social problems of students who are removed from their regular classes for part of the school day. However, simply providing direct intervention to secondary students with learning problems is insufficient. The resource room teacher should also be a teacher-consultant. The teacher-consultant offers support to regular educators so that a secondary student can succeed in the mainstream. Without the indirect services of a teacher-consultant, direct remediation by the resource room teacher may be insignificant.[9] Each aspect of the total resource program, which is outlined in Figure 9–2, is described in the sections that follow.

Figure 9–2 A Comprehensive Resource Room Program for High School Students

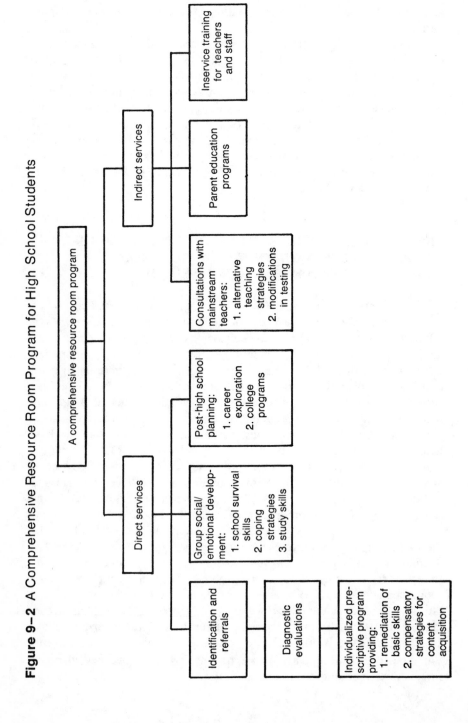

Direct Services

The direct services provided by the resource room teacher include the identification of the appropriate population, choosing screening devices, in-depth diagnostic evaluations (both psychological and educational), and ongoing remediation of basic skill deficits. Basic skills, however, are only one area of concern for the older handicapped adolescent. The resource room teacher must also supply these youngsters with tools for coping with academic subject matter in order to "make it" in their mainstreamed classes. Remedial instruction, therefore, must be integrated with compensatory learning strategies for academic subjects.

A compensatory approach encompasses instruction in "how to learn" in order to help maintain the older handicapped adolescent in the regular classroom. Implementation of these instructional methods provides the student with learning tools that must involve the classroom teacher. In this way, mainstream teachers become involved, and a faculty support system begins to evolve. A direct service model also encompasses the social and behavioral-management problems of the older handicapped adolescent. Group meetings and discussions can provide for these needs as well as post-high school preparation.

Identification, Referrals, Screening, and Diagnosis

Many students who need support services at the senior high school level have been identified in their previous years of schooling. The resource teacher at the high school level is then required to follow through with the recommendations made by previous resource teachers. When a resource system has not been in place and students new to the school must be identified, direct services begin with referrals and a system for referrals. The referral is a request for an investigation by the special educator and building committee (or child study team) to decide if a particular student needs to be evaluated. This can be coordinated with the guidance department. Since parents and teachers are often in contact with guidance regarding students' progress, the counselors can act as the initial step in the identification process. Referral forms should be available in the guidance department and in the resource room.

Since identification relies heavily upon referrals from mainstream teachers, appropriate inservice training is necessary to acquaint teachers and guidance counselors with characteristic symptoms of handicapped adolescents. If the building subcommittee determines to approve the screening procedure, parents are notified, and consent is obtained. The student is then processed through the screening procedure. A suitable screening battery for handicapped students at the secondary level includes:

- the Stanford Diagnostic Reading Test (SDRT)
- the Stanford Diagnostic Math Test (SDMT); (blue or brown levels should be used accordingly for either the SDRT or SDMT)
- the Specific Language Disability Test by Neva Malcomesius (Subtests I, VI, IX)
- an informal writing sample[10]

Appropriate diagnostic tests for evaluating secondary handicapped students include:

- the Woodcock-Johnson Psycho-Educational Battery—Part One: Tests of Cognitive Ability (Teaching Resources, 1977)
- the Detroit Tests of Learning Aptitude (The Bobbs-Merrill Co., Inc., 1968)
- the Specific Language Disability Test (Grades six, seven, and eight) by Neva Malcomesius (Educators Publishing Service, Inc., 1967)
- the Key Math Diagnostic Arithmetic Test (American Guidance Service, 1971)

Informal assessment of written language skills must complete the diagnostic profile of the secondary student. There are few standardized tests available to measure these skills. A skilled clinician must use clinical judgment and compare the performance of the secondary handicapped student to other students at the same grade level. An informal analysis of the secondary student's writing ability is essential and should include:

- ability to express ideas or thoughts clearly or coherently
- sentence structure and length (syntax)
- appropriate grammatical usage
- vocabulary usage
- spelling skills
- capitalization and punctuation

Once the secondary handicapped student has been diagnosed and assessed in terms of particular learning strengths and weaknesses, the IEP can be developed and instructional services can begin. Resource room instruction encompasses remediation of basic skills and teaching compensatory strategies for content acquisition.

Remediation vs. Compensatory Instruction

The potential strengths of remediation are that basic skill instruction: (1) should increase functional literacy; (2) may have particular relevance for secondary students who have received no or poor special/remedial instruction in previous schooling; and (3) should enable better performance in content classes. The potential weaknesses of this approach, however, appear to outweigh its strengths: (1) due to limited time to work with students in the high school, it is highly unlikely that significant progress can be made to reduce the gap between the student's grade and instructional level; (2) motivating older students to work on basic decoding and computational skills is difficult; and (3) this approach focuses on the limited number of skills.[11]

To resolve the dilemma of appropriate individual instruction at the secondary level, the major thrust of direct services should be compensatory learning strategies.

In comparison to basic skills remediation, compensatory instruction focuses on teaching handicapped adolescents strategies that will facilitate their acquisition, organization, storage, and retrieval of information, thus enabling them to cope with the demands of the secondary curriculum.[12] This type of instruction teaches the handicapped high school student how to learn rather than teaching specific content (a tutorial approach). For example, Alley and Deshler describe a "learning strategies" approach for all the basic skills: reading, writing, math, thinking, social interaction, speaking and listing skills. Their book, *Teaching the Learning Disabled Adolescent: Strategies and Methods* is an excellent presentation of detailed methods for teaching learning strategies in each of these areas, and the authors identify specific techniques and rules that the student can use in coping with the demands of the secondary curriculum.[12] This approach teaches students skills that will not only enable them to acquire content material successfully, but will also allow them to generalize skills to other situations over time.

Helen and Martin Weiss, pioneers in the field of adolescents with learning disabilities, present a variety of techniques for teaching basic skills by adapting classroom materials.[13] Many of their suggestions include worksheets and checklists that help the handicapped adolescent organize information and learn "how to learn." They provide organizational structure by presenting notebook organization techniques, note-taking suggestions, language "retraining" tips (basic spelling rules and language principles), directed reading techniques, developmental writing approaches, and so on.

Additional compensatory strategies include alternative methods for acquiring course content. Since reading is typically a primary medium for presenting course content in the secondary school, many handicapped students miss much of the content needed to succeed. An alternative approach to reading is to acquire textbook content through listening.

Listening to the sophisticated content of secondary textbooks may have the additional benefit of stimulating language growth. Tape-recording class textbooks and other reading materials can be time consuming. Recording for the Blind, Inc. records textbooks on tape for blind students and has, in recent years, extended its services to the perceptually handicapped youngster (dyslexic or learning disabled).[14] (See Exhibit 9–1 for a listing of modified or alternate resource materials.)

The resource room teacher should include a unit on study skills as a means to supplement compensatory learning. Skills such as note taking, organization, listening, reference work, planning, report writing, and test taking are essential for the secondary handicapped student. The resource room teacher must also make accommodations to help the handicapped student pass the minimum competency exams. This can be accomplished with a well-structured programmed approach. The resource room teacher must therefore teach compensatory skills and at the same time remediate specific deficits in the handicapped high school student. Uses of calculators and tape recorders can be taught to the student as additional compensatory strategies. The tape recorder can be used as a compensatory tool for listening (that is, lectures/note taking) and for structuring written expressive language (dictation of essays, compositions, and reports). Therefore, compensatory strategies must encompass modifications in the basic model of information processing: (1) input (reception); (2) integration

---

Exhibit 9–1 Modifications, Alternatives, and Resource Materials

- *A National Directory of 4 Year Colleges, 2 Year Colleges and Post High School Training Programs for Young People With Learning Disabilities,* 2d ed., P.M. Fielding, ed. Published by Partners Inc. Pub. Co., P.O. Box 50347, Tulsa, OK.
- ATP, Services for Handicapped Students, Box 592, Princeton, NJ (for modifications in administration of SAT exams).
- Division of Education Testing, University of the State of New York, State Education Department, Albany, NY 12234 (for modifications in taking New York State Regents Competency Tests).
- *Grolier Study Skills,* Grolier Educational Corp., 575 Lexington Avenue, New York, NY 10022.
- Recording for the Blind, Inc., 215 East 58th Street, New York, NY 10022; (212) 751-0860 (for school textbooks recorded on tapes—special provisions for dyslexic students).
- Helen G. Weiss and Martin E. Weiss, *A Survival Manual: Case Studies and Suggestions for the Learning Disabled Teenager,* Treehouse Assoc., Great Barrington, MA 01230.
- Helen G. Weiss and Martin E. Weiss, *The Basic Language Kit* (A teaching-tutoring aid for adolescents and young adults), Treehouse Assoc., Box 568, Great Barrington, MA 01230.

(association); and (3) output (expression). The compensatory strategies must coincide with the handicapped learner's individual strengths and weaknesses. Teaching these students how to think helps them survive the senior high school and prepares them for life. Thinking also involves setting priorities, setting goals, being aware of time, planning, evaluating, and modifying plans. The resource room teacher must include these skills in the senior high school resource room program.

Although a major emphasis of resource room instruction for secondary students with handicapping conditions is the facilitation of the student's ability to function in the regular classroom setting, the resource room teacher should try to avoid a "tutorial" approach by providing direct instruction in academic content areas. Although this approach addresses the handicapped student's immediate academic needs, and regular teachers readily accept this technique, instructional goals are dictated by regular classroom requirements that may present problems. A primary weakness of this approach is that tutoring is a short-term solution: it does not provide the student with skills that will enable independent functioning or with generalized skills for other assignments. Second, the major responsibility for delivery of content material is shifted from the regular classroom teacher to the resource room teacher. Finally, the resource room teacher is not equipped to tutor adequately in all content areas, and the student may still be lacking the prerequisite skills to acquire content information.[15]

It is important, therefore, that the resource room teacher develop a familiarity with both the curriculum goals of the regular classrooms and the materials used. By developing this familiarity, the resource room teacher will be able to give support to the student by adjusting the curriculum demands so that the student will be better able to meet them. Adjustments can be made by helping the student focus on the key elements of an assignment, by breaking down the assignment into smaller units, and by changing the manner of presentation or response. The resource teacher, then, can help the handicapped student function in a regular classroom by providing structure.

To function in the regular classroom, handicapped high school students must be taught compensatory skills that they will be able to apply and generalize in all their content area courses, as well as in life situations. Reading, writing, mathematics, and communication skills are four major areas that require significant attention. Students should be taught the skills in which they are individually deficient. Obviously then, not all subskills of these four major skill areas must be taught to all handicapped students in a resource room program.

Reading Skills. Reading skills include vocabulary development and decoding skills. The high school adolescent learner needs to be taught compensatory systems for word attack and word recognition, such as structural analysis, basic phonic analysis, use of context clues, and use of the dictionary. Vocabulary should broaden to include word meanings that are both within and outside the student's experience, including specialized or technical vocabulary in the sciences, math, or vocational areas. Reading comprehension skills, of course, are essential to surviving a high school curriculum. Comprehension, however, requires more than the literal understanding of main ideas and detail facts at this level. Senior high school students must be taught how to read critically, that is, how to draw conclusions, make inferences, and apply information they read. They must be taught how to organize what they read and how to locate information. Skimming and scanning for information, then, become key compensatory strategies for the handicapped learner in the senior high school. These students must be taught how to survey reading material, organize and locate information they need to answer questions, and to study.

Writing Skills. Adequate writing skills are of equal importance for the high school student to survive. These skills include not only expression of content mastery, concept formation, and personal opinions and judgments, but also many detailed subskills involved in the art of writing. Sentence structure, vocabulary usage, and mechanics (punctuation, capitalization, spelling) are just a few subskills involved in the writing process. Compounding the difficulties involved in this skill are the many forms the writing skill takes at the senior high level. Note taking from class lectures or from reading texts is taken for granted. Students are often asked to write spontaneous summaries or short answers in class, not to mention written essays in test taking. The skill of writing is essential in senior high school. It is mandatory that all handicapped learners be provided with techniques to master this important tool so that they can cope with demands from writing a short answer question on an exam to writing a term paper or research report.

Math Skills. Math skills necessary for surviving a high school curriculum are highly dependent on basic skills taught in the elementary and junior high school grades. Subskills, such as understanding numbers and numeration, place value, and the four basic operations and their computations, are taken for granted as "learned" at this level. Many math courses at the senior high school level rely upon knowledge (both conceptually and computationally) of fractions, decimals, and percentages. Verbal problem solving involving geometry, measurement, and graphs is emphasized in high school by combining and applying concepts and computations taught in earlier years. The resource room teacher must often fill in the gaps, teaching handicapped students concepts, and more often, computations, that are usually learned at an earlier age. At the same time, the resource room teacher must help the handicapped adolescent "make it" through the particular mainstream math class. This task can be overwhelming, both to the student and the teacher. However, with systematic and structured teaching strategies, both needs can be met.

Communication Skills. The last general area, communication skills, involves both listening and speaking skills. Often the handicapped high school adolescent's perception of what to listen to and how to communicate effectively is amiss. Listening skills are critical in the senior high school. Listening comprehension, so necessary for note taking and following lectures or discussions, involves many of the subskills in reading comprehension. Handicapped students must be taught how to listen for main ideas and their supporting details, how to sequence ideas and details, and how to summarize what they hear. Following directions accurately is also critical at the senior high school level.

By this time, teachers expect students to be able to follow complex demands after stating them only once. Listening, however, goes beyond understanding main ideas and following directions at the senior high level. Critical listening, as in critical reading, is often required of these students. They are expected to recognize absurdities, distinguish fact from opinion, detect bias, draw inferences, and make judgments. Handicapped adolescents need to be taught how to listen, by recognizing tone, mood, style, and gestures, and by visualizing what they hear. Moreover, handicapped adolescents must be taught how to apply what they have heard and to utilize this information in their oral speaking.

Speaking skills, then, combine many of the subskills in reading, writing, and listening. Students must learn how to use appropriate vocabulary and abstract concepts, and how to speak in correct sentence structure with good organization and coherence of thought. Skills involved in speaking formally, as compared with speaking spontaneously, often present problems for handicapped adolescents, who tend to be acquainted only with the latter. These students must be taught these skills as they must be taught those involved in reading, math, and writing, for these are the essentials in order to survive in senior high school.

Implicit in a learning strategies approach is cooperative planning and programming between the regular classroom teacher and the resource room teacher. The strengths of this approach are that handicapped students are taught skills that promote adjustment in a mainstreamed setting and that the instructional goals of the resource room teacher tend to be consistent with regular curriculum goals. Although emphasis is placed on the student's strengths and potential for learning, this approach does not address the basic skills approach. Moreover, an inherent weakness in this approach is the difficulty of implementing cooperative planning between the resource room teacher and regular classroom teachers.

The instructional responsibilities of the resource room program, therefore, include not only the attempt to remediate, to make problems disappear, but to compensate, to find ways of getting around problems.

Social/Emotional Adjustment

The sphere of personal-social development is characterized by an unfortunate paradox. Although there is tremendous agreement among professionals about the importance of this domain, there are few models of intervention that have been proposed or developed. Moreover, the line between counseling and personal-social instruction is often difficult to draw. For example, programs for handicapped adolescents can center on group problem-solving and role-playing techniques. Other "social perceptual training" programs involve teaching handicapped adolescents social signals, such as tone of voice, gestures, and motor expression. Behavior modification approaches are additional techniques that can be used to increase the task-oriented behavior of handicapped students, improve their social interacting skills, and reduce their frequency of emitting maladaptive behaviors. If resource room teachers are to implement this type of program successfully, they must learn counseling skills and collaborate with school counselors and psychologists in the design and implementation of such programs.[16]

Teaching handicapped adolescents social skills, however, is necessary if not mandatory at the senior high level. These students must be taught self-awareness of their own behavior, personal values, and society's values, and self-awareness of their perceptions of the environment around them. They need to be taught personal problem-solving techniques, acceptance of responsibility, and appropriate social relationships with peers and adults. This can be encompassed within the direct services of the high school resource room program.

Direct services in the resource room should provide group meetings to develop the social and emotional skills necessary to survive in the senior high school and in life. In addition to deficit skills, many handicapped adolescents lack the ability to cope with the academic and social demands placed on them. Group meetings are provided to help handicapped adolescents deal more effectively with problems in these areas.

School survival skills emphasize exploring and developing coping skills. Since the senior high school faculty is typically large and diverse, learning disabled students must acquire patterns that are appropriate to many kinds of adults. Most students usually learn typical teacher-pleasing behaviors without specific instruction. Many handicapped adolescents, however, do not, and instruction in the positive value of these behaviors may be essential to school survival. For example, these group meetings can emphasize the importance of getting to class on time, having a pencil and the right books, sitting straight and looking attentive, making eye contact with the teacher, responding to questions, and so on.[17] Handicapped students can be helped to be aware of what behaviors make classroom situations more positive. Moreover, students learn to recognize the impact of their behavior on teacher and student attitudes toward them. Teaching handicapped students school survival skills can effectively improve their attitudes toward mainstream classes and the attitudes of mainstream teachers toward handicapped learners, as well as reduce the amount of detentions, suspensions, and absenteeism.

A comprehensive social skills curriculum must include training sequences for improvement of both social perception and social behavior skills. Teaching coping skills (teacher-pleasing behaviors), such as rules (having materials, handing in assignments) and classroom requirements (working quietly, answering questions) are also appropriate for the resource room teacher. Role playing, modeling, discussion, and charting are good ways of teaching and reinforcing social skill acquisition. The complications involved in the interpersonal relations of the handicapped high school student and the individuals with whom they interact make teaching social skills critical and at times quite difficult. However, teaching social/life coping skills to attain satisfactory adult adjustment in the community for the handicapped high school student can neither be omitted nor its importance taken too lightly.

Post-High School Planning

A final component of direct services includes career exploration and/or information about college programs for handicapped students. Adolescents need guidance to find worthwhile and satisfactory careers. Many handicapped students do not pursue academic training beyond high school. It is important that these students use their high school years in a practical and realistic way.

To be effective for handicapped students, career education must be adjusted to meet their needs. Career education, however, must not replace basic academic skills training. Nevertheless, as time is running out in the upper grades, the handicapped adolescent must be prepared to make realistic decisions about the future. Many factors should be considered: current levels of achievement in academic subjects, growth rate over the past years, career goals, and parent aspirations.[18]

Career education must prepare handicapped high school students for a successful work life by enhancing their options for occupational choice and maximizing their learning achievement in all subject matter areas. Career education can be viewed as a lifelong, continuous process that begins in preschool or in the home, and continues through formal educational channels into adulthood.

Resource room teachers are faced wtih the difficulty of determining the amount of time to be devoted to direct occupational preparation. While compensatory and academic instruction cannot be abandoned and replaced with career preparation, the demands of society and the needs of the handicapped student strongly suggest the need for career education preparation.

Career education suggests preparation for a broad range of possible occupations or clusters of occupations. Some careers require two, three, four, or more years of college preparation, while many other careers require no college preparation but may involve some form of special training. Resource room teachers must be cautious not to stereotype career possibilities because of misconceptions of the potential of handicapped adolescents.

The handicapped high school student requires career and vocational counseling according to his or her individual needs. The resource room teacher must be informed and inform the handicapped student about work-study programs, vocational education programs, and specific courses in vocational training (printing, mechanics, clerical, computers, and trades). When available, life skills programs, for example, the Adkins Life Skills Programs, can be quite advantageous for the handicapped high school student.[19] There are college programs that have modified programs for the handicapped learner (LD, physically handicapped). It is the resource room teacher's responsibility, working in conjunction with the school's guidance department, to inform the student, whenever applicable, of the possibilities of these choices. Program modification and dissemination of post-high school alternatives are key components of a comprehensive resource room program.

Indirect Services

The teacher-consultant role incorporates indirect services into the structure of a comprehensive resource room program. Consultation with mainstream teachers to develop jointly alternative teaching and assessment strategies is a vital component of a senior high school program. The teacher-consultant and the regular classroom teacher must work together to help the learning disabled and other handicapped high school students survive mainstream classes.

The teacher-consultant's responsibilities include researching additional or alternative materials for content-area teachers, and devising modified curriculum instruction and testing procedures. This element of the resource program is a tenuous and complicated process. However, achievement of this goal is essential to attain full faculty support.

This support system must be an integral part of the resource program for the older handicapped adolescent. It will offer the student the resources and tools necessary to learn at the senior high school level. The teacher-consultant should work directly with mainstream teachers to help them accommodate the needs of handicapped adolescents in the regular classroom. The dual service-delivery approach, which offers direct and indirect services to handicapped high school students, complies with the concept of the least restrictive environment. Students are maintained in regular classrooms for the maximum of their school day, most of them seen by the resource room teacher for one class period a day. While the resource room teacher provides direct instruction to handicapped students, the teacher-consultant works on a one-to-one basis with content-area teachers to explore alternatives in teaching strategies for these mainstreamed students. Parent education programs and inservice training are additional responsibilities of the teacher-consultant.

Consultations with Mainstream Teachers

The problems of the secondary student with learning problems are compounded because the curriculum at this level is developed, interpreted, and presented by content-area specialists. These teachers often lack the time for individual psychoeducational orientation, which is useful for designing alternative teaching assessment strategies. This results in a need for a liaison between the student and the content-area teacher to help the student succeed in the mainstream.[20]

This type of indirect approach enhances the delivery of services in the least restrictive environment. The difficulty lies in staff involvement when general educators are forced to assume responsibilities for the instruction and management of handicapped children. The consultant role must provide information without directing and demanding it. The general and special educator must work together in planning alternative curriculum methods and materials at the secondary level. The use of written memos and questionnaires must be regarded with caution so as not to create resistance. The form presented in Exhibit 9–2 has proved helpful in gathering information from mainstream teachers about disabled children in their classes.

Exhibit 9–2 Sample Form for Use with Mainstream Content
Teachers

Date _____

To: Teachers of _____

From: _____ , Resource room teacher

Re: Progress of students presently receiving services in the Learning Center or
       students referred to the Learning Center.

Dear _____

The student(s) named above

☐ is presently in the Learning Center.

☐ is *not* now in the Learning Center, but is considered a student with regard to
follow-up by the Resource Room Program.

I would appreciate a brief summary of _____ 's progress in your _____ class.

1. Is the student currently passing for this quarter?
2. If not, what seems to be the difficulty?
   a. attitude
   b. completion of assignments
   c. attendance
   d. failure of tests due to
      ____ poor memorization of facts
      ____ poor grasp of concepts
      ____ poor retention of new vocabulary
      ____ poor spelling
      ____ poor ability to express self in writing
   e. other
3. Miscellaneous observations, student's strengths, and so on.

Thank you in advance for your cooperation.

_____
(signature)
Resource room teacher

Resistance can easily result at the secondary level when teachers are
directed to implement change without providing the prerequisites to ensure
supports for such change. General educators tend to retain old patterns of
behavior or expectations based on past experience. The consultant must
not create resistance by causing the general educator to feel threatened.

A major goal of working with mainstream teachers is to help them
recognize that they control the learning environment. With the aid of the

teacher-consultant, the mainstream teacher can be shown means to restructure classroom content and course requirements, thereby providing alternatives. Recent evidence suggests this difficult job can be done, but only by a careful and systematic approach.[21]

Laurie et al. describe three prerequisite steps to ensure the support for working with mainstream teachers. First, since teachers' attitudes toward making change often reflect their administrator's attitudes, administrators are the key to facilitating such change. Therefore, the regular and special education administrators at the district and building level must view the task of making changes in mainstream classes as important as possible. Second, preparation and planning time must be scheduled for regular and special educators to make these changes. Time is also needed for mainstream teachers to meet with the teacher-consultant to discuss students, identify problems, design instructional alternatives, modify materials, and so on. The third prerequisite is that regular and special educators learn to work cooperatively. Historically, many mainstream teachers resent the special education teacher, who has fewer students, more materials, and so on, while many special educators view regular teachers as uncaring, unskilled, and the source of their students' failures. These attitudes are often barriers to cooperative planning. Although changing the attitudes of educators is a long and tedious process, it is a necessary prerequisite to mainstream handicapped students successfully into high school content-area classes.[22]

The results of a four-year project in the Pittsburgh public schools outline a systematic approach to ensure support for the changes necessary for the teacher-consultant and general educator to work and plan cooperatively.[23] They must follow a sequence of eight steps for determining appropriate modifications:

1. Determine requirements for making it in the mainstream class.
2. Specify which course requirements the student is not meeting.
3. Hypothesize causes of failure.
4. Brainstorm possible classroom modifications.
5. Reject alternatives.
6. Select an action plan.
7. Implement the change.
8. Evaluate the changes.

The relationship between the resource room teacher and the mainstream teacher must be cooperative. The resource room teacher cannot tell the mainstream teacher what to do, but instead, can brainstorm possible solutions and help the teachers select from among possible options. Table 9–1 presents several of the alternatives that may be considered.

In addition to helping the mainstream teacher modify classroom organization and management and methods of presentation, practice, and testing, the resource room teacher should help the mainstream teachers modify their particular content areas. This new team approach is a vital aspect of successful teaching of handicapped learners. Without such cooperative efforts, the disabled students will not be able to profit from their high school education.

Parent Education Programs

Parent involvement is another important factor to be included in a comprehensive resource room program. The resource room teacher-consultant should establish parent-school contact early in the school year and act as a liaison between the handicapped student, the resource room program, mainstream classes, and the student's parents. The role of parents at the secondary level is significant. Often parents have been familiar with their child's learning problem since elementary school years. Sometimes, however, the problem remains unrecognized until junior or senior high school, when academic demands change and the handicapped student can no longer cope or get by. These parents, therefore, must be provided with important information related to their child's learning and development. They need to be informed about the services available to handicapped students within the high school and about post-high school alternatives. Moreover, these parents must be provided with help to understand themselves and their feelings. Many parents feel guilty about their child's disability, which often results in defensive reactions regarding their role in the situation. Parent education programs can be effective in establishing positive parent-school relations.

The parent education program should have two purposes. First, parents should be worked with individually. The teacher-consultant's initial contact should be by phone, introducing the program and presenting the positive effects for their child. The phone call should then be followed up with conferences. These conferences should deal with the student's strengths and weaknesses, and with the educational services being provided for both in the resource room and in the mainstream. Parent conferences can be coordinated with the guidance department, since each counselor plays an important role in regular class selection and in helping to see that content-area teachers carry out specific goals, objectives, and support services stipulated in the student's IEP.

The second purpose of the parent education program is parent group meetings. These meetings should focus on the parents themselves, rather than on the student. These meetings should provide parents with an opportunity to share and explore solutions to common problems. They should

Table 9–1 Realistic Alternatives for a Mainstream Teacher

Classroom Organization	Classroom Management	Methods of Presentation	Methods of Practice	Methods of Testing
Vary grouping arrangements • large group instruction • small group instruction • individual instruction • peer tutoring • independent self-instructional activities • learning centers Vary methods of instruction • teacher-directed • student-directed	Vary grading systems • homework • tests • class discussion • special projects Vary reinforcement systems • praise • notes sent home • grades • free time • special activity • progress charts • tangibles Vary rules • differentiated for some students • explicit/implicit	Vary content • amount to be learned • time to learn new information • conceptual level Vary general structure • advanced organizers • previewing questions • cues, mnemonic devices • provide immediate feedback • involve students actively Vary type • verbal-lecture, discussion • written texts, worksheets • demonstration • audiovisuals • tape recorders • filmstrips • movies • opaque projectors • transparencies	Vary general structure • amount to be practiced • time for practice • group/individual • teacher-directed/independent items ranging from easy to difficult Vary level of response • copying • recognition • recall with cues • recall without cues Vary type of materials • worksheets • texts • audiovisual equipment	Vary type • verbal • written • demonstration Vary general structure • group/individual • amount to be tested • time for completion Vary level of recognition • recognition • recall with cues • recall

Source: T. E. Laurie et al., "Teaching Secondary Learning Disabled Students in the Mainstream," *Learning Disability Quarterly* 1, no. 4 (Fall 1978):68.

also help parents understand their anger and frustration, and learn new ways of dealing with their child's learning problems. Parents can be helped to cope with problems of management and control at home, and to learn how to set realistic expectations and objectives for their children.

Therefore, by providing behavior management principles and practical solutions to problems, parents can be helped toward a realistic appraisal of the student's strengths and weaknesses, and assisted in developing realistic short-term and long-term goals and career objectives for their child.

Inservice Training

Inservice training is an equally important component of a comprehensive resource room program at the secondary level. It may be offered to both regular and special teachers. General educators, especially, need to be backed up with good support services. Since most of the instructional service at the secondary level is carried on within the regular classroom, teachers must be provided with technical information regarding handicapping conditions and specific content areas. Handbooks can be devised and handouts circulated to content-area teachers to assist them in assimilating and applying this new body of information, as well as assisting them in providing alternative means to managing the diverse needs of these students.

The essence of inservice training includes modifications in teaching-learning styles and materials used in mainstream classes. Inservice courses should offer teachers practical suggestions for modifying: (a) the presentation of their course content; (b) assessment of the acquisition of the content; and (c) the nature and type of homework assignments.

The teacher's mode of presenting concepts can vary widely (that is, lecture, written outlines, silent reading, role playing, and so on) and can often match the student's preferred mode of response (that is, oral answers, tape-recording, lectures, selecting answers from written choices, drawing diagrams, and so on). Test-taking accommodations can also be made to meet the needs of handicapped students. Essay answers can be dictated orally. A tape recorder can be used, or the student can take the test in the resource room, where the resource room teacher administers the test orally and records the student's responses. Homework assignments can be modified by reducing the length of the assignment, or outlining or listing the entire term's assignments in calendar form to develop an overview of the course. Teaching students how to read chapters and answer questions at the end of chapters is an additional suggestion that teachers cannot take for granted.

These are just a few suggested guidelines for inservice training courses. These suggestions hopefully will serve as a catalyst for the teacher trainer in developing and devising curriculum and teaching modifications for subject area teachers.

CONCLUDING REMARKS

The special needs of the handicapped adolescent at the senior high school level are compounded by academic demands, social expectations, and post-high school career choices. Realistic solutions to these problems and fears of establishing secondary resource programs exist. To help mainstream teachers meet the challenge of PL 94-142, special educators must assume new roles and new responsibilities.

The resource room teacher, who provides direct services, is part diagnostician, remedial specialist, and learning strategist. The role of teacher-consultant broadens to assume administrative functions, coordinating services among special and regular educators and guidance counselors. The teacher-consultant also serves as the advocate for handicapped students within the secondary school setting.

Ideally, two special education teachers could fulfill the dual role of the resource room teacher at the senior high school level. If a second special education teacher cannot be hired to work in the resource room program, alternative staffing patterns can be made. For example, a fulltime teaching assistant to the resource room teacher can carry on direct instruction to handicapped students within the resource room. In addition, regular classroom teachers can voluntarily request assignment to the learning center in place of study hall, cafeteria, or homeroom responsibilities. In this way, the resource room teacher is afforded additional time to meet with classroom teachers to plan cooperatively alternative teaching-learning strategies. Student teachers in special education, peer tutors (honor students in the mainstream), and volunteer aides can also help the resource room teacher in carrying out direct service instruction.

If these staffing adjustments are made, the resource room teacher will have time to work with mainstream teachers, guidance counselors, administrators, and parents to provide the indirect services essential to meeting the needs of the handicapped high school student.

In order to meet the needs of handicapped students at the secondary level, a dual service resource program model can be effective. The program necessitates indirect services with general educators, in order to coordinate efforts with special educators. Both special and general educators assume new roles under this model, and together they can increase the probability of successfully mainstreaming these youngsters in the least restrictive environment.

NOTES

1. Gordon Alley and Donald Deshler, *Teaching the Learning Disabled Adolescent: Strategies and Methods*, (Denver, Col.: Love Publishing Co., 1979), pp. 3–4.

2. D.D. Deshler, "Psychoeducational Aspects of Learning Disabled Adolescents," In L. Mann, L. Goodman, and J.L. Wiederhold, eds., *Teaching the Learning Disabled Adolescent* (Boston, Mass.: Houghton Mifflin Co., 1978), p. 68.

3. Naomi Zigmond, "A Prototype of Comprehensive Services for Secondary Students with Learning Disabilities," *Learning Disability Quarterly* 1, no. 1 (Winter 1978): 40.

4. R. Bradfield, "Preparation for Achievement," In L.E. Anderson, ed., *Helping the Adolescent with the Hidden Handicap* (San Rafael, Cal.: Academic Therapy Publications, 1970), p. 89.

5. John M. Dillard, Lloyd R. Kinnison, and Barbara Caldwell, "Some Developmental Concerns for Strategies in Counseling Learning Disabled Adolescents," *Counseling and Human Development* 10, no. 2 (June 1978): 4.

6. Margaret F. Hawisher and Mary L. Calhoun, *The Resource Room* (Columbus, Ohio: Charles E. Merrill Publishing Co., 1978), pp. 6–7.

7. Gordon Alley and Donald Deshler, *Teaching the Learning Disabled Adolescent*, pp. 5–6.

8. Naomi Zigmond, "A Prototype of Comprehensive Services," p. 41.

9. Lester Mann, Libby Goodman, and J. Lee Wiederholt, eds., *Teaching the Learning Disabled Adolescent* (Boston, Mass.: Houghton Mifflin Co., 1978), pp. 281–82.

10. Stanford Diagnostic Reading and Math Test, Harcourt Brace Jovanovich, Inc., New York, N.Y., 1976; Specific Language Disability Test, Educators Publishing Service, Inc., Cambridge, MA 02138.

11. D. Deshler, N. Lowrey, and G.R. Alley, "Programming Alternatives for LD Adolescents: A Nationwide Survey," *Academic Therapy* 14, no. 4 (March 1979): 393.

12. Gordon Alley and Donald Deshler, *Teaching the Learning Disabled Adolescent*, p. 8.

13. Helen Weiss and Martin Weiss, *The Basic Language Kit* (Great Barrington, Mass.: Treehouse Associates).

14. Recording for the Blind, Inc., 215 East 58th Street, New York, NY 10022; (212) 751-0860.

15. D. Deshler, N. Lowrey, and G.R. Alley, "Programming Alternatives," p. 394.

16. Andrew S. Halpern, "Adolescents and Young Adults," *Exceptional Children* 45, no. 7 (April 1979): 519.

17. Lester Mann, Libby Goodman, and J. Lee Wiederholt, eds., *Learning Disabilities in the Secondary School*, pp. 284–5.

18. Libby Goodman and Lester Mann, *Learning Disabilities in the Secondary School (Issues and Practices)* (New York, N.Y.: Grune and Stratton, Inc., 1976), pp. 108–9.

19. W.R. Adkins, "Life Skills: Structured Counseling for the Disadvantaged," *Personal and Guidance Journal* 49 (1970): 108–9.

20. Naomi Zigmond, "A Prototype of Comprehensive Services," p. 45.

21. T.E. Laurie et al., "Teaching Secondary Learning Disabled Students in the Mainstream," *Learning Disability Quarterly* 1, no. 1 (Fall 1978): 64.

22. Ibid., p. 65.

23. Ibid., pp. 65–70.

BIBLIOGRAPHY

Alley, Gordon, and Deshler, Donald. *Teaching the Learning Disabled Adolescent: Strategies and Methods*. Denver, Col.: Love Publishing Co., 1978.

Anderson, Lauriel E., ed. *Helping the Adolescent with the Hidden Handicap*. San Rafael, Cal.: Academic Therapy Publications, 1970.

Burmeister, Lou E. *Reading Strategies for Middle and Secondary School Teachers*, 2d ed. Reading, Mass.: Addison-Wesley Publishing Co., 1978.

Deshler, D.; Lowrey, N.; and Alley, G.R. "Programming Alternatives for LD Adolescents: A Nationwide Survey." *Academic Therapy* 14, no. 4 (March 1979).

Dillard, John M.; Kinninson, Lloyd R.; and Caldwell, Barbara. "Some Developmental Concerns for Strategies in Counseling Learning Disabled Adolescents." *Counseling and Human Development* 10, no. 2 (June 1978).

Goodman, Libby, and Mann, Lester. *Learning Disabilities in the Secondary School (Issues and Practices)*. New York, N.Y.: Grune and Stratton, Inc., 1976.

Laurie, T.E., et al. "Teaching Secondary Learning Disabled Students in the Mainstream." *Learning Disability Quarterly* 1, no. 4 (Fall 1978).

Mann, Lester; Goodman, Libby; and Wiederholt, J. Lee. *Teaching the Learning Disabled Adolescent*. Boston, Mass.: Houghton Mifflin Co., 1978.

Sabatino, David A., and Mauser, August J. *Intervention Strategies for Specialized Secondary Education*. Boston, Mass.: Allyn and Bacon, 1978.

Schloss, Ellen, ed. *The Educator's Enigma: The Adolescent with Learning Disabilities*. San Rafael, Cal.: Academic Therapy Publications, 1971.

"Special Education for Adolescents and Young Adults." *Exceptional Education Quarterly* 1, no. 4 (Fall 1978).

Thomas, Ellen L., and Robinson, Alan H. *Improving Reading in Every Class*. Boston, Mass.: Allyn and Bacon, Inc., 1977.

Wiederholt, J. Lee; Hammill, Donald D.; and Brown, Virginia. *The Resource Teacher: A Guide to Effective Practices*. Boston, Mass.: Allyn and Bacon, Inc., 1978.

Wiig, Elisabeth H., and Semel, Eleanor M. *Language Disabilities in Children and Adolescents*. Columbus, Ohio: Charles E. Merrill Publishing Co., 1976.

Wiseman, Douglas E.; Hartwell, L. Kay; and Hannafin, Michael J. "Exploring the Reading and Listening Skills of Secondary Mildly Handicapped Students." *Learning Disability Quarterly* 3, no. 3 (Summer 1980).

Woodward, Dolores M. *Mainstreaming the Learning Disabled Adolescent*. Rockville, Md.: Aspens Systems Corp., 1981.

Zigmond, Naomi. "A Prototype of Comprehensive Services for Secondary Students with Learning Disabilities." *Learning Disability Quarterly* 1, no. 1 (Winter 1978).

Zigmond, Naomi; Silverman, R.; and Sansome. "Teaching Coping Skills to Adolescents with Learning Problems." *Focus on Exceptional Children* 3, no. 6 (February 1981).

At Issue

THE ROLE OF MINIMUM COMPETENCY TESTS IN THE EDUCATION OF HANDICAPPED STUDENTS

The establishment of minimum competency tests (MCT) has made an impact on a national basis. Presently, three-quarters of the states use minimum competency tests, and in 17 states, passing these tests is required for high school graduation.[1] The imposition of the MCT is undoubtedly a response to the public's outcry that some students are presently graduating from high school without attaining a minimal level of skill competency. Therefore it is felt that the testing of mathematics, reading, and writing is needed to validate the quality of a student's high school education. When such tests are not used as a requirement for high school graduation, they are implemented as a means of evaluating which students are in need of remediation. Many feel that the MCT places a greater responsibility on the local educational institution to evaluate the quality of education that their students are receiving. In some instances the recertification of high schools may depend on the percentage of students passing MCTs.

While the debate about the need for these tests and their validity continues, there is no question that such exams create problems for students who have been identified as handicapped. If all students must pass these tests to graduate, then certainly the curriculum of the resource program must accommodate and prepare exceptional learners for taking these exams. To educate mildly handicapped learners through intensive support services and to have them fail such competency tests would create extreme frustration for students as well as resource teachers.

In her article entitled "Minimum Competence Testing and Handicapped Students," Martha McCarthy provides an excellent overview of the ramifications of such tests for the exceptional learner.[2] The format of the article is that of issues for consideration. The resolution of these issues can only be accomplished by decisions on a state-by-state basis through ruling by state education departments. However, the examination of these issues and tentative answers, proposed by McCarthy, are worth careful consideration by special educators at the secondary level. The following summarizes some of the most pertinent issues with McCarthy's speculative answers.

• *Issue*: If MCTs are used as a requirement for high school graduation, should all students comply, or are there alternatives for the handicapped child?

The meaning of a high school diploma must be evaluated to address this issue. A diploma can be viewed as the satisfactory completion of a course of study (including the concept of completing an IEP), or it can be seen as the completion of a designated number of years of schooling. Others might view the granting of a diploma as attesting to the mastery of certain skills felt to be minimal preparation for postsecondary experiences such as employment or higher education. Going on the assumption that a high school diploma represents demonstrated skill competency, those who do not demonstrate such competency should be denied a diploma. The state is legally empowered to set levels for the evaluation of performance, and, whether or not these levels are based on passing specified courses and number of academic units and passing competency tests, these criteria are valid if applied universally in a nondiscriminatory manner.

McCarthy feels that, unless the awarding of a high school diploma is to be individualized for each student, it would be difficult to justify exempting handicapped children from the MCT requirement, thereby applying more stringent standards to the nonhandicapped population.

If the state education department chooses to deny a student his or her diploma based on an inability to pass MCTs, then such tests must bear close scrutiny as to their validity and reliability.

If the state education department chooses to validate the handicapped child's secondary education with the alternative approach of successful completion of an IEP, problems arise. As a handicapped child may receive at the minimum one IEP for each year of secondary education and such children are required to be educated through their twenty-first birthday, which IEP should be used? If a student receives a diploma based on completion of the IEP but is unable to perform at a minimally competent level and therefore is rejected by higher education or the working community, is the high school diploma a valid document?

Those wishing to pursue the question of incorporating the IEP into the minimum competency program are directed to read "Minimum Competency Testing and the IEP Process" by Kenneth Olsen.[3] Olsen suggests approaches for integrating MCT skills within the IEP. Another article by P. Grisé, entitled "Florida's Minimum Competency Testing Program for Handicapped Students," describes how Florida has implemented ways of testing handicapped children through such means as exemptions, special standards, and modification of testing techniques.[4]

• *Issue*: Should some categories of exceptional learners be excused from the MCT process?

If MCTs are used to identify children in need of remediation, then all handicapped children should take part in this testing program. The MCT will assist in the process of evaluating mastery of objectives and can be incorporated into the diagnosis or evaluation needed for the IEP.

If, however, the MCT is used as a graduation requirement and there is little reason to believe that a handicapped child is able to pass the test, the child should be exempt from the testing program. The decision to exempt the child from the MCT should be specified in the child's IEP and be based on the child's capabilities. Any handicapped child who wishes to attempt the exam should be given the opportunity to do so until he or she reaches 21 years of age.

If exceptional learners are to be exempted from the MCT program and passing such tests is a graduation requirement, then certificates of program completion should be awarded for those exempted. In New York state there is a current controversy regarding a local school district's decision to award a regular high school diploma to handicapped students who did not take or pass the MCT that is currently required for graduation. As of yet, the state education department has not chosen to revoke these diplomas, but the validity of the diploma is in question.

• *Issue*: Should handicapped students receiving attendance certificates rather than diplomas be segregated during graduation exercises?

Handicapped youngsters should be given the opportunity to partake in graduation exercises. Such a ceremony does not validate a student's proficiency in the same manner as does the high school diploma. To deny handicapped students the gratification of commemorating their years of education cannot be defended on any legal or educational basis.

• *Issue*: What technical concerns need to be addressed in using the MCT with handicapped learners?

The federal mandate of PL 94-142 specifies that all tests and evaluation procedures be demonstrated as valid for the specific purposes for which they are intended. As the MCT is a new type of testing instrument and may measure a wide range of academic or functional living skills, it must be scrutinized as to its validity and reliability. In addition, some states have chosen to include a phase-in period of four to twelve years to demonstrate that students have had adequate time to prepare for the MCT.

• *Issue*: What adaptations are available so that the MCT can be used with handicapped students?

Any modification in the testing procedure should be done to ensure that the test is a valid measure of the student's academic competency and does not solely reflect the child's handicapping condition. Florida has made such adaptations as flexible scheduling of the tests, adaptable testing environments, variations in test format, acceptance of alternative modes of response, and the use of auditory aids. Such adaptations must be made on the basis of the child's individual set of handicapping conditions. Caution should be taken to ensure that test modifications do not invalidate the academic purpose for testing.

There are several other issues relating to competency testing programs and handicapped learners. These include methods of integrating the IEP objectives with MCT objectives through programmatic changes, qualifications of those overseeing the administration and interpretation of the MCT for handicapped students, and the vulnerability of the local educational agency to legal suits on the part of nonhandicapped learners who fail the MCT or the handicapped learner who is denied a diploma.

The MCT program needs to be carefully evaluated. It is no panacea for validating secondary education. "Minimum competency testing will not make poor teachers become excellent teachers or dull students become bright."[5] The public needs to be educated as to its true usefulness.

McCarthy concludes her overview of the issue with this admonition:

> . . . if competency tests are used as the basis for awarding diplomas, educators must be able to substantiate that the tests are reliable, valid, and bias free and that students have received adequate instruction as to the required competencies. Indeed, this is a challenging assignment for education agencies contemplating the use of minimum competency tests.[6]

Certainly, the imposition of an MCT can dramatically affect the kind of education received by handicapped students, their ability to receive a regular high school diploma, and the role of the secondary resource teacher.

NOTES

1. M. McCarthy, "Minimum Competency Testing and Handicapped Students," *Exceptional Children* 47, no. 3 (November 1980): 166.

2. Ibid., pp. 166–72.

3. K. Olsen, "Minimum Competency Testing and the IEP Process," *Exceptional Children* 47, no. 3 (November 1980): 176–83.

4. P. Grisé, "Florida's Minimum Competency Testing Program for Handicapped Students," *Exceptional Children* 47, no. 3 (November 1980): 186–91.

5. McCarthy, "Minimum Competency Testing," p. 172.

6. Ibid.

Chapter 10

Developing a Resource Program for College Students

Kathleen Joyce

Handicapped students have always attended universities if they had the mental ability, courage, and stamina to do so. In many cases these individuals had to work doubly hard to maneuver into the classroom, acquire the course information (in or out of class), or produce the required end products. Blind students, physically handicapped students, and deaf students were virtually left on their own to obtain their education.

REHABILITATION ACT OF 1973

Gradually, over the past 20 years, individuals with handicaps have become not only accepted in colleges and the business world, but their presence has mandated many changes in their working environments. Through awareness and acceptance, but mainly through changes in the law, the onus has been placed on the university to adapt itself to the handicapped student. Since the passage of the Rehabilitation Act of 1973, many physical modifications have been mandated. Section 504 of the Act states that each building on a university campus must have one entrance serviced by a ramp to accommodate wheelchairs. If there is no elevator in the building, any class for which the student registers must be offered on the first floor of the building. Even toilets must be reconstructed "barrier free" to accommodate the physically handicapped. This mandate also holds for persons with heart impairments or some other affliction that prevents them from climbing stairs. Handicapped students also have the right to have a note taker and someone to carry their books if they are physically unable to do this themselves. These services are to be provided by the educational institution.

Blind and deaf students have also been afforded many accommodations on the university level. For example, translators are now being provided who translate lectures into sign language for deaf students or who give oral responses for the speech impaired. Extra lighting, Braille textbooks, and taped textbooks are being provided for the visually impaired college student. It is no longer the case that handicapped students may attend college if they can physically; rather, now it is up to the college to "make reasonable adjustments to permit handicapped persons to fulfill academic requirements, and to assure that they are not effectively excluded from programs because of the absence of auxiliary aides" (Section 504—Rehabilitation Act of 1973).

The program accessibility section of this Act includes the term "specific learning disabilities" under the heading of physical or mental impairment. Included are perceptual handicaps, minimal brain dysfunction, dyslexia, and developmental aphasia. Although learning disabilities are often referred to as invisible handicaps, since the evidence of their existence is not as overt as a wheelchair, cane, or hearing aid, nevertheless the law requires these students be provided an equal opportunity to obtain an academic education.

Subsection E of the Act deals with postsecondary education. There is no specific mandate for the establishment of resource rooms or programs for perceptually or physically impaired students, as long as "reasonable adjustments" are made to afford them equality of educational opportunity. These adjustments include modifications in adminstration of admissions tests, any inquiry as to whether a person is handicapped (unless it is to take action to overcome the problems of the handicap), or exclusion of qualified handicapped students from any course of study. However, the response of universities has ranged from token compliance with the law to active and vigorous participation in all aspects of education, from academic to social and emotional.

THE COLLEGE RESOURCE PROGRAM

Although there are scattered programs throughout the country that offer precollege preparation or various forms of auxiliary support services, most of these programs are geared to the physically handicapped, such as the deaf or crippled, and the number of these programs are minimal. For the most part, there has been little choice available for the less obviously impaired students after they finish high school. What happens to those who are intelligent and who desire to further their education, but who have such disabilities as dyslexia, auditory perception disabilities, or written expressive that prevent them from being successful in a regular college setting?

Within the past few years, a number of colleges and universities have started to develop resources to help learning disabled or perceptually impaired students attain a higher education. In many cases, these are either one-year programs or precollege preparatory sessions to help students learn to compensate for their disabilities. This may be quite successful with some students who are capable of functioning independently when given the proper compensatory skills and direction. However, many other students, whether their handicap is physical, perceptual, or neurological, will require continuous support and modification to be able to complete their college education. Since the law mandates that modifications be made for all handicapped students no matter what that handicap may be, long-range decisions must be made as to how to establish the alternative situations within the university to supply long-range compensatory facilities for students who require them.

In many cases, all areas of the learning disabled person's life are affected by the handicap, including the ability to make and maintain friendships, to drive a car, and to form appropriate study habits. College life does not and should not afford the insulation of a self-contained classroom, albeit for a summer, a semester, or a full college program. Handicapped students attending college ought to do so fully, because college offers more than what is learned in the classroom. Many handicapped students are deficient in the area of the extra-academic activities and need support.

On the elementary and secondary level, resource rooms are able to afford the most concentrated and individualized help to all handicapped students, while keeping them in the mainstream. This "least restrictive environment" not only fulfills the mandate of PL 94-142, but also lessens the stigma often attached to the self-contained class in day school programs.

Since each handicap presents its own type of problem, whether it be physical, academic, or emotional, the idea of developing a resource program on the college level would be both innovative and practical. The resource room would not only handle the remedial aspects of the student's education, but would also coordinate all aspects of the college career. This should include offering social and emotional as well as academic supports; arranging for class programming that would be accessible; assigning tutors, interpreters, and translators; and arranging for books on tape. Finally, the resource room should handle a university-wide public relations campaign for recognition, understanding, and ultimate acceptance of all kinds of handicapped students.

Admission

The learning disabled student probably would appear intellectually to be least likely to succeed on the college level. Although the admissions office screens candidates for acceptance, the resource faculty should help establish some criteria, based on the guidelines of the Rehabilitation Act, for handicapped students, particularly those with perceptual or learning impairments. For example, the measured intelligence of a learning disabled student may be somewhat depressed due to difficulty in processing or lack of expressive skills. However, the subscores of the Wechsler Intelligence Scales will aid in the understanding of the nature of students' disabilities and their deficient areas. General knowledge, visual or auditory memory, spatial relations, visual-motor coordination, and some aspects of social intelligence can all be examined qualitatively. These scores enable the examiner and the admissions team to understand the area of the student's deficit and how it affects functioning. A poor Information subscore, for example, may mean poor memory, inability to process information in the way it was received, or insufficient ability to pick out an important fact from given information. Comprehension scores may exhibit deficits in verbal expression, auditory processing, or reasoning ability. Coding scores may demonstrate poor visual memory, poor tracking, or poor visual-motor integration.

These will all affect the way students will handle the work assigned them. Low subscores in some areas do not necessarily mean overall low intelligence, as other areas may be far above average. In addition, there are a few subtests that measure more general or abstract intelligence. These include Similarities, Block Design, and Picture Arrangement. By looking at each response, and at the entire score for each of these subtests, the examiner can ascertain whether this person will be able to form concepts, or abstract and generalize ideas, and thus be able to handle college level work. Without this ability, even if other subtest scores are high, the individual's chances of success would be limited. This information should be shared with admissions officers to help them better understand the nature of a learning disability and how the student could or could not function in college.

Motivation, or a strong desire to attend college, should also be considered for admission, because the long, extra hours of compensatory studying might make the endeavor overbearing. A personal interview is the most effective means to ascertain a student's motivation. A member of the college resource program should be part of the admissions interview to help understand the students, and their skills and deficits. Any input the resource program faculty would have for admissions would be most beneficial not only in screening the students but enlightening the counselors about what to look for and expect from prospective students with visible or discrete handicaps.

Examination of the quantitative and qualitative remedial programs on the elementary and secondary level would be helpful in understanding each student's level of functioning. Certainly the depressed grades of a student whose school was remiss in offering remediation would not be considered as heavily in the admission process as those of a student who has had several years of diligent services.

Precollege Summer Session

Before any learning disabled students are unconditionally accepted into college, there should be an intermediate remedial and diagnostic period, where both students and college get to know and assess each other. Resource rooms on the elementary and high school level spend many weeks at the beginning of each term doing diagnostic testing, assessing, and planning for the individual needs of each student. Although it is necessary, it is often to the detriment of the students to miss out on these weeks of remediation. On the college level, this time for testing and planning should be done before the start of the first-year semester, since students will need all the academic assistance they can get once classes start.

The college level resource program should coordinate a program prior to the opening of classes for the first year, preferably coinciding with one summer session. This period should last approximately six weeks. During this period the handicapped students should be given the opportunity to sample the various aspects of college and decide if it is appropriate for them. At the same time the college, via the resource program, can assess the student formally through diagnostic tests and informally by observing study habits, ability to handle college work, and emotional and social adjustment. The duties of the resource program would be expanded over the summer to handle not only the testing and academic needs of the students, but also their social and emotional adjustment. Summer session would be a time of learning everything from library skills and how to write a college paper to tennis and how to get along with a roommate.

The handicapped students, accepted into college and under the auspices of the resource support, should be requested to live on campus for the summer program. For some, this may be their first experience being away from home and functioning independently. Reactions to their experience might include fear, timidity, mild disorientation or confusion, or over-abundant use of this new freedom. Because of these reactions and because some handicapped people, especially those with learning disabilities or other perceptual handicaps, lack internal controls and feedback systems to ration their time appropriately and understand their feelings, a counseling component of the resource program is necessary, particularly in the summer. A trained resident adviser should be available to handle any problems that arise in the dorms, and to use these experiences to teach or demonstrate how particular social situations can be handled. Informal dorm meetings might even be held to discuss both the theoretical and actual difficulties that are part of group living, such as expression of feelings and opinions, and finding times and places both to study and relax.

More formal counseling should also be available for students, either individually or in small groups, to discuss any personal problems they might be experiencing. The aim of resource counseling is twofold: (1) to assess the student's present ability to handle the social and emotional pressures that college entails, but more importantly, (2) to guide the student over the rough areas of adjustment in all phases of college life and to teach him or her how to handle particular social situations.

Academically, the summer resource program should consist of diagnostic testing, remedial courses in English and study skills, some credited courses in an area of interest that would be nonthreatening and not too demanding, and individualized tutoring. Resource programs are usually given the task of handling all diagnostic testing, but on the college level this testing has a dual purpose. First, any external funding source that supports a resource program would mandate some visible evaluative procedures. Pre- and posttesting would be required to show areas of improvement. Second, these tests can indicate to the educational staff of the resource program not only the student's comparative levels of functioning, but also how information is perceived and processed by the student to arrive at a particular answer. If compensatory skills are going to be taught, the learning channels and processes must be understood.

Since the purpose of the college level resource program is not only to help students with their course work but to prepare them better to function independently, the precollege summer program should include formal training in English usage, particularly written expressive language. A regular course, offered by the resource room staff, should begin with parts of speech and include forming a complete thought and formulating it into a sentence and paragraph. Use of the library and its reference materials must also be covered. Each student should have tutoring in small, homogeneous groups, preferably on a daily basis. These sessions should both complement and supplement the course by providing practical application of classroom theory.

Because students with different handicaps are being offered the services of the resource program, some sessions will have to be strictly individualized to handle the different needs of the students. Some students may need to learn about the nonprint media section of a library so that they can obtain taped or visually presented information. Others may need to learn how to handle the library physically, and where and how to go about obtaining assistance. Still others will have to learn the purpose and use of a card catalog and various types of reference material. In all cases, the tutors should help the students research a topic of their choice, guiding them through the library readers' guides and other references necessary for learning to write a college paper.

The most effective means of learning for anyone, not just a handicapped person, is to experience a situation visually, auditorily, motorically, or kinesthetically. The actual performance of a task will make a more lasting impression on the student's memory. Tutors may also assist the students in getting their notes organized into thoughts, and their thoughts organized and processed into grammatically correct written and verbal form. Since one of the purposes of the resource program is to teach the students to compensate for their disabilities, the student who has written expressive difficulties, whether the etiology is physical or perceptual, may want to learn to dictate a report into a tape recorder. The student can experiment with the amount of taping needed and with determining when a report is ready to be put on paper. The question of whether or not to put a taped report on paper will be discussed later.

Prospective math or business students may want to learn basic math skills on their calculators. Tutors should help with calculator skills, explaining its compensatory ability for dyscalculaic students. These skills would be reinforced later when practical application would be mandated. Previous knowledge and understanding reduces anxiety.

The second nongraded course would involve study skills and would be taught in groups, then individualized by tutors for the special problems of each student. Informal testing and observation by a specialist from the resource program can pinpoint, along with the diagnostic tests, areas of dysfunction and the methods that the student uses to learn. When the dominant learning mode and learning style are understood, specific ideas to help with comprehension, attention span, memory associations, or even the development of an entire new style of learning can be attempted. Classwork may include helpful hints for study organization, such as wearing and using a wrist watch, buying a datebook and keeping it filled in with every daily activity, and having a large calendar where a month's activities can be seen at a glance.

These suggestions may sound almost too simplistic to mention, but it sometimes is the obvious that is most overlooked by many handicapped, particularly the learning disabled. Laying out a daily plan, setting specific times for study, learning how to study each subject, and rationing time are also topics for this course. Finally, for the students who need to hear their textbooks, either due to blindness, dyslexia, a physical impairment, or weak visual memory, class time should be devoted to how to obtain a cassette tape player through the Library of Congress. These play "Talking Books" taped by various voluntary organizations, such as Recordings for the Blind. The intricacies of reading a catalog, checking for the correct edition, and ordering the textbooks on tape need to be demonstrated to the student. The resource faculty should also help those students with hearing impairments to arrange for interpreters who can either sign for them or take notes in class.

A difficult decision for the educational and counseling component of the resource program is how much follow-up there should be for each student. Although people with learning disabilities as well as other handicaps may be forgetful and need to be reminded and prodded, many can be manipulative and wait to have things done for them just to avoid having to do it themselves. The aim is to wean the students from dependent to independent functioning, but in a way that is productive, not destructive.

A resource program is traditionally defined as a place where a student can receive academic assistance. However, on the college level, a number of questions arise, particularly with learning disabled or perceptually impaired students. Such students often require more academic guidelines than the average students and ought to be treated as such. Therefore, should this academic assistance be given only upon request, when the student feels help is needed, or should unsolicited tutorial help be mandated for resource program members? Do anger, frustration, and resentment increase by being forced to go to tutoring? If so, does this decrease academic performance? Should students with learning problems be given the freedom to decide for themselves if and when they want tutorial assistance? Perhaps the most pragmatic solution is to mandate resource assistance for a certain number of hours during the first year of college, and then allow more optional attendance as the students know themselves, their courses, and their needs better.

The question of need, and required versus optional assistance or intervention by the resource program, can be applied to any handicap. Some students want to handle all problems and situations as they arise by themselves. They feel they not only have the self-confidence to do this, but that this is also a growing process for them. This mature attitude may be genuine or may be a form of rationalization, for not wanting to face the limitations that impairments may cause. The resource counseling staff should assess, as best as possible, the emotional attitudes and needs of the college students they are servicing.

Sometime near the beginning of the summer program, a full day should be set aside for an orientation program. In many colleges and universities the counseling department or admissions office arranges this, or, if necessary, it may be handled by the resource staff. In any case, the day should consist of a full tour of the campus, including dorms, library, gym, and various departments and administrative offices. The students should also be taught the function of the different offices, such as bursar and registrar, and be given sample situations of where to go for specific problems on campus. Accessibility of the various buildings and offices should be brought to the attention of the physically impaired students, along with how to go about dealing with situations where their accessibility is limited. Most learning disabled or perceptually impaired students need experience, not just verbal explanation, in order to remember what they have been taught. The more practice they have in using college facilities, the more secure they will be using them.

The students should be evaluated for the summer on their ability and their progress. Much of the evaluation should be done by the tutors and dorm counselors who have seen the students work and perform on a first-hand basis. Criteria used should include the following:

- Is the student exhibiting motivation and desire to improve his or her skills in the summer session?
- Has the student been able to follow a study routine and devote serious time to studying?
- Has the student recognized the disability, be it physical or perceptual, and that this disability will demand more time and effort than is required of the average student?
- Is the student capable of organizing a research paper on the college level?
- Is the student capable of coping with social problems in a socially acceptable manner?

Near the end of the summer session, a written report should be prepared and sent to the parents. This should include an evaluation from each person involved in the student's activities during this period. Tutors, dorm counselors, English and study skills instructors, and faculty members teaching the credit hour courses should all have input.

The goal of helping the student toward independence is not diminished by the report of their progress to their parents. The summer session is a diagnostic period where the student is not only evaluated, but educated and taught compensation skills. The report tells how their child is functioning in this diagnostic college setting.

If either the student or program staff members decide that college is not the correct choice at this time, career counseling should be offered to help the person decide on a more appropriate goal based on abilities and interests. Skill and interest inventories are available to facilitate this.

Matriculation

Students accepted for admission by the college or university should no longer be offered the insulation of the summer program. They become matriculated students who should enter the mainstream of the college, academically and socially when the fall semester begins. Because of their membership in the resource program, the students should be expected to participate in many advice and support systems during the academic year.

Before the students leave for home at the end of summer school, they will have to register for the fall semester, and will be offered advice on their choice of courses for the first year. It is recommended that the minimum number of credits for a full program be taken first semester. The student has to adjust to the amount of work required for each college course, as well as to a tutorial, counseling, and study schedule. By starting with a smaller course load, the chances for success will be increased.

The students may enter any major area of study that they choose, but the resource program should be available to advise them with practical and realistic choices. For example, severely dyslexic students with poor expressive skills should be counseled away from English as a major, as should poor math students be advised against an accounting or business major. It should be strongly recommended to these new students that they declare themselves "undecided majors" and take some basic courses from various departments. This will help the students get an idea of where their interests lie and what type of course they may be best able to handle.

The function of the resource teacher in the program changes somewhat as the students enter their first year. The resource teacher no longer structures the students' days, but now assists them directly through tutoring and counseling, and indirectly through public relations and faculty education. The program now takes on more of the function of a typical resource room. Tutorial work and counseling remain the major portion of the program in order to support the students in their studies. However, these efforts, no matter how dedicated and determined, are not sufficient without the understanding and cooperation of the total school faculty.

In addition, developing independence in these students is not an overnight process. It is a learning and maturing process that comes as a result of skill and practice. Socialization is also a learned process, particularly for the learning disabled, just by the nature of this handicap. Becoming socially accepted is not an automatic event for a large proportion of handicapped students. Counseling is absolutely essential in the resource program, particularly throughout the first year, to help students learn and practice the social skills and nuances that are part of daily living. Many students may continue to live in the dormitory, and may or may not have roommates that are also part of the program. The right to privacy and to individuality, and an understanding and respect for the feelings of others, need to be discussed, reinforced, and practiced. Fears, anxieties, problems with professors and fellow students, and how to deal with particular situations must also be discussed. It should be up to the individual whether he or she wants to be part of a counseling group or meet in private sessions. Both should be available, but the groups should have regular meeting times. If the counselor's available time is posted in the program office, each student may choose times for counseling sessions. Counseling by either method should be mandatory.

Tutors in the resource program should assume a dual role during the academic year. They should also assist the student in course work assignments. Hopefully, as study skills improve, this will become less necessary. Gradually, the tutors should take an increasingly passive role in the student's academic life. However, it should not be assumed that every student will eventually manage without any tutoring, although this is the ultimate aim and success of the resource program. In many cases, the tutor may be needed to help translate information to be acquired into a form that the student can understand, such as with the aid of outlines and diagrams. Not everyone can learn solely by reading or by listening to a tape. Eventually, the academic weaning from dependence to independence will include helping the student develop the skills to translate material into a form that can be studied independently.

Students and tutors should meet daily for 60 to 90 minutes. This amount of time is required to help the student learn to organize material and develop a learning schedule. This also allows for a sufficient period of time for reinforcement of work in each course the student is taking.

For reasons of expedience, efficiency of instructional time, and social growth, students taking the same course should form study groups with the tutor. Discussion and sharing of information by everyone can benefit the group. This has been found to be an effective tool in gaining peer cooperation, and no amount of lecturing can equal the value of peer acceptance. In this case, too, learning by doing is the most effective way of learning.

Public Relations and Faculty Education

It was mentioned earlier that a resource program would indirectly affect the student through public relations and faculty education. The administrators of the program must actively engage in sharing information about their role to the rest of the university. This can be accomplished in a variety of ways. Newsletters announcing the existence of a resource program for handicapped students and its location on campus is a good start. Subsequent newsletters explaining the meaning of the various handicaps, such as learning disabilities and perceptual impairments, their effect on students, and the general purpose of the program can be sent to all staff members. In addition, the educational and counseling directors can jointly visit campus organizations and offices, such as continuing education, career counseling, and Educational Opportunities Program, to exchange information and ideas. Time can be requested at the faculty meetings of various departments, where the directors can personally explain the aim of the resource program and the types of problems encountered in college by the students involved. Once the program and the students are understood for what they are, they will be less feared and more welcomed around the university. There are still many people, even in the field of education, who do not understand the concept of many handicaps, especially learning disabilities and other invisible impairments.

Another function of the program is to inform the university faculty of the students' rights under the law. As mentioned at the beginning of this chapter, these include the right to note takers and translators in class, the right to have books on tape, and even the right to tape the lectures themselves. Also, no rules may be imposed in any class that would in any way limit the participation of the handicapped student. This has vast implications depending on the type of handicap. It has yet to be determined if, legally, students with written language impairments may submit reports on tape. However, it is the right of the faculty to be made aware of the actual and potential implications of the law.

A further responsibility of the educational director is to meet with any faculty members who will have a learning disabled or other impaired student in their class, and discuss with them the specific problems and learning modes of that individual. If the professor is responsive, specific teaching techniques and modifications may also be discussed. This is then followed by a written profile of the student for teacher reference. At no time should the faculty member feel that the student would benefit by lowering expectations or decreasing assignments for that individual. A resource program on the college level involves compensation, not compromise. The faculty must understand that any concessions made to the students should not include academic material, but rather the way the material is presented to them and assimilated by them. If the course work is not equal, then the college degree is not going to be equal, and the purpose of the program is lost. The student must *earn* his or her degree, albeit through compensatory means.

As the semester progresses, the program staff should maintain contact with the involved faculty. The purpose is to monitor student progress and to assist in case of problems or answer any questions that may arise. An instructor may feel a student is missing information imparted in class and may need hints on how to help the person understand the material. Perhaps the professor is requiring a term paper and needs guidelines for the student. As mentioned previously, some learning disabled individuals are so deficient in written expressive skills that no amount of training or practice is going to help. In the summer, these students can be taught to dictate their papers into a recorder and then transcribe it. However, when the student carries nine or twelve academic credits, this process is laborious and time consuming. Program intervention would involve requesting general permission of the faculty for certain students to be allowed to hand in written assignments, such as reports and term papers on tape. This is not an individual request for each student, because this would tend to increase dependency. The resource program is asking for understanding and support of the faculty. It is then the responsibility of each student to decide if this is best and to discuss it with the individual professor.

Further program interventions may include notifying and discussing with the course instructors the need for individuals to have their exams administered orally and to dictate their answers verbally. This will probably involve a large majority of the handicapped students. The administrators of the program must take the responsibility for this process, and for the ancillary duties of scheduling times for the exams that are both agreeable with the instructor and convenient for the student. They must also pick up and return the exams on time. It may be necessary for counselors and directors to become test administrators during final exams or any time when test schedules are tight. The requirements of the instructor must be followed. The integrity of the testing procedure must be upheld.

Advisement and Registration

A final task of the resource program is to help the student with course selection and registration. After one semester, some students may have a general idea of the direction they would like to take. Others may have chosen a particular major and already been assigned faculty advisors. The cooperation between the program and the various academic departments will have already opened communication channels. The program administrator and faculty advisor must discuss both course requirements for the student and the quantitative limitations of the handicapping condition. A workable schedule may combine a course or two that involves much research and writing with some less strenuous credit hours. The department advisor and resource program representative should also candidly discuss the advantages of particular instructors in the department. It is not uncommon for some people to be more understanding of a student with a handicap, and therefore be more amenable to accommodating the class for the student. Conversely, some professors may consider that having a tape recorder present or having to modify teaching techniques is unpleasant and bothersome, even though it is mandated by law. Naturally, the handicapped student would benefit more from the former situation.

There is a possibility that, due to decreased course loads each semester, many perceptually handicapped students may not complete degree requirements in four years. Some may choose to attend summer school, while others may remain in college a fifth year. Although it might seem disheartening for the student at the time, ultimately it is a small price to pay for a college education that may have been impossible to accomplish a few years ago.

Coordinating Tutoring and Counseling

Students are requested to submit a copy of their course programs to the resource program as soon as possible after registration. Tutorial and group counseling times must be arranged so that they do not interfere with class schedules. The individual's right to choose course section and professor should be honored in every feasible circumstance. Only when scheduling is impossible should the student be consulted about a change.

The problem of coordinating tutoring and counseling with each student's course schedule poses a difficult administrative problem. Is it more practical to hire fulltime tutors and counselors, and work the programming on a nine-to-five timetable, or is it more expedient to hire parttime employees or graduate students from special education, psychology, and social work?

There are benefits to both systems. Fulltime staff members would be available to their students for more hours each day. They may also assume some of the responsibilities of dealing with individual faculty members, of scheduling exams for their students, and so on. Hiring a parttime staff would ease the difficulty in arranging schedules since their work time could be spread out into the evening. Naturally, financial considerations are a factor in this decision. If there is a limited budget, meeting the salary requirements of certified psychologists or special education teachers is difficult. Competition from boards of education and from private practice is formidable. Fulltime employees are the less practical solution, both in terms of temporal requirements and monetary considerations.

How can this situation be resolved? In most states, certification requirements in education do not permit individual or group tutoring in lieu of the classroom student teaching requirement. However, many certified learning disabilities teachers may be anxious for parttime work, and both day and evening schedules may be arranged based on the student's needs. Students with late classes can be tutored early in the day, and those whose daytime class and activity schedule is full can have evening tutoring. This will benefit everybody, since for most of the day and evening there will be at least one tutor available on campus in case of any difficulty in studying or homework.

Graduate students in clinical psychology or social work may be used as resident advisors in the dorms. Moreover, they may act as counselors as part of their field work internship under supervision. The cost to the program or college is minimal. Certified tutors are paid on an hourly basis, and only one fulltime psychologist or social worker, probably the program's social service director, is required to supervise the interns.

At the end of the first year, each student should meet with both the education and the social directors to evaluate progress. A decision can then be mutually made as to the amount, if any, of tutoring and counseling that the individual may need in the following semester. This decision should not be irrevocable; the student may request additional assistance from the program at any time during the term. With proper planning, the program can be flexible enough to accommodate any contingencies.

CONCLUSION

In summarizing the highlights of a college resource program, a few points bear emphasizing. First, the precollege summer session is a diagnostic period. The students are taught to use their strongest learning modes and to compensate in areas where they are deficient. They are taught how to study, how to research, and how to organize their time and their work.

Second, the students are offered assistance in the form of counseling to help them develop some of the social skills and some level of emotional maturity necessary to survive in college. Next, the program offers direct academic support to the student through daily tutoring, and indirect assistance by eliciting faculty understanding and cooperation.

Last, and most important, the essence of a resource program on the college level is compensation, not compromise. The bachelor's degree earned by the physically or perceptually handicapped student must have the same worth as every bachelor's degree granted by the university. Anything less destroys the entire value of the program.

At Issue

CAREER EDUCATION FOR THE POSTSECONDARY, HANDICAPPED STUDENT

College resource programs will probably grow more prevalent as higher learning institutions need to comply with the mandate for providing non-discriminatory admissions procedures and equal access to facilities for all qualified handicapped learners. In addition, admitting learning disabled students to community colleges and senior colleges will increase as the demand grows to create special programs for these mildly handicapped students.

What is the role of career education for these postsecondary, handicapped students? There is a growing concern on the part of special educators that career education should be incorporated into the curriculum for handicapped students at the elementary and secondary levels. While little attention has been given to the concept of career education for the handicapped student at the postsecondary level, a higher education degree that is not marketable in the workplace is an injustice.

The most commonly referred to definition of career education was supplied by Hoyt in 1972:

> Career education represents the total effort of public education and the community to help all individuals become familiar with the values of a work oriented society, to integrate those values into their personal value structure, and to implement those values in their lives in ways that make work possible, meaningful, and satisfying to each individual.[1]

In a somewhat more specific fashion, Mori defined career education as:

> A lifelong, continuous process which begins in preschool or in the home and continues through formal educational channels on into adulthood. The learner is exposed to career awareness, career exploration, career preparation, and continuing education in order to understand the relationship between a career and one's life style.[2]

With such definitions, all resource teachers must consider the role of career education in their resource program curriculums. Clark and White have specified a set of seven tasks for resource room teachers of exceptional children with regard to implementing career education. These suggestions can apply at all levels of instruction:

1. Integrate, to the fullest extent possible, the assumptions of career education for the handicapped into their instructional activities.
2. Help pupils develop, clarify, and assimilate personally meaningful attitudes, values, and habits.
3. Help pupils develop and demonstrate behaviors reflecting positive human relationships.
4. Help pupils acquire information on occupational alternatives.
5. Help pupils acquire cognitive and psychomotor skills needed for or related to actual job or daily living performance.
6. Use or devise methods and materials designed to help pupils understand and appreciate the career development implications of whatever subject matter is being taught.
7. Use career-oriented methods and materials in the instructional program, where appropriate, as one means of motivation for learning.[3]

At the present time, many students who have been classified as learning disabled rarely receive career education. A recent survey conducted with resource teachers of secondary learning disabled students reported that 37 percent of the teachers seldom or never use career education programs. Further, only 16 percent use career education on a regular basis.[4] At the college level there is a scarcity of literature that deals with career advisement for physically handicapped or learning disabled students.

An informal interview with a college career counselor indicated that she was aware of the growing need for additional information about career counseling for the handicapped, but she was unable to locate such material. She revealed that college counselors have traditionally dealt with handicapped students in a variety of ways. Her philosophy is that students with physically handicapping conditions should receive the same kind of counseling that is given to all college students. Such an orientation to the world of work consists of the following topics:

- identification of career resources and information guides
- résumé writing
- composing a cover letter
- learning to follow up letters and interviews
- networking to locate job prospects
- interview skills
- learning to answer stress questions

In addition, she counsels handicapped students to explore the reality of their limitations and choose careers where such limitations will not prohibit productive employment. She cited the example of a blind student who was interested in teaching at the elementary school level. This student explored the limitations presented by her handicap and realized that she would have difficulty with such instructional tasks as teaching handwriting. After reflection, the student decided to pursue a teaching career with a content focus at the high school level.

When physically handicapped students are scheduled for employment interviews, the college counselor asks the students if they wish her to intercede in their behalf. Some students request that the counselor advise the prospective employer about their physical handicaps. Some students prefer to discuss their handicapping conditions with the prospective employer during the interview process. If individuals feel that they have been unfairly denied employment, they can register a complaint with the Human Rights Commission. This agency then asks the employer to provide evidence that discrimination based on the physical handicap has not taken place.

When the college counselor works with students in a college program designed for the learning disabled, her techniques are slightly modified. When presenting her curriculum about the world of work, she finds that it is necessary to be extremely concrete and provide many specific examples. In addition, these students need guidance in choosing occupational goals that are realistic, based on their learning and performance limitations.

A comprehensive career education model for the learning disabled proposed by Mori warrants careful examination.[5]

> The model allows for continuous assessment, planning, intervention, modification, and evaluation as the student moves ·
> through indepth exploration of a career cluster, to specialization in one cluster, and finally to an entry-level job or more intensive skill training in a post secondary situation.[6]

Examination of the model, provided in Figure 10–1, reveals that it is a process approach to career education that can be adapted at the postsecondary level. The model begins with assessment, including medical, psychological, work-related traits, and work-related evaluations. These evaluations lead to a career plan with recommendations that the student seek appropriate additional support services from the sectors of education, psychological-social services, work adjustment, vocational skill development, and other support services. The student is next directed to an entry-level position in the area of chosen employment or is advised to pursue

Figure 10–1 A Model for Comprehensive Career Education for the Learning Disabled

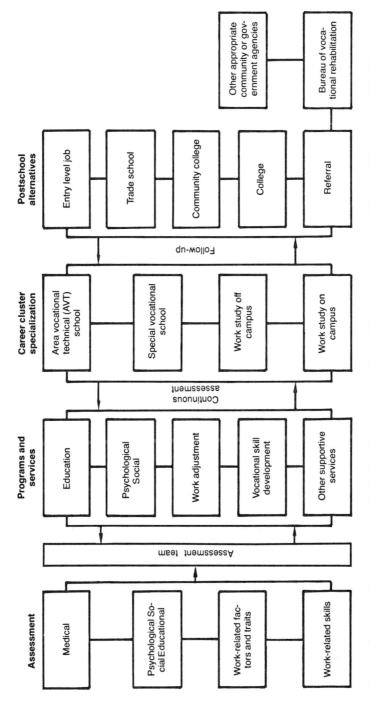

Source: Reprinted from A. Mori, "A Model for Comprehensive Career Education for Learning Disabled," in *Learning Dis. Quarterly* 3 (Winter 1980): 97; by permission of *LDQ.*

postsecondary training at a trade school, community college, or senior college. Additional counseling and support can be obtained from referrals to other community or government agencies such as the Bureau of Vocational Rehabilitation.

All teachers and counselors involved in career advisement and career education should be aware of the variety of possible occupations or occupational clusters that have been enumerated by the U.S. Office of Education. Especially when dealing with handicapped students, it is vital that the career educator consider a wide range of alternative career options. The career clusters involve the following employment possibilities:

- agri-business and natural resources
- business and office
- consumer and homemaking education
- communications and media
- construction
- environment
- fine arts and humanities
- health
- hospitality and recreation
- manufacturing
- marine science
- marketing and distribution
- personal services
- public services
- transportation occupations[7]

There is ample reference material available that details the variety of careers and job descriptions within each of these clusters.

Career education and counseling are important aspects of the handicapped student's education. The responsibility for providing such services is another aspect of the resource teaching model. Obviously, career education must be a cooperative effort on the part of many for it to be effective. It should be integrated throughout the student's education at all levels. Handicapped students who pursue higher education degrees are entitled to the same career services and employment opportunities that are available to their nonhandicapped peers. Inevitably though, it will be the responsibility of the mature student to seek out all career services and to discover methods for accommodating in the employment sector. Admitting handicapped learners to college degree programs without benefit of supportive employment counseling holds false promise for their futures.

NOTES

1. Gary Clark, "Career Education: A Concept," in G. Clark and W. White, eds., *Career Education for the Handicapped: Current Perspectives for Teachers* (Boothwyn, Pa.: Educational Resource Center, 1980), p. 3.

2. A. Mori, "Career Education for the Learning Disabled—Where are we Now?" *Learning Disability Quarterly* 3 (Winter 1980): 92.

3. Clark and White, *Career Education for the Handicapped*, p. 148.

4. Mori, "Career Education for the Learning Disabled," p. 92.

5. Ibid., pp. 91–101.

6. Ibid., p. 94.

7. Ibid., p. 93.

Chapter 11

The Resource Teacher as an Inservice Educator

Elaine Schwartz

Special education is experiencing phenomenal growth and change in knowledge, practices, and educational service systems. Major factors contributing to this are: (1) parent advocacy; (2) the increase in litigation that established the rights of handicapped children and mandated their return to general education classes; and (3) the government commitment to the education of handicapped children as exemplified by federal and state legislation and funding.

The Education for All Handicapped Children Act of 1975, PL 94-142, states that all handicapped children, whatever the nature or degree of the disability, must be educated in the "least restrictive environment" appropriate for the child. Operationally, this means the placement of choice is the regular classroom setting, provided it is instructionally appropriate.

The impact on local school districts has been profound. Early identification and, consequently, preschool and kindergarten programs have been initiated. Pupils identified as requiring special attention, who previously might have been referred for special class placement, are now being mainstreamed with supportive services. In addition, pupils formerly referred to special schools have been returned to the local educational agency. Consequently, the school population is a more heterogeneous student body.

As pupils with special needs are integrated into regular classes, their education falls under the aegis of the classroom teacher, together with supportive instructional staff. Moreover, the law specifically prescribes that there be an IEP as well as nondiscriminatory testing procedures for handicapped children. Consequently, the classroom teacher is centrally involved and shares direct responsibility and accountability with special education teachers.

Handicapped persons now have the opportunity to participate more fully in the mainstream of American education. In formulating PL 94-142, legislators recognized the impact that this imposed integration would have on every public school educator. They, therefore, provided legislation for an inservice component to prepare personnel for this task. This inservice training was to be designed to assist in the acquisition of knowledge, skills, and attitudes necessary for implementing the requirements of the law.

Its success depends on an extensive staff development program. Only as regular education personnel can work effectively with this more heterogeneous population can the intent of PL 94-142 be fulfilled. Inservice training would enable teachers simultaneously to meet the needs of the special student and educate the regular student. Teachers have not previously had the kind and level of preparation required to deal with the full range of differences found among the current, more diverse population of children in the regular school setting.

Given the premise that the demands of the new delivery system can only be accomplished through inservice training, the focus next is on implementation of training.

Since each school staff is unique in professional preparation, level of instructional expertise, and experience, detailing the content of inservice training must be done on an individual basis. However, there are specific guidelines that can serve as a conceptual framework for planning the inservice.

GUIDELINES

Needs Assessment

Initially, the resource teacher should identify those competencies that the classroom teacher, instructional staff, and supportive personnel must have so that they can effectively teach moderately handicapped students. These competencies provide a framework for the teacher needs assessment survey and other activities that will determine the scope of the inservice training.

The impact that mainstreaming has already had has served to provide both the resource room teacher and instructional staff with a realistic perception of these youngsters' needs. Also, teachers probably have already expressed their anxieties and concerns. Contact with the COH and the subsequent task of participating in formulating IEPs has further focused on school staff needs. In addition to the general awareness that has evolved, there are diverse specific procedures by which needs can be assessed. Informal and formal group meetings and conferences provide an opportunity to discuss further relevant issues. Furthermore, a needs assessment survey can be distributed to every staff member. This can be designed to evaluate both instructional strategies and attitudinal factors. Effective teaching of any child, but especially the handicapped, is directly related to the personal perceptions and biases of the teacher.

Two surveys are presented as models. These contain suggested items that can be utilized and/or adapted.

The Everett Public Schools Assessment of Needs for Staff Development evaluates the cognitive aspect of instruction.[1] (See Exhibit 11–1.) It was originally devised to form the basis of inservice workshops at special education centers. (The section in Exhibit 11–1 related to Chapter 766 (#11) can be changed to PL 94-142 and the laws of the state where inservice is being provided.)

The attitude scale in Exhibit 11–2 was constructed to investigate specific factors affecting the attitude of regular classroom teachers toward mainstreaming special needs children.[2]

Data provided by these instruments should be collected and analyzed. Inservice leaders would then be able to appraise attitudes and instructional skills, and devise a program relevant to the needs of the instructional staff.

Staff Involvement

An inservice program can only be effective if the total staff is committed to its stated goals and objectives. Therefore, after topics and priorities are established by the school staff members, resource room teachers, and the special education administrator, this list would then go to a curriculum committee composed of district teachers and administrators, who would select, modify, and approve the final product.

School-Based Training

Any inservice training should be held within the school and conducted by the staff of the school and district. Research has demonstrated that programs that actually make a difference are those that are conducted at the teachers' school, and use both teachers and university faculty as trainers.[3] Coordinating school and university resources and articulation between the two produces more effective delivery of services.

Education of the mildly handicapped, specifically of the learning disabled, is a comparatively new field in education and one that has experienced phenomenal growth within the past decade. Growing pains of controversy regarding etiology, symptomatology, and treatment have accompanied this. Since the colleges have the advantage of involvement in research and accessibility to up-to-date information, they should serve as a resource that schools can tap for training.

Exhibit 11–1 Assessment of Needs for Staff Development Activities

Personal information:

A. Please check the box that most accurately describes your present professional responsibility:

   1. Central office administrator ☐
   2. Central office supervisor or coordinator ☐
   3. Secondary school administrator (9–12) ☐
   4. Secondary school teacher (9–12) ☐
   5. Junior high school administrator (7–8) ☐
   6. Junior high school teacher (7–8) ☐
   7. Elementary school administrator ☐
   8. Elementary school teacher ☐
   9. Guidance/counseling services ☐
  10. Special needs
     a. substantially separated ☐
     b. moderately separated ☐
  11. Other: _____

B. Secondary teachers (7–12) check your field or the closest item to it:

   1. English ☐
   2. Social studies ☐
   3. Mathematics ☐
   4. Sciences ☐
   5. Occupational/vocational education ☐
   6. Physical education ☐
   7. Modern language ☐
   8. Other: _____

The purpose of this section is to gather information that may be utilized to plan and offer inservice courses and workshops for teachers.

Instructions:

Are there some things you would like to learn to do more effectively? What are they? Please review the teacher responsibilities listed below and indicate the extent to which you have a desire to become more effective in that role by marking a number from 1 (low desire) to 4 (high desire).

	Low		High	
	1	2	3	4
1. Diagnosis of pupil needs				
a) Gathering information of individual difference among students	☐	☐	☐	☐
b) Collecting information about student learning styles	☐	☐	☐	☐
c) Diagnosing academic problems	☐	☐	☐	☐

Exhibit 11–1 continued

	Low		High	
2. Assessment of student performance	1	2	3	4
a) Designing and using teacher-made tests	☐	☐	☐	☐
b) Administering and integrating formal assessment techniques	☐	☐	☐	☐
c) Appropriate use of norm-referenced and criterion-referenced measures	☐	☐	☐	☐
3. Organizing classrooms for instruction	1	2	3	4
a) Handling multi-age-level groups	☐	☐	☐	☐
b) Grouping pupils	☐	☐	☐	☐
c) Organizing classroom resources and material for effective instruction	☐	☐	☐	☐
d) Planning for classroom management, establishing routines, rules, daily procedures, and orderly operation of classroom	☐	☐	☐	☐
4. Planning for instruction	1	2	3	4
a) Organizing instruction around goals and objectives	☐	☐	☐	☐
b) Sequencing learning activities and experiences	☐	☐	☐	☐
c) Using resource room, materials, and personnel	☐	☐	☐	☐
d) Selecting and modifying materials for the instruction of the mildly handicapped child in the regular classroom	☐	☐	☐	☐
5. Building interpersonal relationships with colleagues	1	2	3	4
a) Developing better working relationships between classroom teachers and specialists	☐	☐	☐	☐
b) Interaction and communication between teachers and administrators	☐	☐	☐	☐
c) Working collaboratively inhouse for effective problem solving and decision making	☐	☐	☐	☐
6. Building interpersonal relationships with students	1	2	3	4
a) Building an environment to encourage self-awareness and self-concept in students	☐	☐	☐	☐
b) Reacting with sensitivity to the needs and feelings of students	☐	☐	☐	☐
c) Providing for the appropriate use of a variety of communication patterns within the classroom	☐	☐	☐	☐

Exhibit 11-1 continued

	Low		High	
7. Utilizing goals and objectives	1	2	3	4
a) Identifying goals and objectives appropriate to student needs	☐	☐	☐	☐
b) Selecting and stating appropriate objectives for specific pupils and groups of pupils	☐	☐	☐	☐
c) Daily planning to organize instruction around goals and objectives	☐	☐	☐	☐
d) Prescribing material for individual children based on learning strengths and needs	☐	☐	☐	☐
e) Individualizing direct instructional techniques	☐	☐	☐	☐
8. Facilitating and implementing instructional programs	1	2	3	4
a) Utilizing a variety of instructional materials and strategies	☐	☐	☐	☐
b) Using appropriate questioning techniques	☐	☐	☐	☐
c) Modifying materials for instructional programs	☐	☐	☐	☐
d) Sequencing learning activities and experiences	☐	☐	☐	☐
e) Individualizing direct instructional techniques	☐	☐	☐	☐
9. Working with community	1	2	3	4
a) Interacting and communicating effectively with parents and community	☐	☐	☐	☐
b) Utilizing community resources	☐	☐	☐	☐
c) Developing better working relationships with special service personnel	☐	☐	☐	☐
d) Student record regulations (privacy of records)	☐	☐	☐	☐
10. Classroom management	1	2	3	4
a) Developing appropriate techniques for management of pupil behavior	☐	☐	☐	☐
b) Using behavior modification in the classroom	☐	☐	☐	☐
11. Knowledge and skills related to Chapter 766	1	2	3	4
a) Knowledge of handicapping conditions	☐	☐	☐	☐
b) Knowledge of Chapter 766 terminology	☐	☐	☐	☐
c) Understanding appropriate instructional settings for the handicapped	☐	☐	☐	☐
d) Knowledge of procedural safeguards	☐	☐	☐	☐
e) Knowledge of IEP development and implementation	☐	☐	☐	☐

f) Knowledge of state and local guidelines for implementation of Chapter 766	☐	☐	☐	☐
g) Knowledge of least restrictive placement possibilities	☐	☐	☐	☐
h) Knowledge about related services and their availability	☐	☐	☐	☐
i) Referral of students who may need special services	☐	☐	☐	☐
j) Ability to provide goals, objectives, and minimal competence criteria	☐	☐	☐	☐
k) Increasing awareness of parents' role under Chapter 766	☐	☐	☐	☐

Source: From Merrimack Education Center, Chelmsford, Mass. Reprinted by permission of the author.

Practicality

Of the qualities teachers identify as criteria for inservice, practicality is foremost. They want training that is performance based and is designed to increase their skills in helping learners. Research also confirms that staff development that occurs closest to the classroom is seen as most helpful. Practicality implies the following:

- ideas from a person who has applied them successfully;
- program participants transfer new techniques to the classroom;
- staff development addressed to individual needs and immediately applicable to teaching assignments.

Utilization

The culmination of the staff development process is to utilize what has been learned. This is assessed by evidence of follow through within the classroom.

DELIVERY

The guidelines specified serve as a conceptual framework for planning staff development. Next, the inservice developer must address the issue of delivery. This encompasses determining course content, specifying target audience, identifying delivery modes, and conducting evaluation for future activities.

Exhibit 11-2 A Survey of Teachers' Opinions Relative to
Mainstreaming Special Needs Children

Recent legislation requires that children with special needs be integrated into the regular classroom to the extent that such integration is possible. Educators have long realized that one of the most important influences on a child's educational progress is the classroom teacher. The purpose of this questionnaire is to obtain information that will aid school systems in maximizing the classroom teacher's effectiveness with special needs children placed in his or her classroom.

Section I: Background variables

Please *circle* your response to the following items:

1. Grade level taught:	K	1–3	4–6	7–9	10–12
2. Number of students in your class:	11–15	16–20	21–25	26–30	31–35
3. Number of students in your school:	1–300	301–600	601–900	901–1200	1200+
4. Type of school:	Urban		Suburban		Rural
5. Degree of success to date in dealing with special needs students in the regular class-room has been:	Very low	Low	Average	High	Very high
6. The level of administra-tive support I have received relative to special needs students has been:	Very low	Low	Average	High	Very high
7. The availability of addi-tional support services for accommodating special needs students, such as resource room, resource teacher, remedial reading teacher, counseling, and appropriate instructional materials has been:	Very low	Low	Average	High	Very high

Section II: Teacher opinions

Please circle the number under the column that best describes your agreement or disagreement with the following statements. There are no correct answers: the best answers are those that honestly reflect your feelings.

Scale: SA = Strongly Agree   D = Disagree
         A = Agree   SD = Strongly Disagree
         U = Undecided

Exhibit 11-2 continued

	SA	A	U	D	SD
1. Many of the things teachers do with regular students in a classroom are appropriate for special needs students.	1	2	3	4	5
2. The needs of handicapped students can best be served through special, separate classes.	1	2	3	4	5
3. A special needs child's classroom behavior generally requires more patience from the teacher than does the behavior of a normal child.	1	2	3	4	5
4. The challenge of being in a regular classroom will promote the academic growth of the special needs child.	1	2	3	4	5
5. The extra attention special needs students require will be to the detriment of the other students.	1	2	3	4	5
6. Mainstreaming offers mixed group interaction that will foster understanding and acceptance of differences.	1	2	3	4	5
7. It is difficult to maintain order in a regular classroom that contains a special needs child.	1	2	3	4	5
8. Regular teachers possess a great deal of the expertise necessary to work with special needs students.	1	2	3	4	5
9. The behavior of special needs students will set a bad example for the other students.	1	2	3	4	5
10. Isolation in a special class has a negative effect on the social and emotional development of a special needs student.	1	2	3	4	5
11. The special needs child will probably develop academic skills more rapidly in a special classroom than in a regular classroom.	1	2	3	4	5
12. Most special needs children do not make an adequate attempt to complete their assignments.	1	2	3	4	5
13. Integration of special needs children will require significant changes in regular classroom procedures.	1	2	3	4	5
14. Most special needs children are well-behaved in the classroom.	1	2	3	4	5
15. The contact regular class students have with mainstreamed students may be harmful.	1	2	3	4	5
16. Regular classroom teachers have sufficient training to teach children with special needs.	1	2	3	4	5
17. Special needs students will monopolize the teacher's time.	1	2	3	4	5

Exhibit 11-2 continued

18. Mainstreaming the special needs child will promote his or her social independence.	1	2	3	4	5
19. It is likely that a special needs child will exhibit behavior problems in a regular classroom setting.	1	2	3	4	5
20. Diagnostic-prescriptive teaching is better done by resource room or special teachers than by regular classroom teachers.	1	2	3	4	5
21. The integration of special needs students can be beneficial for regular students.	1	2	3	4	5
22. Special needs children need to be told exactly what to do and how to do it.	1	2	3	4	5
23. Mainstreaming is likely to have a negative effect on the emotional development of the special needs child.	1	2	3	4	5
24. Increased freedom in the classroom creates too much confusion.	1	2	3	4	5
25. The special needs child will be socially isolated by regular classroom students.	1	2	3	4	5
26. Parents of a special needs child present no greater problem for a classroom teacher than those of a normal child.	1	2	3	4	5
27. Integration of special needs children will necessitate extensive retraining of regular teachers.	1	2	3	4	5
28. Special needs students should be given every opportunity to function in the regular classroom setting, where possible.	1	2	3	4	5
29. Special needs children are likely to create confusion in the regular classroom.	1	2	3	4	5
30. The presence of special needs students will promote acceptance of differences on the part of regular students.	1	2	3	4	5

Source: Reprinted from B. Larrivee and L. Cook, "Mainstreaming: A Study of the Variables Affecting Teacher Attitude," *Journal of Special Education* 13, no. 3 (1979): 321–23.

Content

Meeting the requirements of PL 94-142 necessitates that extensive preparation be provided for those entrusted with the education of handicapped students. Since the training encompasses many areas and is unique to each district, it is only feasible to identify certain topics of focus. These are suggested modules. However, specific content must be detailed by the local educational agency.

Historical Perspective of Special Education

A brief history of the field should be presented to develop a broad awareness of trends and new directions. This would provide staff members with background to understand why current federal legislation for the handicapped has been enacted. The mandates of PL 94-142 should be reviewed with emphasis on those provisions that are directly applicable to school personnel. In this way, staff members would know what their responsibilities are in reference to the law, and they would become knowledgeable about concepts such as "least restrictive alternative" and "due process."

Nature of Handicapping Conditions

An overview of the areas of exceptionality should be introduced, emphasizing the learning disabled and those with mild emotional and intellectual handicaps, since this is the population that will be primarily mainstreamed. Classification of major areas for disability should be presented with specific behaviors involved in each of these broader categories delineated. These include motor activity, visual and auditory perception, language and symbolization, attention and memory, and behavior and emotionality.

Identification Process

The instructional staff should familiarize itself with the complete assessment procedure, beginning with the referral to the school CST and the district COH, and leading up to the construction of the IEP. Sources of data gathering, specifically the case history, cumulative records, formal and informal testing, and systematic observation, that transmit important information about a learning deficit child should be reviewed. Techniques, procedures, and instruments that provide diagnostic information necessary to prescriptive planning should be introduced. Areas assessed should be academic ones as well as the identifiable generic factors—physical, social, emotional, intellectual—that contribute to affect learning as well.

Teaching Strategies

Teachers should be introduced next to applying diagnostic input data to prescriptive teaching. This implies adapting general educational goals and methods to individual needs and abilities. This includes modification of existing curriculum materials, development of alternative instructional strategies, and utilization of innovative curriculum materials and media. Academic areas stressed would be reading, mathematics, and expressive language, both oral and written. An example of an alternative instructional strategy and a suggestion for introducing workshop topics is presented at the end of this chapter. (See Exhibit 11-4.)

Behavior Management

Inappropriate behavior and conduct problems are frequently a concomitant of learning problems. There is rarely an instance where remediation of children with learning problems is not complicated by these factors. Therefore, to promote desirable behavior and maintain attention to learning activities, it is frequently necessary to manipulate the environment. Staff members should be exposed to management systems for structuring the learning environment and techniques for behavior management.

Special Education Delivery Systems

The school instructional staff will probably only be directly involved with the program for the learning disabled and moderately handicapped in their own school setting. However, an array of organizational systems and placement facilities have been developed to provide for the diverse education needs of handicapped children. These would include resource room and self-contained classes in district schools, special day schools, residential schools, child guidance clinics, mental health agencies, and community agencies. If staff members are provided with an overview of this continuum of services, they will be better equipped to recommend referral to appropriate programs or agencies.

Home Management

Parents of the learning disabled or mildly handicapped child have serious questions, concerns, and anxieties that can become overwhelming. The special education staff members can schedule periodic meetings with parents of their pupils to convey information and facts, and to counsel parents about their role and responsibilities so that parents can have a positive effect on the outcomes of remediation. This would be ongoing throughout the school year. Information might be presented in the following areas:

- manifestation and identification of a learning disability;
- school academic programs and specialized remedial techniques and materials being utilized;
- articulation of classroom and resource room programs;
- homework assignments and parents' roles;
- community resources and agencies where more detailed information can be obtained;
- vocational training, college programs, and career preparation;
- familial relationships.

Target Audience

As stipulated by PL 94-142, in order to develop and implement a comprehensive inservice training project, all personnel who contribute to the education of handicapped youngsters—professional, paraprofessional, and nonprofessional persons—must be involved. All of these persons must have the necessary skills, knowledge, and attitude to implement their responsibilities under PL 94-142. Comprehensive inservice programs produce distinct behavioral changes in the personnel receiving training, and the training will have a direct effect on services provided to handicapped children, as well as ultimately on the exceptional youngsters themselves.

An inservice matrix that specifies the precise pairing of modules and target audience is presented in Table 11-1. By this administrative procedure, delivery of content can be tailored to the individual needs and group concerns.

Delivery Modes

As the content will vary according to the particular audience, so too will the mechanisms through which inservice is delivered. The more highly educated and experienced personnel may require different inservice models than those that meet the basic needs of paraprofessionals and support personnel. Delivery mode will also be contingent upon the nature of the topic. No individual inservice vehicle is inherently more desirable than any other. The particular mode will vary according to the specific objective. However, the key is staff involvement.

Harris and Bassent present a design grid that demonstrates the articulation of inservice activities and specific objectives.[4] (See Figure 11–1.) This model can be applied to the models enumerated in Table 11–1.

For example, the following workshops would be considered in the cognitive domain: (1) Historical Perspective of Special Education; (2) Nature of Handicapping Conditions; and (3) Special Education Delivery Systems.

Table 11-1 Inservice Delivery System Matrix

	Administrators	General Education Staff	Guidance Counselors	Nurse-Teachers	Bus Drivers	Teacher Aides	School Psychologists	School Physicians	Parents
1. Historical Perspective of Special Education	X	X	X	X	X	X	X	X	
2. Nature of Handicapping Conditions	X	X	X	X	X	X	X	X	
3. Identification Process	X	X	X	X			X		
4. Teaching Strategies	X	X		X			X		
5. Behavior Management	X	X			X	X			
6. Special Education Delivery Systems	X	X	X	X			X	X	
7. Home Management									X

Outcomes are concerned with recall and recognition of information. Utilizing the design grid, the lecture and demonstration would be selected as instructional activities.

The workshops Identification Process, Teaching Strategies, and Behavior Management demand that the participants not only obtain knowledge, but also apply what they have learned to their own teaching situation. According to Harris and Bassent's model, the activities suggested by the objectives would be varied, ranging from lecture to guided practice. Emphasis, however, would be on direct group participation, interaction, and application of concepts in order that teachers are placed in an active role.

Implicit in all the workshops is that for mainstreaming to be effective the affective dimension must be considered. An underlying goal is to heighten teacher awareness and sensitivity toward special needs students. Some objectives, however, necessitate procedures that directly affect feeling tone. For example, utilizing the model, role playing, might be

Figure 11–1 Inservice Design Grid

Activities	Knowledge	Comprehension	Application	Synthesis	Values and attitudes	Adjustment
Lecture						
Illustrated lecture						
Demonstration						
Observation						
Interviewing						
Brainstorming						
Group discussion						
Buzz sessions						
Role playing						
Guided practice						

Objectives

Design I
Cognitive
objectives

Design II
Affective
objectives

Design III
Broad
spectrum
objectives

Source: Reprinted from B. Harris and W. Bassent, *In-Service Education: A Guide to Better Practice* (Englewood Cliffs, N.J.: Prentice-Hall, 1969), p. 37; by permission of the authors.

included as part of the Home Management workshop. A hypothetical situation might be presented where a child expresses concerns about his or her ability to learn. Parents would spontaneously enact how they would behave and the dialogue that might ensue. Following this, alternative ways of dealing would be discussed, and guided practice for modification of actions would be provided.

Evaluation

The precise relationship between the inservice intervention and improved services to handicapped students cannot be evaluated definitively. The validity can be judged primarily on teacher performance empirically demonstrated. For example, this can be achieved by observing the number of workshop ideas applied in the classroom and the emulation of behaviors similar to those advocated. Ultimately, the basis for judging effectiveness will be pupil performance.

Tangible criteria for evaluation can include an assessment survey completed by workshop participants as well as teacher attendance at workshops.

A reaction sheet, as shown in Table 11–2 , may include major categories and subcategories as applicable.

CONTINUING INSERVICE

Instructional Staff

Conducting formal inservice workshops is only one aspect of the professional education that the resource room teacher provides. Inservice is ongoing on almost a daily basis. Wiederholt, Hammill, and Brown rec-

Table 11–2 Inservice Reaction Sheet

	Excellent	Good	Fair	Poor	Not Applicable
Presentation Organization of subject matter	4	3	2	1	N
Instructor's knowledge of subject	4	3	2	1	N
Effectiveness of instructional procedures	4	3	2	1	N
Illustrative materials	4	3	2	1	N
Time and length of class	4	3	2	1	N
Content Relevance to classroom instruction	4	3	2	1	N
Course plans consistent with objectives	4	3	2	1	N
Encourages critical thinking	4	3	2	1	N
Discussion Opportunity for discussion	4	3	2	1	N
Responsiveness to questions	4	3	2	1	N
Opportunity for individual help	4	3	2	1	N

ommend that the following should be included in the resource room teacher's responsibilities:

(1) discussing the educational problems of specific children with teachers; (2) describing the methodology being used in the resource room; (3) presenting ideas that the teachers can use in their classes to reinforce and supplement the resource effort; (4) acquiring information on how separate resource activities can mesh with the child's regular class program; (5) following up on the progress of children who no longer attend the resource program; (6) observing the classroom performance of children who have been referred for resource help; (7) demonstrating techniques by which the teacher can improve the classroom climate, individualize instruction, or manage group misbehavior; and (8) sharing sundry professional information regarding their respective operations, new programs on the market, and new methods of reading.[5]

The implication is that there must be continuous consultation with the school staff to communicate information on topics similar to those of the workshops. However, the vehicle need not be a formal program.

There are times when a more formal presentation might be warranted. For example, instructional staff might manifest a specific need, or the resource room teacher might want to impart information on a particular technique or discuss relevancy of new research. A minicourse of short duration or single session might be a viable means for this inservice training.

Inservice needs will most likely never be completed. Rather, they will change and evolve to reflect the impact of current training and new knowledge.

Administrators

As stated previously, the education of pupils with special needs is in a state of flux. Some older ideas are being questioned, while research and experimentation are expanding upon current information. This has led to controversies within the field. For example, there are the issues of remediation versus compensation and process training, identification of diverse etiologies, and advocacy of different materials and methods. A further complication is the recognition that educators are dealing with a heterogeneous population that includes the learning disabled segment. Still, an additional pressure is presented when the communications media highlight the sensational, whether it is a nonprofessional touting a particular panacea or recent litigation.

With expanding professional demands, it is not feasible for administrators to stay abreast of new developments in the field of special education, specifically in the specialized areas of knowledge, techniques, and curriculum. Therefore, resource teachers should assume the role of providing administrators with the appropriate information that will enable them to understand and support the resource room program. This can be implemented by: (1) formal districtwide inservice sessions for the administrators; (2) informal discussions on current research and practices; (3) summary of a relevant journal article; or (4) preparation of an annual report summarizing the year's activities and changes in program, as well as stating recommendations for next year.

A PROFESSIONAL LIBRARY

A collection of reference materials is a further component that can effectively provide:

- information sources related to the content of the inservice course;
- solutions for teachers for specific and immediate classroom problems;
- ongoing inservice;
- current validation of information since the education of the handicapped, and particularly the learning disabled, is a comparatively new field.

Copies of journals and texts, available for circulation, might be located in the resource room. This would provide an opportunity for individual consultation and allow special education staff members to direct teachers to relevant sources. It would also serve as informal follow-up sessions to the inservice and provide continued teacher guidance.

JOURNALS

- *Exceptional Children,* 1920 Association Drive, Reston, Virginia 22091. This journal is directed toward the teacher of children with special needs and encompasses a wide range of exceptionality. Included are research reports, professional book reviews, and a conference calendar.

- *Teaching Exceptional Children,* 1920 Association Drive, Reston, Virginia 22091. This "how-to" magazine has practical suggestions for instructional methodology.
- *Journal of Learning Disabilities,* 101 East Ontario Street, Chicago, Illinois 60611. This journal contains primarily research studies and articles that address critical evaluation of current practices. Included also is practical information for the special education teacher, such as reviews of programs, materials, techniques, a course and conference calendar, and professional book reviews.
- *The Learning Disability Quarterly,* Department of Special Education, University of Kansas Medical Center, 435 H. C. Miller Building, 39th and Rainbow, Kansas City, Kansas 66103. This new journal is published by the Division for Children with Learning Disabilities of the Council for Exceptional Children. Articles emphasize practical application and cover techniques in assessment and remediation, interpretive reviews of the literature, discussion of pertinent issues, practical research, and personnel preparation.

TEXTS

General References

- Lerner, Janet W. *Children with Learning Disabilities: Theories, Diagnosis, Teaching Strategies.* 2d ed. Boston, Mass.: Houghton-Mifflin Company, 1976. This text provides a comprehensive overview of the field. Various theories are surveyed and diagnostic procedures and instructional strategies discussed. Organizational models for delivery services are presented.
- Lynn, Roa, with Gluckin, Neil and Kripka, Bernard. *Learning Disabilities: An Overview of Theories, Approaches, and Politics.* New York, N.Y.: The Free Press, 1979. Based on interviews with professionals and practitioners, this volume contains up-to-date information of interest to teachers without a technical background. Included are characteristics of the learning disabled student, federal legislation, evaluation and remediation, and research findings.

Curriculum

The following texts offer practical instructional information pertaining to major curriculum areas:

General References

- Hammill, Donald D., and Bartel, Nettie R. *Teaching Children with Learning and Behavior Problems.* Boston, Mass.: Allyn and Bacon, Inc., 1978. This book presents basic information for assessment and instruction in reading, arithmetic, language, perception, handwriting, and behavior. The appendix provides a list of specific instructional materials with general evaluative comments.
- Alley, Gordon, and Deshler, Donald. *Teaching the Learning Disabled Adolescent: Strategies and Methods.* Denver, Col.: Love Publishing Company, 1979. This publication advocates a learning strategies model as the approach to the learning disabled (LD) adolescent. For example, techniques to organize, store, and retrieve information in content areas are emphasized rather than instruction in the actual subject content. Characteristics of the LD adolescent, assessment procedures, and learning strategies in the academic areas of reading, writing, mathematics, thinking, listening, and speaking, as well as in social interaction, are described.

Mathematics

- Underhill, Bob; Uprichard, Ed; and Heddens, Jim. *Diagnosing Mathematical Difficulties.* Columbus, Oh.: Charles E. Merrill Publishing Company, 1980. This text describes diagnostic-prescriptive instruction based on a task analysis and task process model (a synthesis of ability training and task analysis). Specific case studies illustrate this process utilizing the task process model. The appendix includes a taxonomy of mathematical concepts for evaluating performance.
- Reisman, Fredricka K., and Kaufman, Samuel H. *Teaching Mathematics to Children with Special Needs.* Columbus, Oh.: Charles E. Merrill Publishing Company, 1980. This volume explains the impact of generic factors, specifically cognitive, psychomotor, physical, social, and emotional factors on mathematics learning. Assessment activities and instructional strategies are presented practically. Appendixes include a screening checklist, case studies, and guides interfacing general influences described with instructional strategies.

Reading

- Gillespie-Silver, Patricia. *Teaching Reading to Children with Special Needs.* Columbus, Oh.: Charles E. Merrill Publishing Company, 1979. This book presents an ecological or environmental perspective for reading instruction. The interchange between the environment and special child is considered, and reading programs are advocated that are relevant to the child's total life experiences. The characteristics of special children and models for teaching reading are presented in order that practitioners may select a methodology congruent with unique needs. The psycholinguistic model of reading is the conceptual framework for the assessment and programming approaches described.

Language

* Wiig, Elisabeth Hemmersam, and Semel, Eleanor Messing. *Language Assessment and Intervention for the Learning Disabled.* Columbus, Oh.: Charles E. Merrill Publishing Company, 1980. Comprehensive information is presented in this text describing characteristics, assessment, and remediation for the curriculum language components morphology, syntax, and semantics. The effect of deficits in these areas on reading and content area subjects is detailed, along with suggested strategies for adaptation of instruction.

RESOURCE MATERIALS FOR WORKSHOPS

The books recommended for the professional library would serve as a major source of materials for workshops. Additionally, *Mediagraphy on Mainstreaming* provides a reference for media materials.[6] This is a bibliography of audiovisual instructional materials (slides, cassettes, films, and videotapes) on mainstreaming of handicapped children, which includes a brief description of each item. The following references might also be useful to guide teachers in preparing individual modules. However, these listed materials can only serve as a core. Workshop leaders must then adapt and supplement for individual requirements.

* Historical Perspective of Special Education—Book: *Exploring Issues in the Implementation of PL 94-142: Developing Criteria for Evaluation.* U.S. Bureau of Education for the Handicapped, Research for Better Schools, Inc., 1979; Filmstrips/Cassettes: *Public Law 94-142: The Education for All Handicapped Children's Act of 1975.* Reston, Virginia: The Council for Exceptional Children.
* Identification Process—Document: Green, Mary, and the Midwest Regional Center. *The Individualized Educational Program: A Team Approach,* ED 169712. Des Moines, Iowa: Drake University, 1978.
* Teaching Strategies—Document: Massey, Sara, and Henderson, Robert, eds. *The Range of Variability: Inservice Design in Special Education,* ED 168234. Durham, New Hampshire: New England Teacher Corps Network, 1977; "Prediction Guide," (See Exhibit 11-3 and "Alternative Instructional Methodology," Exhibit 11-4.).

Exhibit 11-3 Prediction Guide

To foster greater involvement by participants and to provide thoughtful consideration of the topics, a guide can be provided in which participants are asked to predict answers to issues that will be presented. The workshop presentation will provide feedback about the accuracy of their responses. For example, to introduce a workshop on reading and perception, the following might be included in the anticipation guide:

1. In a study reported in the *Journal of Learning Disabilities,* high frequency, low discriminability words (for example, saw/was, where/there, went/want) were presented to poor and normal readers under the conditions listed below. When would you expect to find a difference between poor and normal readers?
   ____ Matching the word to another in the line
   ____ Remembering the word presented to find it in a line of three words
   ____ Reproducing the words from memory
   ____ Reading the words in isolation
2. Increasing evidence from research in the field of learning disabilities attributes reading disorders to:
   ____ Language or linguistic deficits
   ____ Perceptual deficits

- Behavior Management—Document: *Project Team: Teacher Encouragement to Activate Mainstreaming. Administrative and Resource Personnel Kit,* ED 140494. Fullerton Union High School District, August, 1977; Book: Sulzer, Beth, and Mayer, C. Roy. *Behavior Modification Procedures for School Personnel.* New York, N.Y.: Holt, Rinehart, and Winston, 1972.
- Special Education Delivery Systems—Books: Gollay, Eliro, and Bennett, Alwira. *The College Guide for Students with Disabilities.* Cambridge, Mass.: Abt Books, 1976; Ellingson, Coreth, and Cass, James. *Directory of Facilities for the Learning Disabled and Handicapped.* New York, N.Y.: Harper & Row, 1972.
- Home Management—Books: Freeman, Stephen W. *Does Your Child Have a Learning Disability?* Springfield, Ill.: Charles C Thomas, 1974; Buscaglia, Leo. *The Disabled and Their Parents: A Counseling Challenge.* Thorofare, N.J.: Charles B. Slack, Inc., 1975.

Exhibit 11-4 Alternative Instructional Methodology

Example of a strategy that can be presented to demonstrate alternative instructional methodology for secondary students:

Science 8

Name _____ Date _____
Period _____

Assignment sheet—Wednesday, November 12

Check each item as it is completed.

Classwork
___ 1. Check last night's homework.
___ 2. Go over questions from current *Science* magazine.
___ 3. Begin Investigation 12—igneous rock formation.

Homework
___ 1. Bring pen.
___ 2. Bring notebook.
___ 3. Bring blue book.
___ 4. Bring current *Science* magazine.
___ 5. Bring Workshop I.
___ 6. Read pp. 15-19 in blue textbook. Put correct heading on paper and label it blue textbook, pp. 15-19.

Questions to Answer
(Sample questions with provision for structuring answers)
1. What is magma?
   _____
   _____

2. Explain two ways igneous rocks form.
   a. _____
      _____
   b. _____
      _____

3. Which cools faster, lava or magma?
   _____

4. Name four forces that break igneous rocks into pebbles, sand, and clay.
   a. _____ c. _____
   b. _____ d. _____

Conclusion
(To foster organization and summary of materials for long-term recall.)
Write four "I learned that" statements.
1. _____
2. _____
3. _____
4. _____

NOTES

1. Jean E. Sanders, *Training Complex Model for Appraising and Programming. Summary Report,* ERIC ED 157866 (Chelmsford, Mass.: Merrimack Education Center), 1977.
2. B. Larrivee and L. Cook, "Mainstreaming: A Study of the Variables Affecting Teacher Attitude," *Journal of Special Education* 13, no. 3 (1979): 321–23.
3. J.C. King, "Some Requirements for Successful Inservice Education," *Phi Delta Kappan* 59 (1977): 686–87.
4. Ben M. Harris and Wailand Bassent, *In-Service Education: A Guide to Better Practice* (Englewood Cliffs, N.J.: Prentice-Hall, Inc., 1969), p. 37.
5. J. Lee Wiederholt, Donald D. Hammill, and Virginia Brown, *The Resource Teacher: A Guide to Effective Practices* (Boston, Mass.: Allyn and Bacon, Inc., 1978), p. 29.
6. Burbank, Lucille, *Mediagraphy on Mainstreaming,* ED 144297 (King of Prussia, Pa.: Eastern Pennsylvania Regional Resources Center, 1977).

At Issue

WHAT DOES THE REGULAR CLASS TEACHER EXPECT FROM THE RESOURCE TEACHER?

Inservice education is documented as being a necessary component for the success of a team approach in the education of mainstreamed children. An appropriate inservice model provides knowledge, increases skills, and develops positive attitudes for the teachers in attendance. Much attention has been paid to teachers' attitudes about exceptional children. Perhaps more stress should be placed upon regular classroom teachers' attitudes as they perceive their roles and responsibilities in relationship to resource teachers. If resource programs are to work effectively, classroom teachers and resource personnel must engage in a new kind of partnership. If there is misunderstanding about the nature of their roles and the resulting responsibilities for providing services, hostility can result. Inservice education can be an excellent vehicle for clarifying roles and responsibilities.

What are the attitudes that regular classroom teachers hold toward the education of handicapped children placed in the mainstream? In a study conducted by Hudson, Graham, and Warner, 151 regular elementary classroom teachers from 28 school districts were polled about six categories of teacher attitudes and needs in relationship to educating mainstreamed exceptional children.[1] The following is a summary of the areas of inquiry and the results of the study:

- "Are regular classroom teachers' attitudes supportive of mainstreaming exceptional children in their classrooms?"[2] In general, these teachers did not demonstrate support of the principle of mainstreaming exceptional children. While teachers were willing to accept an exceptional learner in their classes, they felt that this would have a deleterious effect upon the education of the other children or that the exceptional learner profits more fully from special class placement.
- "Do regular classroom teachers feel that they have enough time to be able to teach exceptional children in their classrooms?"[3] An overwhelming majority of the teachers felt that they did not have sufficient time to provide for the exceptional learner.
- "Do regular classroom teachers feel that they have the necessary materials to teach exceptional children in their classrooms?"[4] There was "moderate agreement" among the teachers that they could locate sufficient instructional materials, but the majority felt that they did not have access to adequate materials.

- "Do regular classroom teachers feel that they have the necessary skills to teach exceptional children in their classrooms?"[5] The majority of teachers felt that they had the competency to teach exceptional children with regard to identification of learning needs, ability to individualize instruction, and to meet with parents. However, almost half the teachers reported that they had misgivings about their abilities to remediate specific deficits.
- "Do regular classroom teachers feel that they have the necessary support services to teach exceptional children in their classrooms?"[6] Teachers reported that sufficient support services were not available.
- "Do regular classroom teachers feel that additional training would aid them in teaching exceptional children in their classrooms?"[7] Teachers felt that additional training either through preservice or inservice models would be necessary before they could meet the needs of exceptional children in their classes.

In conclusion, the researchers feel that this study documented that the attitudes of teachers in the mainstream do not support the placement of handicapped children in their classes. Further, they call for a deeper understanding of the needs and attitudes of regular educators so that effective instructional teams can be created.

What specific services do regular classroom teachers expect from resource personnel? In a study conducted by Speece and Mandell, an Index of Support Services was developed based on an investigation of the research on mainstreaming.[8] Two hundred twenty-eight regular elementary classroom teachers were polled about the importance of each of the 26 specific support services rendered by resource teachers and the frequency in which the services were actually delivered.

An examination of the findings reported in Table 11-3 reveals that "resource room teachers were not providing those support services rated as most important by regular teachers to teach learning disabled students."[9] The researchers have provided several explanations about the lack of congruence between teachers' expectations and the resource services provided. For example, state education department guidelines may dictate the role of the resource teacher as to amount of planning time and contact hours with children. In addition, many resource teachers have not been trained to develop consulting skills with regular classroom teachers.

How important are these findings for the education of handicapped children? Mainstream educators and resource personnel must learn to work together to educate handicapped children. "If a regular teacher's needs are not being fulfilled by the resource room teacher, it is doubtful that maximum educational benefits are being reaped by the handicapped

Table 11-3 Percentage of Regular Teachers Rating Support Services as *Important, Frequent,* and *Infrequent*

Support Service* (Important)**	Frequent***	Infrequent****
The resource room teacher:		
1. attends parent conferences (74.2)	6.6	93.4
2. meets informally to discuss student progress (74.2)	86.2	13.8
3. provides remedial instruction in the resource room (67.0)	73.0	27.0
4. provides information on behavioral characteristics (54.5)	43.7	56.3
5. provides academic assessment data (53.9)	25.8	74.2
6. schedules meetings to evaluate student progress (52.7)	32.9	67.1
7. provides materials for classroom use (52.1)	34.2	65.8
8. suggests materials for classroom use (52.1)	35.3	64.7
9. provides written reports of students' activities and progress (51.5)	20.4	79.6
10. helps evaluate instructional techniques (49.7)	36.0	64.0
11. aids in educational programming for nonhandicapped (48.5)	25.8	74.2
12. offers classroom management techniques (46.7)	37.1	62.9
13. helps adapt instructional techniques for classroom use (46.7)	36.0	64.0
14. schedules meetings for planning (41.9)	29.4	70.6
15. demonstrates use of materials (39.5)	33.0	67.0
16. explains purpose and procedure for IEP (28.8)	9.0	91.0
17. provides techniques to evaluate student progress (28.2)	10.8	89.2
18. asks for assistance in writing IEP (27.0)	10.1	89.9
19. observes students in classroom (24.6)	8.9	91.1
20. provides ideas to facilitate peer acceptance (24.0)	12.6	87.4
21. plans inservice to explain instructional techniques (22.2)	4.2	95.8

*Items are in abbreviated form.

**Numbers in parentheses indicate percentages from "most important" and "vital" categories.

***Summation of percentages from "monthly," "weekly," and "more than once per week" categories.

****Summation of percentages from "not provided," "twice or less per year," and "once per grading period" categories.

Source: Reprinted from D. Speece and C. Mandell, "Resource Room Support Services for Regular Teachers," *Learning Disability Quarterly* 3 (Winter 1980): 52; by permission of *LDQ.*

Table 11-3 continued

22. plans inservice to explain LD/BD characteristics (21.6)	5.3	94.7
23. trains peer tutors (16.2)	12.0	88.0
24. suggests classroom environment modifications (13.8)	4.2	95.8
25. helps with class trips and parties (12.6)	6.0	94.0
26. teaches handicapped/nonhandicapped students in regular class (10.8)	3.0	97.0

students in the regular class setting."[10] Resource teachers must be trained to assist the regular classroom teacher with the education of the handicapped child in the mainstream. Simply providing tutorial services in the resource program is not sufficient. Resource teachers and classroom teachers must work cooperatively in an interactive model so that each other's roles and needs are identified and understood. Without such cooperative efforts, the education of mainstreamed exceptional learners is doomed to fail.

Discussing the impact of PL 94-142 from the perspective of the regular educators, John Ryor, president of the National Education Association, has commented on the feeling of "unpreparedness to educate handicapped students" by the regular teacher.[11] He says that teachers feel that inservice training must take place before handicapped children are placed into mainstream education. In addition, teachers' criticism of inservice education emanates from the feeling that people other than classroom teachers choose the content of inservice courses. Teachers feel that they must be directly involved in practices that affect them. Ryor states that "the potential for conflict is clearly present during this time of changing professional roles and relationships" and that "the enmity which has existed between regular and special educators was generated by both parties."[12]

The inservice program provides the opportunity for a meeting ground between resource teachers and regular educators. Inservice education must prepare teachers in advance of the placement of handicapped children. The roles and responsibilities on the part of both sets of educators must be fully explored and discussed. Teachers must have direct responsibility for the content of inservice courses so that their self-perceived needs are met. The potential of PL 94-142 is great, but it can only be met when all educators work cooperatively to ensure its success.

NOTES

1. F. Hudson, S. Graham, and M. Warner, "Mainstreaming: An Examination of the Attitudes and Needs of Regular Classroom Teachers," *Learning Disability Quarterly* 2 (Summer 1979): 58–62.

2. Ibid., p. 60.

3. Ibid.

4. Ibid.

5. Ibid.

6. Ibid., p. 61.

7. Ibid.

8. D. Speece and C. Mandell, "Resource Room Support Services for Regular Teachers," *Learning Disability Quarterly* 3 (Winter 1980): 49–53.

9. Ibid., p. 51.

10. Ibid.

11. J. Ryor, "94-142—The Perspective of Regular Education," *Learning Disability Quarterly* 1 (Spring 1978): 7.

12. Ibid., p. 13.

Chapter 12

Administration of a Resource Program

Joseph Zacherman

BACKGROUND AND NEED

With the passage of PL 94-142, special education entered a new phase. The significance of this legislation has affected the educational process considerably. First, it mandates that all local education agencies provide free and appropriate education in the least restrictive environment. The key phrase in this law is "the least restrictive environment." Its emphasis is both on special education and regular education.

No longer concerned with just the profoundly and moderately handicapped, the law now addresses itself to the mildly handicapped. As a result, local educational agencies are now designing alternative educational and social environments to support these mildly handicapped students who are in a regular classroom.

The resource room concept is probably the best alternative for mildly handicapped students, regardless of their handicapping condition. For learning disabled, socially-behaviorally, or physically disabled students who are in a regular classroom, the resource room provides an alternative to the self-contained class. The resource room provides students with individualized and small group instruction while they remain in the regular classroom.

DEVELOPING A RESOURCE ROOM

The selection of personnel for the resource room is one of the most important aspects for making a successful program. It is the responsibility of the school administration to select the best qualified teachers for the resource room assignment.

Because of the neediness, difficulty, and diversity of handicapped problems present in a resource room, a dedicated and highly skilled teacher is necessary to make the program successful.

Teacher Selection

To work in a resource room program, a teacher should possess the following credentials:

- a master's degree, preferably in a field of special education;
- state accreditation or certification in special education;
- six credits in reading;
- six credits in math;
- three credits in speech.

The selection of teachers to serve in the resource room should be made by the central program office. It is the responsibility of the program office to screen all candidates and their credentials, and to see that they meet the minimum requirements before they are sent to a school.

Further, the principal of a school should be involved or have input in the selection of the resource room teacher. The office of special education makes the final selection and assigns the teacher to a local school.

Teacher Competencies

The following is a list of teacher competencies developed by the New York City Board of Education—Resource Room Program:[1]

Diagnostic-Evaluative

- Interpret a psychological report and identify the educational relevance of findings in the report.
- Administer and interpret formal, informal, and criterion-referenced tests for educational programming.
- Conduct and interpret interviews with students and observations of them in and out of class.
- Prepare a written report of testing results as a member of the evaluative team, including appropriate placement and planning recommendations.
- Participate as educational member of the evaluative team in multidisciplinary team conferences to develop recommendations for individualized educational programming.
- Develop procedures to monitor the placement and programming recommendations for mid-year and end-term review.

Direct Services

- Develop individualized educational (instructional and/or behavioral) programs, utilizing assessment data.
- Develop data-based programming for instructional areas specified from diagnostic evaluation.
- Establish criteria for instructional periods daily, weekly, and monthly objectives, and establish level of mastery required to achieve instructional goals that lead to appropriate grade (or age) level achievements.
- Develop appropriate time series data charts showing instructional expectancies and mastery developments.
- Teach in the basic skill areas of language (written and oral expression), reading, and mathematics.
- Select commercially available instructional programs for the educational objectives as well as for age and interest of students.
- Develop appropriate teacher-made materials (as in preceding competency).
- Use classroom management techniques to reduce interfering maladaptive behaviors and enhance the student's peer and adult interactions.
- Use applied behavioral analysis to establish criteria for daily, weekly, and monthly objectives, and levels of mastery.
- Develop appropriate time series data charts showing behavioral expectancies and mastery developments.
- Develop contingency contracts and appropriate reinforcement schedules to achieve mastery of behavioral goals and objectives.

Indirect Services (Consultation with Teachers)

- Communicate effectively with other teachers and assess their receptivity for change.
- Analyze the "system" operating within the school and recognize constraints under which the regular teacher must function, including prescribed curriculum class size, time limitations, and limitations of materials.
- Analyze the teaching styles in the regular classroom, including the management strategies and the ways in which student achievement is being assessed.
- Understand the content of the curriculum well enough to be able to make suggestions for changes in methods of presentation of information and evaluation.
- Suggest and model modifications of management strategies for individuals or groups of students and modifications in teaching

approaches (information delivery and knowledge assessment) to accommodate students with different learning styles and skill levels.

Indirect Services (Consultation with Parents)

- Communicate with parents to help them to understand the implication of the student's learning styles in school, home, and community.
- Help parents find effective strategies for dealing with their children in conflict situations.
- Assist parents in developing realistic expectancies for their children.
- Direct parents to community and governmental volunteer and parent organizations that provide support services for themselves and their children.

In summary, the functions of the resource room teacher are centered around three important objectives: (a) to assess the educational needs of children in order to plan for their instructional objectives; (b) to provide individualized instruction in curricular and behavioral areas in order to support the student's mainstream experiences; and (c) to consult with mainstream teachers in the development of their skills and attitudes toward resource room students for a more effective resource room environment.

Supervision of Resource Teachers

The supervision of the resource room teachers is similar to that of mainstream teachers, with one exception. Resource room teachers are also responsible to the special education supervisor and the building principal. It is the responsibility of both the principal and special education supervisor to monitor the progress, IEPs, and programming of these classes.

It is the responsibility of the principal and special education supervisor to observe and rate the teacher. For a final rating at the end of the school year, the building principal and supervisor work in conjunction on the rating report.

Exhibit 12–1 is a form used in the New York City schools' resource room program. It contains suggestions for observing the teacher and the functions of the resource room.

Administration

As with any new program, a great deal of planning and consultation must take place between the program office and the school principal.

Exhibit 12-1 Sample Teacher Observation Form

Teacher's name: _____ License: _____ Status: _____
School:_____ District: _____ Room number: ____
Date: _____ Register: _____ Attendance: _____

I. **Administrative Responsibilities**

	Yes	No	Comments:
A. **Planbooks** 1. Is there evidence of individualization?			
2. Does the written plan reflect IEP objectives?			
3. Are the paraprofessional plans indicated?			
4. Do the plans indicate ongoing group work?			
B. **IEP** 1. Are objectives written in observable, measurable terms?			
2. Are criteria for performance stated?			
3. Is there evidence of pupils' progress, measured at least weekly?			
C. **Recordkeeping** 1. Are individual folders prepared for each child?			
2. Is there evidence of: a. samples of children's work?			
b. anecdotal records?			
c. behavioral checklists?			
d. informal and formal tests?			
e. parent contact summary sheets?			

Exhibit 12-1 continued

	Yes	No	Comments:
D. General pupil accounting 1. Is the rollbook current and complete?			
2. Are individual cumulative records on file?			

II. **Classroom Design**
   A. Learning centers
   B. Evidence of pupils' work
   C. Routines established
   D. Learning materials

III. **Teaching Methods on Observed Lesson**
   A. Classroom and behavior management techniques
   B. Teacher-pupil relationships
   C. Evidence of planning
   D. Materials used
   E. Motivation techniques
   F. Goals and/or objectives
   G. Development of lesson
   H. Degree of individualized instruction
   I. Evaluation

IV. **Suggestions and Recommendations**

V. **Summary**

Date of Postobservation conference:
Overall performance _____ Satisfactory _____ Unsatisfactory

Teacher trainer's signature _____

Supervisor's signature _____

I have read and received a copy of this report.

_____
        (Signature of teacher)   (Date)

Source: Reprinted with permission from Jed P. Luchow, *Plan for the Development of the Resource Room Program* (New York, N.Y.: New York City Board of Education, 1979).

Guidelines for the selection of students and teachers must be established. Parents must be notified. The school staff should be notified and prepared that a resource room is being established.

The administration of the resource room becomes a joint effort between the central program office and the school principal. To ensure accountability and uniformity in all the resource rooms in the district, the district administrator/supervisor of the program should develop the following procedures:

- teacher selection
- notification of parents
- pupil selection
- teacher training
- curriculum development
- public relations

This will ensure that each resource room program in the district is the same in each school.

It is difficult to administer the day-to-day operation of a resource room from a central office. Therefore, the daily operation and direct supervision of the resource room program falls under the school principal. The principal should have the flexibility and authority to modify the program to fit the needs of the students and school. Although many of the responsibilities of the central district administrator/supervisor and school's principal overlap each other, the principal is at an advantage since he or she is onsite for the daily decisions. The principal has the authority of scheduling, programming, and designating room assignments to both the students and resource room teacher.

Monitoring the resource room, then, becomes the responsibility of the central program office. Providing support personnel is also the responsibility of the central program.

Depending on the number of resource rooms in a school, support personnel, such as paraprofessional, guidance counselor, school psychologist, social worker, speech teacher, and other support service professionals, should be provided for the students.

The main administrative/supervisory concern in the resource room program centers around the following seven issues:

1. inservice training
2. allocation of space (physical facility)
3. financing the resource room
4. public relations

5. integration of regular and special education
6. grading practices and accreditation
7. legal guidelines

In order for the training of resource room teachers to be successful, planning between district-wide administration and the building principal is essential. The district administrator/supervisor should provide the technical (legal) knowledge on the principles of programming, curriculum modification, and the nature and needs of youngsters with mild learning disabilities.

Principals should supply essential information on the needs of the students in their school. The special education administrator/supervisor and principal should jointly plan to meet the needs of the students in the school by modifying the school's curriculum and instructional material to be used in the resource room.

Teacher Training

For a program to succeed, ongoing training must be provided for the teachers involved. An effort of cooperation between special educators and regular educators must also be undertaken for the resource room to succeed. The program office should provide qualified trainers to visit schools with resource rooms on a regular basis. An ideal situation would be to have one teacher trainer for 35 resource room teachers.

The training sessions should be held in each school where a resource room exists or where one is planned. The training sessions should be geared to prepare regular administrators and teachers for students with special needs. The areas of training should focus on classroom management techniques, screening procedures, instructional objectives, and instructional alternatives. The mainstream staff should assimilate the training process.

Part of the ongoing training process for resource room teachers should be to visit existing resource rooms and meet with other members of the program. Teachers new to the resource room program should receive written guidelines and testing materials to be used from the program office. The new teacher should also have an opportunity to visit an existing program to see its operation.

Orientation workshops for new teachers should focus on areas such as IEP development, PL 94-142, diagnostic assessment, behavior management, teaching strategies, instructional designs and materials, curriculum development, staff relations, and parent/community involvement.

In addition to the training provided by the program office, a joint effort should be undertaken by the program office and local universities to develop new research and training projects.

Allocation of Space

In selecting the room, the following should be noted:

- state regulations concerning per pupil classroom space, lighting, and ventilation should be kept in mind.
- the room should not have been used as a special education class in order to avoid any unnecessary stigma.
- the room should be in a central location in the school building. On the other hand, it should not be in a high traffic area (for example, cafeteria or gym).
- an area that houses a materials center and library or both might be quite appropriate.
- the room should be large enough to permit student movement.

In designing the physical space for the resource room, the following principles should be adhered to:

- adequate space for individual and small group instruction;
- adequate space for individual carrels;
- provision for learning center areas, for example, reading, mathematics and language;
- portable chalkboard;
- room dividers;
- adequate educational materials and provision for storage;
- desks should be movable;
- an area in the room should be set aside for the teacher's work space.

Financing

Financing the resource room depends on the school district's budget. This amount varies from state to state or district to district. Cost factors play an important role in how much funding a program will get.

The amount of money allotted to the resource room program depends on busing, number of students to be served, materials to be bought, and personnel. If a district has to pay for busing students to a resource room, its allotted budget will be reduced. The escalation in cost of materials, personnel budgets, and number of students enrolled all are major factors in determining the resource room budget.

Most funding for the resource room is tax levy, and state education departments usually reimburse only a small percentage that the district has to spend. Yet on a cost effectiveness basis, it seems less expensive to run a resource room than a self-contained special education class, since more pupils can be served in a resource room than a special education class. The accountability of the students becomes the responsibility of the district, and therefore, these students are counted into the district's entire pupil enrollment.

District budgets are computed by number of students enrolled. Besides saving money, there is an obvious educational advantage for keeping students in neighborhood schools in their home districts.

The resource room teacher is funded through tax levy. However, certain ancillary services, such as paraprofessionals, guidance counselors, social workers, psychologists, and instructional materials, may be funded through various federal programs (Title I, EHA-B).

Public Relations

One of the problems with the concept of resource rooms has been the unfortunate relationship between regular and special educators. To a great extent, the enmity that has existed has been generated by both parties. Special educators have felt that regular educators not only fail to understand the pupil with special needs, but that special classes were developed as a dumping ground for these students. The regular classroom teacher, on the the other hand, with less training in this area, looks to the special educator, whose pupil to teacher ratio is smaller and whose resources are often greater, and wonders why even more progress cannot be made in the self-contained special class.

With the passage of PL 94-142, which provides a free and appropriate education in the least restrictive environment, it has become more apparent that the services of a resource room can be most effective the closer they are to the child. The Gartner report on educational services for students with special needs states:

> . . . we recommend that heavy emphasis in every school be placed on early screening of all children, the development of

resource room programs and flexible support staff utilization patterns. Only those children with profound and/or severe handicaps, who cannot profit from "regular" classroom placement, including programs of in-class and out-of-class support services, would be sent to special placements in a "hub" school in their own communities.[2]

Whenever a new program is started in a school, and this holds true of the resource room program, both the staff and parents must be informed. It becomes the responsibility of the special education administrator/supervisor and building principal to communicate with all parties involved.

Wiederholt, Hammill, and Brown also emphasize that in conducting a public relations campaign the staff and parents must be informed:

> As with most proposals for change, there may be some resistance to various aspects of this new program, at least at first. Some regular and special classroom teachers may be reluctant to work with the resource teacher, for reasons that may not be fully known or articulated. Some support personnel (counselors and/ or psychologists), especially those who have been oversold on the merits of previous innovative approaches and have been disappointed with the results, may consider the resource idea to be just another panacea. In addition some parents may not want to expose their children to the resource program. A few parents of handicapped children may prefer segregated instructional support in the form of self-contained classes because they fear that their children might be lost in the mainstream. Some parents of normal children may be reluctant to have their children educated in such close proximity to deviant children. Whatever the objections, the principal, resource teacher, and other responsible professionals should prepare thoroughly the school staff and parents for the program and should make every effort to enlist their support in its behalf.[3]

A controversy that may arise in selling the resource room program to the district and parents is the status of the children. The question of whether or not these children are labeled handicapped and whether this notation will become part of their school record is a matter of great concern.

Another concern for both the building principal and resource room administrator/supervisor is that parents of children referred for evaluation to the resource room program should be alerted to the possibility that a more restrictive setting may be recommended. Careful explanation at the start of the process may avoid any controversy and ensure better public relations for the resource room program.

Integration of Regular and Special Education

The term mainstreaming is journalistic in nature. It does not even appear in PL 94-142; rather, the law concerns itself with placing students in the least restrictive environment. With the student participants in the resource room program, this means that students in the regular school program who are in need of special academic or behavioral assistance will stay in that regular school program, except during those assigned time periods when they are in the resource room class. The intensive, individualized instruction provided for these students in their resource room classes helps them stay up to par academically in their regular subject classes. By going over difficult concepts, by helping to make homework assignments more clearly understood, and by adding to the student's information base in different subject areas, the resource room teacher gives the specific needed support the student needs to remain in regular classes as a contributing class member. In a curious way, the resource room is sometimes viewed as a reverse mainstreaming process, with the student moving from the least to a more restrictive environment. This has been misconstrued. The more the student adjusts emotionally and academically to the regular classroom learning environment, the less time is needed in supplementary instructional services such as resource room classes. The goal is to move resource room students progressively from the position where, through resource room participation, they are sustained in their regular classes to the point where they become fulltime regular students.

As the resource room program moves toward a generic model, students with mild emotional and other learning problems will remain in their regular classes, as opposed to the traditional self-contained class.

A controversy that arises from the mainstream concept is that a more difficult behavior-disordered student will now remain in the regular class. Opposition has been voiced by parents, regular teachers, and building principals for not placing these youngsters in a more restrictive setting.

Whether this child will be successful depends on the resource room teacher in maintaining these children in the educational mainstream.

Accreditation

A problem arises for the resource room student in the area of grading and earning school credits. While the resource room teacher keeps careful track of a student's strengths and weaknesses, and diligently charts and measures the mastery level of acquired skills, the actual progress a student makes (behavioral and academic) is not graded within any traditional letter grade system. While a student may make significant progress in resource room classwork, this success many times goes unrecorded in the regular school records (for example, the student is not granted any credits toward the completion of a school program).

There should be a district-wide uniform policy regarding the crediting of resource room work, so that students have an equitable opportunity to complete school programs no matter where they attend school. As it is now, accreditation policies differ from district to district and, at the high school level, from school to school. Besides providing for the resource room students' special needs to achieve academically and behave appropriately in their regular subject classes, the resource room class does something additional: it significantly increases the students' basic knowledge. This increase in the resource room student's knowledge base should be awarded half a credit for the exact same period of school time that a full credit is earned in the regular classes. This would be a fair practice, and it would not unduly penalize a special needs student who requires resource room assistance. There are only so many school hours a student spends in school each day, and if the resource room classes do not receive the half accreditation status they deserve, then the completion of a school program—especially at the junior and senior high school level—can become problematic. Perhaps resource room teachers, acting with consistency wherever they are assigned, could give their students either a pass or fail grade when considering work for credit. This would be easy enough to implement, and this practice would contribute both to the success and the attractiveness of the resource room program.

Issues on accreditation have caused much controversy on the secondary level. The first of these issues questions whether credit can be given for resource room participation. If the students are not granted credit, they and the parents may decline the service of the resource room.

If students are programmed for the resource room, they are then pulled out of another subject. Will this necessitate losing credit from that subject class? To make up for this, should the school day be increased, or should the four-year high school program be increased to more than four years or five years? There are many social and legal ramifications concerning the issue of accreditation. At this time, there is little uniformity, and local educational agencies set their own policy.

Legal Guidelines

Before a resource room is started in a particular school, eligible students must be identified. The process for identifying eligible students follows the guidelines set by PL 94-142 carefully. All referrals for the resource room must be clinically evaluated and have parental consent, and final recommendation for placement must be made through the COH.

Using the guidelines of PL 94-142, priority should be given to students who have not been served. The resource room should consist of no more than 20 students. All must be enrolled in the mainstream and receive no more than 50 percent resource room service. If a student needs more than 50 percent service of a resource room, he or she should be reevaluated by the clinical team for possible placement into a regular special education class.

In following guidelines set up by local educational agencies, groups no larger than five students should be taught at any one time. Students enrolled in a resource room should receive at least one instructional period a day.

In further keeping with guidelines, a resource room teacher should serve no more than 20 students. If that number should be exceeded, the service that is provided becomes insufficient, and the needs of the students are not met.

The following are subsections of the *Regulations of the Commissioner of Education* (New York state) that refer to resource room programs:

Section 200.4(d) Resource Programs (general)

1. The formation of resource programs as instructional service options shall depend upon the nature of the child's capabilities and individual needs.

(i) The total enrollment in a resource room program serving children with different handicapping conditions shall not exceed 20.

(ii) Each handicapped child in a resource room program shall receive at least one hour of individual or small group instruction, five days a week. Pupils shall spend not more than fifty percent of their time during the day in a resource program.

Section 200.4(d) Resource Programs (specific)

5. Resource programs for children with combined handicapping conditions.

Children with different handicapping conditions, i.e., educable mentally retarded and neurologically impaired, combined for service shall be provided instruction within a caseload not to exceed 20 pupils. School districts having fewer than 20 handicapped children may have the resource program teacher provide service to children who are not handicapped, provided that the handicapped and non-handicapped pupils shall receive instruction at different times. Handicapped children shall receive instruction in groups not exceeding five, for a minimum of one hour per day, five days per week.[4]

Issues on accreditation have caused much controversy on the secondary level. The first of these issues questions whether credit can be given for resource room participation. If the students are not granted credit, they and the parents may decline the service of the resource room. This chapter covers many administrative aspects for developing a resource room. There is no "one fit all" administrative policy that can be applied uniformly to all resource rooms. Variables, such as social, economic, and geographic, must be considered. The special education administrator/supervisor should look at all the variables that are needed to develop an effective resource room and enlist the support of the school staff, parents, principal, and district office personnel.

NOTES

1. J. Luchow, "Plan for the Development of the Resource Room Program," unpublished document (New York: New York City Board of Education, 1979).

2. A. Gartner, M. Taylor, and L.A. Truesdell, "Executive Summary," *Educational Services for Students with Special Needs: A Study of their Delivery and Recommendations* (New York, N.Y.: Center for Advanced Study in Education, The Graduate School and University Center, City University of New York, 1979), p. 11.

3. J.L. Wiederholt, D. Hammill, and V. Brown, *The Resource Teacher* (Boston, Mass.: Allyn and Bacon, 1978), p. 37.

4. Regulations of the Commissioner of Education, Subchapter P—Pursuant to Secs. 207 and 4403 of the Education Law—Part 200 (Albany, N.Y.: New York State Education Dept., 1980).

BIBLIOGRAPHY

Carroll, A.W. "The Classroom as an Ecosystem." *Focus on Exceptional Children* 4 (1974): 1–12.

Christolopos, F., and Renz, P.A. "A Critical Examination of Special Education Programs." *Journal of Special Education* 3 (1969): 371–79.

D'Alonzo, B.J.; D'Alonzo, R.L.; and Mauser, A.J. "Developing Resource Rooms for the Handicapped." *Teaching Exceptional Children* (Spring 1979), pp. 91–96.

Deno, E. "Special Education of Developmental Capital." *Exceptional Children* 37 (1970): 229–37.

Dunn, L.M. "Special Education for the Mildly Retarded—Is Much of it Justifiable?" *Exceptional Children* 35 (1968): 5–22.

Frampton, M.E., and Gall, D.E., eds. *Special Education for the Exceptional.* Boston, Mass.: Porter, Sargent, 1955.

Frampton, M.E., and Rowell, H.G. *Education of the Handicapped, Vol. 2.* Yonkers, N.Y.: World Book, 1940.

Garrison, M., and Hammill, D. "Who are the Retarded?" *Exceptional Children* 38 (1971): 13–20.

Gartner, A.; Taylor, M.; and Truesdell, L.A. "Executive Summary." *Educational Services for Students with Special Needs: A Study of their Delivery and Recommendations.* New York, N.Y.: Center for Advanced Study in Education; The Graduate School and University Center; City University of New York, February 1979.

Hammill, D., and Bartel, N. *Teaching Children with Learning and Behavior Problems.* Boston, Mass.: Allyn and Bacon, 1975.

Hammill, D., and Wiederholdt, J.L. *The Resource Room: Rationale and Implementation.* New York, N.Y.: Grune and Stratton, 1972.

Keogh, B., and Levitt, M. "Special Education in the Mainstream: A Confrontation of Limitations?" *Focus on Exceptional Children* 8, no. 1 (1976): 1–11.

Lilly, S.M. "Special Education: A Teapot in a Tempest." *Exceptional Children* 37 (1970): 43–48.

Luchow, J. "Plan for the Development of the Resource Room Program." Mimeographed. New York, N.Y.: New York City Board of Education, 1979.

Wiederholt, J.L.; Hammill, D.; and Brown, V. *The Resource Teacher.* Boston, Mass.: Allyn and Bacon, 1978.

At Issue

TEACHER BURNOUT—WHAT CAN THE ADMINISTRATOR DO?

A new concept has been introduced into the literature on effective teaching. This concept has been identified as "teacher burnout." Various definitions of burnout have ensued, but essentially burnout is described as "becoming exhausted from excessive demands on energy, strength, or resources,"[1] and "emotional exhaustion resulting from the stress of interpersonal contact."[2] Regarding burnout among special educators, the term can be measured by "not only the rate of staff turnover, but also the number of persons who are remaining in their positions, but who have literally 'given up the struggle' out of sheer frustration and fatigue."[3]

All teachers, and in particular special educators, have been dramatically affected by the problem of burnout. While no data presently exists on the number of teachers leaving the field because of burnout, a recent study indicated that "many teachers are frustrated with teaching and would prefer leaving the profession."[4] The negative effects of teacher burnout can be felt on education, the teacher's own physical and mental health status, and on services provided to children. In addition, such other groups as the entire school staff, the student population, parents, and the teachers' families can be the indirect victims of teacher burnout.

Reviewing the literature on this phenomenon, Weiskopf cites that teacher burnout is the result of occupational stress resulting from: (1) personal characteristics ("i.e., work overload, time pressures, responsibility for people, poor relationships at work, physical danger, etc."); (2) stress occurring in the work environment; and (3) sources of stress outside the organization ("i.e., family problems, life crises, financial difficulties, etc.").[5] While the special education administrator can do little to ensure that the teaching faculty possesses only the most desirable mental health traits and that no additional stress is brought to bear from outside of the school setting, the administrator should understand the particular stresses endemic to special education teaching.

Weiskopf summarizes stresses that affect special educators in particular:[6]

- Work overload: The heavy job demands of the special educator include such tasks as developing IEPs, working with parents, attending meetings, teaching children, and consulting with regular educators. "Due to this heavy work load, job tension increases as job satisfaction decreases," and "special educators . . . suffer from enormous environmental pressures."

- Lack of perceived success: "Special educators . . . can become disenchanted, disillusioned, angry, and burned out while working with children in special need. Teachers often perceive only the child's problems and fail to see any progress or success within their relationship." If the teacher perceives that progress is not being made, then that person's self-esteem deteriorates.
- Amount of direct contact with children: "Special children require constant adult supervision in school environments," and studies have demonstrated that burnout increases with the number of hours of direct contact with children.
- Staff-child ratio: "In high-ratio centers, the staff experienced greater pressure and emotional stress and, overall, liked their jobs less than did staff in low-ratio centers." Teachers of exceptional children in the mainstream are especially vulnerable to this factor.
- Program structure: "While an open and nondirective approach to education may be ideally suited to some children, it is emotionally exhausting for the teacher." It is recommended that "the prevailing tone of certain structure and moderate control is necessary to alleviate excessive emotional stress."
- Responsibility for others: In the helping profession, the professional is expected to be the caregiver and the client, the receiver. Teachers are expected to provide services for children for most of their school day. "Unless supportive services are provided to teachers to replenish their ego needs, then gradually their caring and concern for students diminishes and burnout occurs."
- Other factors: The special educator is vulnerable to stresses that might occur from: lack of administrative support, misdiagnosis of exceptional children, uncooperative parents, impingement of lawsuits, confused or hostile colleagues, tremendous amounts of paperwork, and poorly trained aides.

Weiskopf goes on to describe in detail the symptomatic progression of teacher burnout.[7] At the outset, the teacher may feel personal distress and desire not to go to work. As burnout continues, other factors, such as fatigue, irritability, mild depression, boredom, and feelings of overwork, become evident. Such symptoms can persist for several weeks, but can be reduced or alleviated with a short vacation. However, if the teacher does not get a respite, other changes take place. Increasing rigidity, cynicism, and negativism may occur in the direct contact with children. At this point, teachers are likely to retreat from social contacts with other colleagues, and they avoid school meetings, group lunches, and they come to school late or leave early. A decrease in teaching effectiveness may be apparent to administrators, children, colleagues, and parents. Paradoxically, teachers experiencing burnout may work longer hours to overcome their perceived lack of effectiveness, but in the end they make a less positive contribution. If these symptoms of stress continue, more severe problems can occur. Other problems that have been noted include alcoholism, drug and other substance abuse, absenteeism, marital conflict, mental illness, and depression.

A study conducted by a group of researchers attempted to determine the methods that teachers currently use to deal with job related stress.[8] Approximately 140 experienced regular and special educators were asked to respond to the question: "What do you now do to deal with stress on the job?" Seven methods of reducing stress and the percentages of teachers reportedly using these techniques accounted for 83 percent of all responses made. These techniques and percentages utilizing them were:

1. Rap and learn about it (35 percent).
2. Organize and prioritize it (11 percent).
3. Stay cool and diversify (9 percent).
4. Snooze and forget it (9 percent).
5. Call time out or quit (8 percent).
6. Jog it away (6 percent).
7. Snack it out (5 percent).[9]

Interpreting this study, Dixon, Shaw, and Bensky find it distressing that less than half of the responses cited for dealing with stress (categories 1 and 2) actually get at the underlying problem. They characterize the other responses as "avoidance behavior" and comment that such responses are not indicative of people with good mental health. They conclude that "it is likely that this approach to the problem of stress for educators can only result in a reduction in the quality and the level of services provided for handicapped students."[10]

Another study conducted by a group of researchers in Connecticut found that resource teachers and regular teachers of mainstreamed children were more likely to suffer from occupational stress than were special education teachers of self-contained classes.[11] The researchers attribute this phenomenon to the lack of clear role definition for both mainstream teachers and resource teachers, who in addition are required to perform a multitude of new services. Administrators are therefore cautioned to note that stress is not likely to affect all staff members in the same manner. Administrators should be aware of the symptoms of burnout to be able to identify those affected and deal with specific problems. In the same study, it was determined that of all the occupational roles that may potentially contribute to stressful conditions, diagnosis and assessment were found by teachers to be highly stressful activities. In addition, among special educators stress from pupil load and teaching duties were higher than that of regular class teachers.

There are many recommendations for helping teachers learn to identify stress and deal with it. Ensuring that the following recommendations for preventing burout are followed is within the role of the administrator overseeing the special education functions: (These recommendations are abstracted from the work of the researchers cited earlier.)

- Special teachers should be made aware of the emotional stresses their work involves before they begin teaching.
- Teachers must learn to set realistic goals both for themselves and their students.
- Special teachers should learn to delegate work to others wherever possible; for example, paperwork and nonteaching services can be performed by aides or volunteers.
- It is important that special educators not be isolated from other staff.
- Special teachers should diversify their methods through the use of such systems as team teaching and learning centers to break up the time spent in continuous, direct contact with children.
- Teachers of special children should seek outlets for mental growth and stimulation away from the workplace.
- Physical activity helps to relieve stress and tension.
- To avoid boredom, special educators should be encouraged to use creativity and innovations to create high interest for themselves and their students. Repetitive routines should be avoided.
- Developing hobbies, skills, or interests not involved with teaching helps to make teachers feel better about themselves and raise their self-confidence, as well as providing opportunities for rejuvenation.
- Inservice and preservice skill development should focus upon methods of diagnosis and assessment.
- Emphasis should be placed on helping teachers with direct teaching skills.
- Teachers with a high degree of role uncertainty where the system is only marginally compliant with the mandates of PL 94-142 need a great deal of support.
- Teachers with a high degree of role uncertainty where the system is only marginally compliant with the mandates of PL 94-142 need a great deal of support.
- Administrators should provide opportunities for increasing the number and kind of interpersonal and professional relationships among staff.

- School systems should investigate the possibility of incorporating a multilevel intervention strategy to reduce burnout.

The major goals of stress management are to both develop a stress management technique that works for each person involved and to teach a school system how to build upon its own resources to provide such techniques. Models of stress management developed for other helping professions can be looked at for guidance.

In conclusion, the problems of stress reduction and teacher burnout require additional competencies on the part of special service administrators. To avoid the effects of burnout and stress, they must be confronted directly and systematically. The actions of the administrator must be viewed as credible and obvious by the teachers involved. Administrators must be concerned with the differentiated problems of each teacher as well as with the entire special service system. While no specific approach will work in every situation, research emphasizes that it is the administrator of special education who is directly responsible for addressing the mental health needs of the teachers involved in special education. Not to do so indicates potential disaster both for the individuals involved and for the ability of the system to provide appropriate special education.

NOTES

1. J. Freudenberger, "Burn-Out: Occupational Hazard of the Child Care Worker," *Child Care Quarterly* 6 (1977) pp. 90–98.
2. P. Weiskopf, "Burnout Among Teachers of Exceptional Children," *Exceptional Children* 47, no. 1 (September 1980), p. 19.
3. B. Dixon, S. Shaw, and J. Bensky, "Administrator's Role in Fostering the Mental Health of Special Services Personnel," *Exceptional Children* 47, no. 1 (September 1980), p. 36.
4. Weiskopf, "Burnout Among Teachers," p. 18.
5. Ibid., p. 19.
6. Ibid., pp. 19–20.
7. Ibid., p. 21.
8. Dixon, Shaw, and Bensky, "Administrator's Role," p. 31.
9. Ibid.
10. Ibid.
11. J. Bensky et al., "Public Law 94-142 and Stress: A Problem for Educators," *Exceptional Children* 47, no. 1 (September 1980), p. 27.

Chapter 13

Evaluation of Resource Room Programs

Ruth Gold

Evaluation is an important component of a resource room program. Questions relating to the effectiveness of the program and the services provided are valid evaluation concerns. Ideally, in order to assess program effectiveness and to pinpoint areas of change, all aspects of the program, including pupil progress and program management, should be evaluated. However, because of budget and time factors this is not possible, and the evaluation plan must indicate the priority areas to be assessed. In general, the evaluation results should determine whether the program is effectively providing services to the disabled child and if resources are being used efficiently. The results of the evaluation should indicate those areas that are functioning successfully and those that require modification. Such an evaluation process will provide objective data upon which decisions can be made. After changes are made and reevaluated, future evaluation plans will address other priority areas.

The evaluation procedures discussed in this chapter are derived from the Discrepancy Evaluation Model (DEM).[1] This model focuses on the program as a whole, making it a good framework for providing resource room teachers with specific information for assessing and improving their own programs. The evaluation indicates a standard, which is determined from experience, values, and knowledge, against which performance is compared. The standards are described by the *inputs* (people and resources used in the program, federal and state laws, and school district policy), *processes* (activities that occur), and *outputs* (the changes or products that result). All three aspects make up the program design against which performance is compared. The data collected are used to determine whether the program is working as planned in the original design, to improve the ongoing program, to ascertain the degree to which objectives have been met, and to indicate areas for future change.

A specific level of acceptable performance (standard) should be indicated for each variable being investigated, though some data may be collected for informational purposes.[2] These standards should be made public. For example, in evaluating an inservice training program, an average score of five on a rating scale from one to seven may be considered to be an acceptable performance. When the data from the rating scale are analyzed, if the average score is less than five, the program would not have been at an acceptable level of performance.

To facilitate the evaluation process, a plan is constructed that indicates: (1) the components of the resource room program; (2) the evaluation questions to be answered; (3) the data needed to answer the questions; (4) the respondents who will provide the data; (5) the instruments or methods to be used to generate the data; and (6) a schedule of data collection.

COMPONENTS OF A RESOURCE ROOM PROGRAM

Eight major components of most resource room programs can be identified:

1. environment
2. intake procedures
3. scheduling
4. materials
5. remediation
6. recordkeeping
7. reporting
8. staff relations

Depending on the resource program, other components also may be identified. The components that will be evaluated are determined by the priorites of a particular school or resource teacher. For the evaluation, each major component can be refined still further. For example, the environment includes the physical size of the room, the use of space, arrangement of furniture, work areas, lighting, ventilation, storage, and so on. Table 13–1 shows a further delineation of the other components.

Because each resource room program is unique, resource teachers must identify their own priority areas and develop an evaluation plan based on the programs's philosophy and goals. An effective evaluation plan provides information that is needed to make changes. Depending on the evaluation questions that are addressed, different types of information

Table 13–1 Major Resource Program Components

Environment	Intake procedure	Scheduling
seating, storage, light, sound, size, use of space	referral forms, procedures, testing, report writing	student attendance, planning, team meeting, parent conferences
Materials	Remediation	Recordkeeping
availability, ordering, storage/accessibility, frequency of use, gaps	grouping, individualizing assignments	for self, administration, teachers, parents, storage, format
Reporting		Staff relationships
purpose, type, frequency		homeroom teacher, other special education, ancillary faculty, administration

collection procedures are used. Following are some questions that have been asked (and evaluated) by resource room teachers:

- Does the resource room teacher use time effectively?
- Have the children improved in the targeted skills?
- Are materials being used effectively?
- Are any aspects of the program being neglected?
- Does the diagnostic battery provide adequate information?
- Is the attitude of the school staff positive regarding the program?
- How effective is the inservice training program?

To answer the first question, a resource teacher kept data on the amount of time she spent on the following activities: testing, providing remediation, conferring with teachers, parent conferences, inservice training sessions, preparation for inservice training sessions, report writing, attending COH and building team meetings, planning for instruction, making materials, school assignments, and collecting and analyzing data for program evaluation. (Note: if data collection, planning, and analysis are too time consuming and provide limited data, the evaluation plan may need revision.)

The teacher established a priority listing for each item and then compared the percentage of time spent in terms of its priority. It quickly became apparent that the teacher was spending more time testing and conferring than she was in remediation. Working with the school administration, the teacher was able to have the testing and reporting responsibilities shared with another qualified staff member.

Other quantitative data that are important—indeed such information is needed for federal and state reports—include the number of children served, ages and grades served, types of disabilities, the number of periods children are in the resource room, and the number of regular and ancillary staff members with whom the resource teacher works.

To answer the second question, the resource teacher used not only data from the resource room but also had the homeroom teacher and parents complete questionnaires relating to academic, social, and behavioral performance. In this way, the teacher was able to ascertain which of the improvements noted in the resource room had been generalized.

The evaluation process should be well organized. To coordinate data collection, a chart of the evaluation schedule is helpful. (See Exhibit 13–1.) The chart indicates the aspects of the program to be evaluated, the evaluation questions to be answered, the method of data collection, the type of instrument to be used, the respondents from whom the data will be collected, and the time when it is due. The schedule provides at a glance the status of the evaluation procedure.

EVALUATION INSTRUMENTS

Tests

Evaluation of student progress can be made in many ways depending on the information desired. Pupil progress can be determined by an increase in grade level as measured by a specific test, the extent to which students have attained specific skills as determined by criterion-referenced tests, and the number of long- and short-term goals from the IEP that have been met.

Most often, achievement tests are used to measure the extent to which a student has profited from the resource room program. The tests used,

Exhibit 13–1 Sample Evaluation Schedule

Evaluation Schedule				
Evaluation Question	Method	Respondent	Date Administered	Date Completed

therefore, must reflect the content of the student's individual course of study.

Most achievement tests are norm-referenced. That is, they are standardized using national norms, and they provide information about a student's performance as compared to a national sample of the same age or grade. Generally, the child's scores at the beginning of the school year (or at entrance to the resource room program) are compared with those obtained at the end of the school year.

Criterion-referenced tests, a second type of test used to examine academic progress, are being administered on a widespread basis. These tests are designed to pinpoint performance in specific skill areas and are directly related to the goals of the resource room. The criterion-referenced test is concerned with children's ability to perform particular skills rather than their performances as compared to a national norm. Criterion-referenced testing makes it possible to determine when the child has met the long- and short-term goals that are part of the IEP. Many criterion-referenced programs are currently available.[3,4,5,6]

> It is usually better, however, for resource teachers to make up their own tests. Teacher-made tests can be criterioned to particular instructional programs, specifically constructed to meet the needs of an individual student, and designed to serve areas for which no ready made tests or lists are available.[7]

According to Hofmeister: "Criterion-referenced testing can reach its full potential only when it is so integrated into the day-by-day functioning of the classroom that it cannot easily be separated out as a 'testing' activity."[8]

IEPs

The objectives included in the IEP that relate to the activities of the resource room should be included in the program evaluation. Academic, social, and behavioral objectives should be assessed. By comparing the number of objectives reached by the number established, for individuals and for groups, a quantitative relationship between the program and goals can be stated. For example, if 20 short-term goals were to be met within the program and 16 were reached, the program could be considered 80 percent effective. Such data help to indicate which children benefit most from the program and the effectiveness of the program as a whole.

Questionnaires, Checklists, and Rating Scales

In addition to other uses in the resource room program, questionnaires, checklists, and rating scales can be used to obtain important evaluative information from students, teachers, and parents. They are self-administered and can be completed (within limits) at the respondent's convenience.

When preparing such instruments, several cautions should be observed. The forms should be short, easy for the responder to complete, and easy for the evaluator to tabulate. The forms should be easy to read, with each item numbered. If behaviors are being rated, they should be observable. Each item should be defined so that only one dimension is rated. Provisions should be made for additional comments. Exhibits 13-2 and 13-3 contain sample evaluation forms for parents and teachers.

Exhibit 13-2 Sample Parent Evaluation Form of Resource Room Program

Dear _____

We would like to know how you feel your son/daughter _____
has progressed this year in the resource room program. Your rating of the following statements will help us provide the best education for your child.

Please return this rating sheet by _____.
(date)

Sincerely,

_____
(Signature)

	Strongly Agree	Agree	Disagree	Strongly Disagree
	1	2	3	4
1. My child's attitude toward school is positive.	—	—	—	—
2. My child's attitude toward the resource room program is positive.	—	—	—	—
3. My child's school work is improving because of the program.	—	—	—	—
4. The information provided me about my child is helpful.	—	—	—	—
5. The resource room program is meeting the objectives agreed upon in the IEP.	—	—	—	—

Additional comments and suggestions:

Exhibit 13–3 Sample Homeroom/Academic Teacher Evaluation Form

Dear _____

    Your student _____is enrolled in the resource room program. We would like to know how you feel this student has progressed. Your rating of the following statements will help us improve the program. Please return this form by ___(date)___ . If you would like to discuss the program or this evaluation, please let me know.

Sincerely,

_____
(Signature)

	SA	A	D	SD	U
1. My student has shown improvement in academic areas because of the program.	—	—	—	—	—
2. My student looks forward to time in the resource room.	—	—	—	—	—
3. The written reports provided by the resource room teacher have helped me work with the student.	—	—	—	—	—
4. The resource room schedule has been convenient for my class.	—	—	—	—	—
5. The communication between me and the resource teacher is helpful.	—	—	—	—	—
6. The resource room program is meeting the objectives outlined in the IEP.	—	—	—	—	—
7. The student requires more time in the resource room program.	—	—	—	—	—

Additional comments:

Recommendations:

Key: SA–strongly agree
     A–agree
     D–disagree
     SD–strongly disagree
     U–unsure

Interviews

Interviews are an important information gathering device. Used with planned questions, which provide focus during the interview and ensure that specific topics are discussed, they are also flexible and adaptable. The questions, which should be prepared in advance, should be used as a general guide. Some responses will require follow-up questions. In addition, the interviewees should be given an opportunity to expand into areas of concern that are relevant to the program evaluation. The interview is useful for all respondents, but especially with children since the interviewer can tell whether the question is understood and, if need be, can rephrase it. Because it is conducted on an individual basis, the major shortcoming of the interview technique is the amount of time required.

The results of the evaluation should be compiled into a usable form or report. Feedback should be provided to those who participated in the process. Strengths, weaknesses, and recommendations should be included. When no recommendations for revisions of weaknesses have been made or where those suggested are not appropriate, the resource teacher may suggest the appointment of an *ad hoc* committee to help resolve the problem or come up with alternate solutions. Members of the committee could be other special education teachers, regular classroom teachers, other school support personnel, or parents. Consultants from the state education department, the school district, teachers' organizations, other school districts, or the local university may also be used as resources. The nature of the problem will suggest which approach or consultant to use.

As problem areas are remediated, other evaluation questions can be raised and data collection procedures instituted. Evaluation is an ongoing process and should continue as long as the program is in effect. This adaptation of the DEM has been found to be a useful and efficient method for collecting the data needed by the resource room teacher to improve the quality of the program and the delivery of services.

NOTES

1. Diane Kyker Yavorsky, *Discrepancy Evaluation: A Practitioner's Guide* (Charlottesville, Va.: University of Virginia Evaluation Research Center, 1976).

2. Ibid., p. 70.

3. Donald D. Hammill and Nettie R. Bartel, *Teaching Children with Learning and Behavior Problems* (Boston, Mass.: Allyn and Bacon, Inc., 1975).

4. *Fore Instructional Materials List* (N. Hollywood, Cal.: Foreworks Publications, 1976).

5. *Fore Reading, Fore Language, Fore Mathematics* (N. Hollywood, Cal.: Foreworks Publications, 1977).

6. *System Fore Handbook* (N. Hollywood, Cal.: Foreworks Publications, 1979).

7. J. Lee Wiederholt, Donald D. Hammill, and Virginia Brown, *The Resource Teacher: A Guide to Effective Practices* (Boston, Mass.: Allyn and Bacon, Inc.), p. 17.

8. Alan Hofmeister, "Integrating Criterion-Referenced Testing and Instruction." In W. Havely and M. Reynolds, eds., *Domain-Referenced Testing in Special Education* (Minneapolis, Minn.: Leadership Training Institute/Special Education, University of Minnesota, 1975), p. 77–78.

At Issue

THE PROCESS OF PROGRAM EVALUATION—THE CHOICE BETWEEN OBJECTIVE AND SUBJECTIVE CRITERIA

Evaluation is certainly vital to the ongoing effectiveness of any educational intervention, such as a resource program. However, there is growing evidence that the current mode of program evaluation necessitates a great expenditure of time and money. Such evaluations are causing great distress, and it is unlikely that the effort put into such formal evaluation processes results in more effective programs. In the version of the DEM described by Gold, what seems to be a simpler form of program evaluation is proposed. In this model the teacher and others significantly involved in the resource program are asked to specify a standard of performance against which the program's effectiveness can be compared. Although the statement of these criteria implies an objective standard for the measurement of change, closer examination reveals that this standard is derived solely from opinions. In some sense the process couches "subjective inputs" as "objective criteria," and this makes for a more objective or scientific means of program evaluation. Are there other evaluation models to be employed?

In a recent paper Pierre Woog proposes an approach to program evaluation that shifts from objective data collection to a more "humanistic" approach of monitoring the effectiveness of a project.[1] This model abandons the setting of objective criteria by which to evaluate a project and replaces them with new questions to be asked. In this IKE Model of Evaluation, the new questions by which to evaluate a program emphasize the intent (I), knowledge (K), and energy (E) involved in a human services program. This method of evaluation focuses on the belief that an element of trust is necessary to the process of evaluation and that models that employ objective criteria for evaluation do not contribute as effectively to program success as those that use subjective means. The thought that most people cannot be objective about themselves in an evaluation process is being abandoned. It is being replaced by monitoring the commitment of those most involved in providing services.

There is a growing realization that the process of evaluation is also a form of intervention. The Hawthorne effect—that any treatment or handling condition implies that change will take place—is testimony to the fact that the intervention of evaluation creates an unnatural condition. Those programs scrutinized by an evaluation team are most likely to perform in an unnatural fashion or in a manner atypical to their usual conduct.

In addition, many evaluation projects often result in the collection of contradictory data that are impossible to interpret. Case in point, according to Woog, is the massive evaluation effort in the Head Start program:

> The Head Start program, for example, has been subjected to standard evaluations that have produced entirely contradictory results—which in turn are completely useless as guides, despite the many millions of dollars poured into them. The program continues because way down deep, people know it's just a good thing to do, and because the persons most directly involved have used political pressure to insure its survival.[2]

Particularly in special education, program evaluation should fit a humanistic model. If this is not the case, programs that might be otherwise effective should be abandoned on the basis of criteria such as test-retest scores that do not reach grade equivalency levels. Administrators or mainstream teachers, who may not understand how difficult it is to make significant changes in children who have lifelong disabilities, may set standards that are unrealistic. The process of change in special education is gradual, and in some cases too subtle to be found significantly different when measured with objective criteria.

Persons who must spend time justifying their reasons for existing are often demoralized in the process. Too much time spent on evaluation takes away energy and service. Woog says that recent research has found that some caregivers spend 40 percent of their time justifying their reason for being, rather than providing services.[3]

How then does the IKE model facilitate evaluation? The evaluation model shifts from the concept of looking at the results of programs to the process by which intervention is conducted. The model asserts that "good means can only result in good ends" and that "most of these ends are not discernible within our time frame or our consciousness."[4] The shift becomes that of process evaluation, or monitoring and accrediting an intervention plan. To implement the model the evaluator takes on the role of a monitor and examines the intent, knowledge, and energy of the program participants. Intent is defined as "evidence of the program responding to the mandated need."[5] Knowledge is defined to include "the behavioral analogues of knowledge" such that there is evidence that the program exhibits "state of the art" knowledge in terms of interventional strategies, management, communication, interpersonal and group skills, compassion, and organizational development.[6] Energy can be defined as the existence of "evidence of initiation and follow-through, efficient work patterns, breadth of interest, and the ability of program personnel to take time for themselves."[7]

Woog contends that "if programs for social betterment reflect the above descriptors, good programs will result. These descriptors are discernible and wise evaluators can observe, communicate, and agree upon them."[8] Therefore, program evaluators utilizing the IKE model would be called upon to use their common sense in the monitoring of the program's process and to assist the process when they find a lessening in intent, knowledge, or energy. The accountability for the program's success then falls to the larger domain of those who wish to see success, rather than solely to those who work hard at implementation.

It is vital that the model of evaluation fit the type of interventional strategy to be undertaken. Gold's ideas for evaluating the input from a variety of sources could be extended by calling upon those evaluators to take on some responsibility for ensuring the program's effectiveness. For example, parents who wish to see immediate and objective evidence of resource room effectiveness should be incorporated into the whole resource model; thus, they make a commitment for process changes. This would raise the energy level expended and facilitate greater interpersonal communication between child, parent, and teacher.

As the DEM is presently described, the overwhelming burden of proof falls to resource teachers, who must demonstrate that they are conducting a worthwhile program and meeting the expectations of others not directly involved in providing services. Is this realistic, or can the process of change and concomitant improvement occur when the process of intervention instead of the results of intervention are to be emphasized? As Woog concludes in his article, "The hypothesis offered in the IKE model is that by focusing upon the ingredients that make for successful programs rather than the results of the programs, we will have better programs."[9]

The instructional strategy of specifying measurable goals in a student's IEP and then evaluating the progress toward the attainment of the goals is important. But we should not forget that the process by which change takes place is vital and beneficial, even when those terminal goals are not met.

NOTES

1. P. Woog, "The IKE Model of Evaluation," *CEDR Quarterly,* Winter 1980, pp. 16–20.
2. P. Woog, "Shift to New Evaluation Standards Challenges Government Norms," *Behavior Today,* July 21, 1980, p. 2.
3. Ibid.
4. Woog, "The IKE Model of Evaluation," p. 19.
5. Ibid., p. 20.
6. Ibid.
7. Ibid.
8. Ibid.
9. Ibid.

Publishers of Educational Materials of Interest to Special Educators*

This annotated bibliography was developed from a list of exhibitors at the Council for Exceptional Children's International Convention, April 22–24, 1980. We acknowledge their cooperation and permission to reproduce relevant portions of their list.

Allyn and Bacon, Inc., Atlantic Ave., Boston, MA 02210—New and recently published texts and references.

American Guidance Service, Publishers' Building, Circle Pines, MN 55014—Instructional programs and a wide range of tests in special areas of evaluation.

American Printing House for the Blind, 1839 Frankfort Ave., Louisville, KY 40206—Books and educational aids for visually impaired.

Ann Arbor Publishers, P.O. Box 7249, Naples, FL 33940—Programmed instructional materials to aid the slow learner.

Arista Corporation, NDE Division, 2440 Estand Way, P.O. Box 6146, Concord, CA 94524—A multimedia language arts program for exceptional children, grades elementary through high school.

Aspen Systems Corporation, 1600 Research Blvd., Rockville, MD 20850—Books and journals.

Barnell Loft & Dexter Westbrook Publications, 958 Church St., Baldwin, NY 11510—Individualized reading and language arts series, K–12.

Bemiss-Jason Corporation, 3250 Ash St., Palo Alto, CA 94306—Creative paper products for art, classroom, and home.

Benefic Press, 1900 N. Narragansett, Chicago, IL 60639—Art materials, maps, workbooks, and textbooks.

---

*Prepared by Gloria Wilson.

BFA Educational Media, 2211 Michigan Ave., Santa Monica, CA 90404—Classroom and individualized support curriculum material: kits, print materials, and so on.

Bigtoys, 3113 South Pine St., Tacoma, WA 98409—Children's play structures and play areas.

Binney & Smith, Inc., 1100 Church Lane, Easton, PA 18042—Early childhood teaching aids and art education materials.

Dick Blick Company, P.O. Box 1267, Galesburg, IL 61401—Art and craft materials, and educational playtools for the exceptional child.

Book-Lab, Inc., 1449 37th St., Brooklyn, NY 11218—Materials in the areas of special education, learning disabilities, remedial reading, and high interest, low grade level readers.

Borg-Warner Educational Systems, 600 W. University Dr., Arlington Heights, IL 60004—System 80 individualized AV learning system; includes AV unit and programmed self-instructional materials in basic skills.

Bowmar/Noble Publishers, Inc., 4563 Colorado Blvd., Los Angeles, CA 90039—Educational material, books, kits, filmstrips, records, and cassettes.

Brodhead-Garrett Company, 4560 East 71st St., Cleveland, OH 44105—A special needs program for vocational assessment and occupational training.

C. C. Publications, Inc., P.O. Box 23699, Tigard, OR 97223—Programmed direct instruction materials for the learning handicapped.

Calvin Communications, Inc., 1105 Truman Rd., Kansas City, MO 64106—Educational films; complete motion picture production from script through release printing; and audiovisual sales and rental.

Cambridge Book Company, 888 Seventh Ave., New York, NY 10019.

Campus Film Distributors Corporation, 2 Overhill Rd., Scarsdale, NY 10583—Educational films and filmstrips for the profession.

Carson-Dellosa Publishing Company, Inc., P.O. Box 369, Clinton, OH 44216—Teaching aids; series of learning center activity books.

Center Enterprises, P.O. Box 1361, Hartford, CT 06101—Special education curriculum-oriented rubber stamps.

Centurion Industries Inc., 167 Constitution Dr., Menlo Park, CA 94025—Programmed microcomputers used for diagnostic and basic instruction in arithmetic and for teaching basic word attack skills in English language; elementary, secondary, and special education.

Childcraft Education Corporation, 20 Kilmer Rd., Edison, NJ 08817—Early childhood learning materials plus learning materials for children with special needs.

Clearvue, 6666 N. Oliphant, Chicago, IL 60631—Filmstrips, cassettes, and duplicator masters.

Cognitive Developmental Designs, Inc., 11 Wyman St., Boston, MA 02130—Symbolic Accentuation Reading Program, Symbolic Playthings, Sign and Spoken Language Program, Edge of Awareness documentary.

Cole Supply, 103 E. Bird, Pasadena, TX 77501—Edu-Carpet, Multi-Sensory Mats; introducing Woody Wobbler and his friends.

The Combined Book Exhibit, 12 Saw Mill River Rd., Hawthorne, NY 10532—Books and periodicals from publishers here and abroad.

Consulting Psychologists Press, Inc., 577 College Ave., Palo Alto, CA 94306—Diagnostic and training materials for children with speech and language problems, educationally handicapped, or mentally retarded.

The Continental Press, Inc., 520 E. Bainbridge St., Elizabethtown, PA 17022—Preprinted masters for liquid duplicators, individual pupil books, filmstrips, and boxed instructional material.

Crane Publishing Company, 1301 Hamilton Ave., P.O. Box 3713, Trenton, NJ 08629—Beginning reading; readers, practice books, manuals, management materials, pre/post tests; Spanish reading also.

Creative Publications, P.O. Box 10328, Palo Alto, CA 94303—Books, games, puzzles, posters, and manipulatives for enriching mathematics education.

Croft, Inc., 4922 Harford Rd., Baltimore, MD 21214—Readiness assessment and instruction in comprehension, teacher training, and diagnostic testing.

Curriculum Associates, Inc., 8 Henshaw St., Woburn, MA 01888—Brigance diagnostic inventories of basic skills, early development, essential skills; language arts materials; learning centers.

Phyllis Damon Fiber Co., Inc., 374 Congress St., Boston, MA 02210—Yarn and accessories for weaving; stitchery for use with children with learning disabilities; techniques for best results.

Danmar Products, Inc., 2390 Winewood, Ann Arbor, MI 48103—Helmets, face guards, and chin guards for persons with special needs; also swim aids and head floats.

Developmental Learning Materials, 7440 Natchez Ave., Niles, IL 60648—Manipulatives and supplementary materials in the areas of early childhood, reading, math, language arts, and bilingual.

Didax Educational Resources, 3 Dearborn Rd., Peabody, MA 01960—Manipulative materials for mathematics, sense training, reading and language skills, preschool and K–6.

Ebsco Curriculum Materials, 1230 First Avenue North, Birmingham, AL 35203—IEP kits: Blissymbols, prevocational training kits for collating, sorting, filing, and mail sorting; time incentive program.

Edmark Associates, P.O. Box 3903, Bellevue, WA 98009—Tested programs for severely handicapped, deaf, and learning disabled in reading, language skills, and student management.

Educational Activities, Inc., P.O. Box 392, Freeport, NY 11520—Records, cassettes, filmstrips, audiovisual/multimedia kits; reading, language arts, and math materials; micro-computer software.

Educational Design Inc., 47 West 13th St., New York, NY 10011—Skill Book, multimedia programs in career education/life skills, reading, and math for secondary special needs students.

Educational Dynamics Corporation, Morrison Bldg., King of Prussia, PA 19406—Animated media for direct viewing and overhead projection.

Educational Insights, 20435 S. Tillman, Carson, CA 90746—Charlie, the lovable teaching robot; other programs for special students.

Educational Patterns, Inc., 63–110 Woodhaven Blvd., Rego Park, NY 11374—Retrieval system of educational information for IEP, TV comprehension program.

Educational Performance Associates, 600 Broad Ave., Ridgefield, NJ 07657—Filmstrips, creative playthings, test materials, and workbooks.

Educational Progress Corporation, 4235 S. Memorial, Tulsa, OK 74145— Test materials and workbooks.

Educational Teaching Aids, 159 W. Kinzie St., Chicago, IL 60610— Educational teaching aids and manipulatives.

Educators Publishing Service, 75 Moulton St., Cambridge, MA 02138— Teachers' manuals, student workbooks designed for language learning disabilities; Orton-Gillingham-Slingerland materials.

EMC Corporation/Changing Times Ed. Service, 180 E. 6th St., St. Paul, MN 55101—Educational multimedia materials in many curriculum areas, particularly language arts, reading, career, and consumer education.

Encyclopaedia Britannica Educational Corporation, 425 No. Michigan, Chicago, IL 60611—A full line of EBE educational materials.

Erca-Enrichment Reading Corporation of America, Iron Ridge, WI 53035—Elementary and special education teaching aids.

Everest & Jennings, Inc., 1803 Pontius Ave., Los Angeles, CA 90025— Wheelchairs, walkers, commodes, Hoyer patient lifts, and other patient aids.

The Exceptional Parent, 20 Providence St., Boston, MA 02116—A bimonthly magazine offering practical guidance to parents and professionals concerned with disabled children.

Experience Education, 401 Reed St., Red Oak, IA 51566—Career Exploration System.

Fearon Pitman Publishers, Inc., 6 Davis Dr., Belmont, CA 94002—Educational textbook material: special, business, and adult education with teacher aids.

Flaghouse, Inc., 18 W. 18th St., New York, NY 10011—Motor activity equipment for perceptual gross, fine, and sensory motor development; eye-hand, socialization, and body image.

Follett Publishing Company, 1010 W. Washington Blvd., Chicago, IL 60607—Educational materials: visual/auditory perception, and cognitive development programs.

Gamco Industries, Inc., Box 1911, Big Spring, TX 79720—Filmstrips, cassettes, books, and manipulatives for teaching exceptional children.

Good Apple, Inc., Box 299, Carthage, IL 62321—Materials for elementary teachers, activity books, idea books, records, and a newspaper.

Great Ideas, Inc., 40 Oser Ave., Hauppauge, NY 11787—Manipulative mathematics programs.

Grolier Educational Corporation/E1 Division, Sherman Turnpike, Danbury, CT 06816—Reference and curriculum materials for grade school through high school.

Grune & Stratton, Inc., 111 5th Ave., New York, NY 10003.

Hampden Publishing Company, Box 4873, Baltimore, MD 21211.

Hausmann Industries, Inc., 130 Union St., Northvale, NJ 07647—Manufacturer of equipment for the medical and rehabilitation professions.

Hayes School Publishing Co., Inc., 321 Pennwood Ave., Wilkinsburg, PA 15221—Publishers of duplicating workbooks and related classroom teaching aids.

Hawkins & Associates, Inc., 804 D Street, NE, Washington, DC 20002—Books and published materials.

Education Division, Department of Health, Education and Welfare, 200 Independence Ave., SW, HHH Bldg., 307-H, Washington, DC 20202—Publications/information from the U.S. Office of Education and National Center for Education Statistics.

Highlights for Children, Inc., 2300 W. Fifth Ave., Columbus, OH 43216—Children's educational periodical, supplementary reading handbooks on a variety of topics, and multimedia involvement materials.

Hopewell Books, Inc., 1670 Sturbridge Dr., R.D. # 1, Sewickley, PA 15143—Life skills curriculum for high school students and adults written on a second-grade reading level.

Horton Handicraft Co., Inc., P.O. Box 330, Farmington, CT 06032—Arts and crafts materials.

Houghton Mifflin Company, One Beacon St., Boston, MA 02107—Textbooks.

Howe Press of Perkins School for the Blind, Watertown, MA 02172—Braille materials.

Hubbard, 1946 Raymond Dr., Northbrook, IL 60062—Materials from Project I Can, Me Now Project More, Mr. Rogers, and Project Stretch.

Humanics Limited, 881 Peachtree St., NE, Atlanta, GA 30309—Books and forms in areas of social service, education, parent involvement, and other human relations materials.

ICT-Instructional Communications Technology, Inc., 10 Stepar Place, Huntington Station, NY 11746—Reading, listening, decoding, vocabulary, comprehension, and study skills programs for students requiring special education.

Ideal Developmental Labs, 3044 South 92nd St., West Allis, WI 53227—Vocational training program for special needs students in the maintenance trade area.

Ideal School Supply Company, 11000 So. Lavergne Ave., Oak Lawn, IL 60453—Teaching aids and manipulatives for the educable retarded, learning disabled, emotionally disturbed, physically handicapped, and so on.

Imperial International Learning Corp., P.O. Box 548, Kankakee, IL 60901—K–8 multimedia programs in early childhood education reading, math, science, and social studies , to extend and reinforce the basic curriculum.

Incentives for Learning, 600 W. Van Buren St., Chicago, IL 60607—Instructional materials and programs for children and adults.

Instructional Industries, Inc., Executive Park, Ballston Lake, NY 12019—The PAL System; a new auditory processing program added to over 800 filmstrips and cassettes in the areas of perceptual training, language, math science, and social studies.

Instructor Publications, Inc., 7 Bank St., Dansville, NY 14437—Instructor Curriculum Materials, *Instructor Magazine*.

Interpretive Education, 2306 Winters Dr., Kalamazoo, MI 49002—Multimedia programs for special needs students; high interest/low vocabulary.

Jane Ward Co., Inc., 1642 So. Beech St., Lakewood, CO 80228—Laminated and/or reproducible word attack, comprehension, and math reinforcements.

Janus Book Publishers, 28488 Hesperian Blvd., Hayward, CA 94545—Practical skills workbooks for secondary and adult slow readers.

Ja-Son Div., The Scott & Fetzer Company, 217 Long Hill Cross Rds., Shelton, CT 06484—Snip-Loop Scissors for handicapped, training scissors, school scissors, teachers' shears, and sewing and household shears.

Jastak Assessment Systems, Wilmington, DE 19806—Wide Range Test Series.

Jayfro Corp., P.O. Box 400, Waterford, CT 06385—Manufacturers of athletic, recreation, physical education, playground, and special educational equipment.

Judy Company, 310 N. 2nd St., Minneapolis, MN 55401—Wooden puzzles with/without knobs, educational games, manipulatives for early childhood, and duplicating masters.

Kids Come in Special Flavors Company, Box 562, Forest Park Station, Dayton, OH 45405—Kits, books, and audiovisual materials for classroom and inservice to change attitudes toward the handicapped.

Kimbo Educational, Box 477, Long Branch, NJ 07740—New materials for self-care, music therapy, and adaptive physical education.

Lakeshore Curriculum Materials Centers, local centers throughout the U.S.—Curriculum materials K–12.

Lead Educational Resources, Inc., 32 Colony Rd., Lexington, MA 02173—A total reading, writing, and spelling programs for all ages, "styles and rate" of learning.

Learning Guidance Systems, 1505 Black Mountain Rd., Hillsborough, CA 94010—A phonetic reading program for learning handicapped.

Learning Tree Filmstrips, 934 Pearl St., Boulder, CO 80302—Programs on mainstreaming, values, reading, and writing skills.

National Library Service for the Blind and Physical Handicapped Library of Congress, 1291 Taylor St., NW, Washington, DC 20542—Free books and magazines recorded and in braille for blind and physically handicapped individuals.

Los Angeles County Test Development Center, 9300 East Imperial Highway, Downey, CA 90242—Los Angeles County Test Development Center provides services to districts to meet pupil proficiency assessment in basic skills.

Lotto Talk, Inc., 115 King St., Alexandria, VA 22314—Language program including manual with lesson plans, readiness workbooks, reader, and color video training tapes.

Love Publishing Company, 6635 E. Villanova, Denver, CO 80222—Books, reference and professional, duplicator materials, and journals.

Maddak, Inc., Pequannock, NJ 07440—Aids for daily living.

Mafex Associates, Inc., 90 Cherry St., Johnstown, PA 15902—Books for education of exceptional persons, texts, workbooks, professional guides, and testing materials.

Market Linkage Project—Linc Services, Inc., 829 Eastwind Dr., Westerville, OH 43081—Arranges distribution of BEH/USOE funded programs and products with publishers and producers for national and international distribution.

Keystone View Civ. of Mast/Keystone, 2212 E. 12th St., Davenport, IA 52803—Vision screening and development equipment and materials.

Charles Mayer Studios, Inc., 168 E. Market St., Akron, OH 44308—Visual aids and exhibits for presentation, training, promotion, display, and visual control.

CTB/McGraw-Hill, Del Monte Research Park, Monterey, CA 93940—Special education, criterion-referenced tests, minimum competency tests, and early childhood tests.

EDL/McGraw-Hill, 1221 Avenue of the Americas, New York, NY 10020—Basic skills in reading and mathematics; diagnostic/prescriptive skills programs for elementary and high schools.

Instructo/McGraw-Hill, Cedar Hollow and Matthews Hill Rd., Paoli, PA 19301—Learning centers, spirit duplicating books, desk tapes, mobiles, walk-on-number lines, handbooks, and so on.

McGraw-Hill Book Company (College Division), 1221 Avenue of the Americas, New York, NY 10020—New, revised, and previously published tests in every field of special education.

Publishers' Test Service (a service of CTB/McGraw-Hill), 2500 Garden Road, Monterey, CA 93940—A selection of testing and instructional materials from a wide variety of publishers.

Webster/McGraw-Hill, 1221 Avenue of the Americas, New York, NY 10020—Texts, workbooks, and related aids including diagnostic and prescriptive material for the special education student.

McKnight Publishing Company, P.O. Box 2854, Bloomington, IL 61701—Textbooks and other instructional materials for vocational education and career guidance.

Rand McNally & Company, School Map and Globe Department, Box 7600, Chicago, 'L 60680—Maps, globes, map skills programs: color/sound filmstrips and audio cassette programs, including auditory perception program.

Rand McNally & Company, School Department, Box 7600, Chicago, IL 60680—"Hands-on" materials for programs in science, language arts, and mathematics, including bilingual mathematics.

Media Materials, Inc., 2936 Remington Ave., Baltimore, MD 21211—
Supplemental, basic skill teaching aids: sound filmstrips, cassette learn-
ing packages, giant size duplicating masters, and cassette activity books.
Melton Peninsula, Inc., 1949 Stemmons Frwy.,# 690, Dallas, TX 75207—
Curricular materials for severely/profoundly mentally retarded children
and adults; special survival skills program.
Charles E. Merrill Publishing Company, 1300 Alum Creek Dr., Columbus,
OH 43216—College textbooks and audiovisual materials.
Midwest Publications, P.O. Box 129, Troy, MI 48099—Thinking skill
supplementary materials nongraded K–12.
Milliken Publishing Company, 1100 Research Blvd., St. Louis, MO
63132—Duplicating and transparency books.
Milton Bradley Company/Playskool, Inc., Springfield, MA 01101—Supplementary materials for special education, early childhood, language,
reading, and math.
Mind, Inc., 181 Main St., Norwalk, CT 06851—AV programs for special
education students in reading, math, and prevocational.
Modulearn, Inc., P.O. Box 635, San Juan Capistrano, CA 92693—Reading
programs that use music.
Monroe, the Calculator Company, The American Rd., Morris Plains, NJ
07950—Educationally-oriented hardware/software systems including
skill-drill computers.
Montevideo Follow Through Resource Center, 6th and Grove, Montevideo, MN 56265—Individualized basic skills curriculum K–6.
The C.V. Mosby Company, 11830 Westline Industrial Dr., St. Louis, MO
63141—Mosby reference books, textbooks, and workbooks.

Nasco, 901 Janesville Ave., Fort Atkinson, WI 53538—Pre-K thru 3 early
learning and special education materials and equipment.
National Audiovisual Center, National Archives & Records Service,
Washington, DC 20409—Distributor and central information point for
U.S. Govt. produced audiovisual materials; varied collection, diverse
subject matter.
National Teaching Aids, Inc., 120 Fulton Ave., Garden City Park, NY
11040—Visual and manipulative teaching aids for life science, earth
science, and health education.
Newby Visualanguage, Inc., Box 121, Eagleville, PA 19408—A collection
of language materials.
New Readers Press, Box 131, Syracuse, NY 13210—High interest texts
for low level readers; basic reading, writing, coping skills, and curriculum materials.

Open Court Publishing Company, P.O. Box 599, LaSalle, IL 61301—Language arts program K–6.

Opportunities for Learning, Inc., 8950 Lurline Ave., Chatsworth, CA 91311—Instructional materials for special education, including speech, language development, reading, guidance, and social studies.

Ortho-Kinetics, Inc., 1610 Pearl St., P.O. Box 436, Waukesha, WI 53187—Adaptive wheelchairs.

Pathescope Educational Media, Inc., 71 Weyman Ave., New Rochelle, NY 10802—Multimedia kits and books in the area of special education.

Pendulum Press, Inc., Saw Mill Rd., West Haven, CT 06516—Illustrated books (classics, biographies) and history; filmstrips, Read-A-Long Program.

The Portage Project, 412 East Slifer St., Portage, WI 53901—Early childhood/parent involvement program, including products for teachers, parents, and children.

Prentice-Hall, Inc., Sylvan Ave., Englewood Cliffs, NJ 07632—College textbooks.

Prentice-Hall Learning Systems, Inc., P.O. Box 47X, Englewood Cliffs, NJ 07632—Teacher resource materials.

Prentice-Hall Media, 150 White Plains Rd., Tarrytown, NY 10591—Audiovisual instructional materials on career development and skills for exceptional children.

Prentke Romich Company, RD 2, Box 191, Shreve, OH 44676—Nonverbal communication aids using symbols, letters, words, and capable of signaling, displaying, and printing.

Prep, Incorporated, 1575 Parkway Ave., Trenton, NJ 08628—Audiovisual programs in vocational, occupational, career assessment, psychological testing, and skill development.

J.A. Preston Corporation, 71 Fifth Ave., New York, NY 10003—Special education materials and communication devices.

Project Maine Stream Outreach, Cumberland, ME 04021—Manuals, slides, and tapes.

The Psychological Corporation, 757 Third Ave., New York, NY 10017—Educational and psychological tests and services plus supportive curriculum programs for use with exceptional children.

Quercus Corporation, 2768 Pineridge Rd., Castro Valley, CA 94546—Special education workbooks for high school and junior high students with reading levels of second to third grade.

Reader's Digest Educational Division, Pleasantville, NY 10570—Supplementary language arts materials K–9.

Reading Joy, Inc., P.O. Box 404, Naperville, IL 60540—Reading handbooks, games, K–8 levels.

Relevant Productions, Inc., Heron Publishers, Inc., 1123 Seminole St., Clearwater, FL 33535—Middle through high school multimedia materials dealing with values and basic skills.

Research Press, 2612 N. Mattis, Champaign, IL 61820—Books, films, and multimedia kits for special educators.

Rhythm Band, Inc., P.O. Box 126, Fort Worth, TX 76101—Musical instruments designed for special education.

Frank E. Richards Publishing Co., Inc., P.O. Box 66, Phoenix, NY 13135—Books and workbooks.

Roslyn Equipment Company, 1645 Bustleton Pike, Feasterville, PA 19047—Automatic elevating table for wheelchair confined students.

S & S Arts and Crafts, Colchester, CT 06415—Arts and crafts materials and supplies.

Salco Toys, Inc., Rt. 1, Nerstrand, MN 55053—Wooden products, large-handled puzzles, threading systems, body puzzles, and so on.

Sax Arts & Crafts, 316 N. Milwaukee, Milwaukee, WI 53202—Line of arts and crafts materials, equipment and tools.

Frank Schaffer Publications, 23770 Hawthorne Blvd., Torrance, CA 90505—Support materials for learning basic skills; high interest, low vocabulary.

Scholastic Testing Service, Inc., 480 Meyer Rd., Bensenville, IL 60106—Screening 0–6, assessment 3–15, comprehensive language program, policy and procedures; handbooks for teachers and parents for PL 94-142.

Science Research Associates, Inc., 155 N. Wacker Dr., Chicago, IL 60606—Basal and supplemental instructional materials, career education, guidance tests, and test scoring.

Silver Burdette Company, 250 James St., Morristown, NJ 07060—Educational materials for reaching the special learner through music; SB music for special education.

Singer Career Systems, 80 Commerce Dr., Rochester, NY 14623—Vocational Evaluation System, Career Awareness Lab., Life Skills, Career Entry, Occupational Inforamtion, Skills Orientation Series.

Sing 'N Do Co., Inc., 26 Goffle Rd., Midland Park, NJ 07432—Educational recorded song stories with illustrated guidebooks for teachers.

Skill Development Equipment Company, 1340 North Jefferson St., Anaheim, CA 92807—Inflatable and foam-filled equipment for therapy and special education.

Charles B. Slack, Inc., 6900 Grove Rd., Thorofare, NJ 08086—Books and journals in the field of special education.

Society for Visual Education, Inc., 1345 Diversey Parkway, Chicago, IL 60614—Filmstrips, modules, book-cassettes, puppet kits, and picture-story study prints.

Special Education Materials, Inc., 484 South Broadway, Yonkers, NY 10705—Developmental materials for handicapped, career awareness, and survival skills; secondary level materials.

Special Press, P.O. Box 2524, Columbus, OH 43216—Publications, professional books, journals, and newsletters.

Stanley Tools, 600 Myrtle St., New Britain, CT 06050—Stanley hand tools (Surform); Stanley educational aids and films.

Steck-Vaughn Company, 807 Brazos, Austin, TX 78768—Educational materials.

Step, Inc., South Complex—Paine Field, Everett, WA 98204—Self-correcting manipulative teaching aids for math, language, and visual perception development; primary/elementary level.

Syracuse University Press, 1011 East Water Street, Syracuse, NY 13210—Books on special education subjects.

Teachers College Press, 1234 Amsterdam Ave., New York, NY 10027—Professional and reference materials.

Teaching Resources Corporation, 50 Pond Park Rd., Hingham, MA 02043—Educational materials for special education, language development, communication disorders, and early childhood.

Telesensory Systems, Inc., 3408 Hillview Ave., Palo Alto, CA 94304—Devices for people with disabilities.

Telex Communications, Inc., 9600 Aldrich Ave. So., Minneapolis, MN 55420—FM wireless auditory training systems for education of hearing impaired children.

Training Services, Inc., 2501 Silverside Rd., Suite One, Wilmington, DE 19810—Learning systems, academic and vocational, all grade levels; multimedia/multimodal approach.

Trend Enterprises, Inc., P.O. Box 43073, St. Paul, MN 55164—Learning materials for preschool, early, and special education.

Troubador Press, 385 Fremont St., San Francisco, CA 94105—Enrichment books for science, math, reading, social studies, and art contained in display racks.

UCS, Inc., 155 State St., Hackensack, NJ 07601—Manufacturers of motor development equipment, play furniture, parachutes, and air flow mats.

University of Illinois Press, 54 E. Gregory Dr., P.O. Box 5081, Sta. A, Champaign, IL 61820—Professional books, tests, and films.

University Park Press, 233 E. Redwood St., Baltimore, MD 21202—Textbooks, reference books, tests, and curriculum materials in all areas of exceptionality.

University of Washington Press, Seattle, WA 98105—Sequenced inventory of communication development; a diagnostic test for children functioning between four months and four years.

University of Wisconsin Extension Programs in Education, 610 Langdon St., Madison, WI 53706—Twelve-program videotape series, book of readings, study guide to series, and other educational television work.

Valpar Corporation, 3801 E. 34th St., Tucson, AZ 85713—Career and Vocational Assessment Programs: Valpar Work Samples; Valpar Occupational Interest Choice (VOICE); and Pre-Vocational Readiness Battery.

Vocational Research Institute, 1700 Sansom St., Philadelphia, PA 19103—VIEWS assessment system uses work samples to evaluate the vocational potential of mentally retarded populations.

Vort Corporation, P.O. Box 11132, Palo Alto, CA 94306—Tools for assessment, IEP planning, staff development, and program management.

Voxcom Division Tapecon, Inc., 100 Clover Green, Peachtree City, GA 30269—Card/cassette recorders and Sound Card programs and materials.

Walker Educational Book Corp., 720 Fifth Ave., New York, NY 10019—Instructional programs, professional books, and parent involvement materials for learning disabilities and special education.

Walt Disney Educational Media Company, 500 South Buena Vista St., Burbank, CA 91521—Film strips, 16mm films, and kits.

Wayne Engineering, 4120 Greenwood, Skokie, IL 60076—The TALKING PEN and related accessories for training visual and perceptual motor skills.

Webster's International, Inc., 5729 Cloverland Place, Brentwood, TN 37211—A parent involvement program with parent books, filmstrips, and cassettes, in Spanish and English.

Western Psychological Services, 12031 Wilshire Blvd., Los Angeles, CA 90025—Tests, test scoring services, and textbooks.

Albert Whitman & Company, 560 W. Lake St., Chicago, IL 60606—Children's supplemental and enrichment library books.

B.L. Winch and Associates, 45 Hitching Post Dr., Bldg. 2, Rolling Hills Estates, CA 90274—Educational systems to develop intellectual skills and emotional maturity: diagnostic (BESI), Prescriptive (PMRS), IEP

Development, Parent Involvement, Staff Development, and Self-Concept, age range 0 and up.

Xerox Education Publications, 245 Long Hill Rd., Middletown, CT 06457—Multimedia, filmstrip, and reading programs plus instructional games.

Youngheart Records, 2409 Hyperion Ave., Los Angeles, CA 90027—Educational records featuring the "We All Live Together" series.

ADDENDUM OF OTHER PUBLISHERS

Academic Therapy Publications, 20 Commercial Boulevard, Novato, CA 94947.

Beckley-Cardy, 1900 N. Narragansett Ave., Chicago, IL 60639.

Bernell Corporation, 422 E. Monroe Street, South Bend, IN 46601.

Calloway House, Inc., 451 Richardson Drive, Lancaster, PA 17603.

Career Aids, Inc., 8950 Lurline Ave., Dept. S8340, Chatsworth, CA 91311.

Closer Look, Special Education Information Center, Box 19428, Washington, DC 20036.

Communication Skill Builders, 3130 N. Dodge Blvd., P.O. Box 42050-J, Tucson, AZ 85733.

Creative Teaching Associates, P.O. Box 7766, 5629 E. Westoves, Fresno, CA 93747.

The Economy Company, P.O. Box 25308, 1901 North Walnut, Oklahoma City, OK 73125.

Education for Special Needs, 85 Main St., Watertown, MA 02172.

Foreworks, 7112 Teesdale Ave., N. Hollywood, CA.

Garrard Publishing Co., Champaign, IL 61820.

Globe Book Company, Inc., 50 West 23rd St., New York, NY 10010.

Guidance Associates, 757 Third Avenue, New York, NY 10017.

I.E. Products, Inc., 2306 Winters Drive, Kalamazoo, MI 49002.

Jamestown Publishers, P.O. Box 6743, Providence, RI 02940.

National Easter Seal Society, 2023 West Ogden Ave., Chicago, IL 60612.

New England Supply Co., P.O. Box 1581, Springfield, MA 01101.

Publishers Test Service, 2500 Garden Road, Monterey, CA 93940.

Reinforcement Learning, Inc., 87 Dimmig Road, P.O. Box 562, Upper Saddle River, NJ 07458.

The Supply Room, P.O. Box 96, Great Neck, NY 11022.

Teacher's Pet, P.O. Box 325, Suffern, NY 10901.

Index

About the Author

JUDITH COHEN is presently an assistant professor of education at Adelphi University, Garden City, New York, where she is also a coordinator of student teaching and field placement services. She teaches methods courses both in elementary and secondary education, along with reading and special education courses at the graduate level. Dr. Cohen received her Ph.D. from Hofstra University, Hempstead, New York. She has taught at both the elementary and secondary levels, publishes curriculum materials with Educational Activities, and serves as a consultant and inservice educator on a variety of reading and learning problems.

About the Contributors

JOAN BOSSIS is a specialist in learning disabilities and cofounder of the North Shore Learning Center, a private facility for learning disabled children on Long Island. She has worked as a senior learning diagnostic specialist at Long Island Jewish-Hillside Medical Center and as an adjunct instructor at Adelphi University, Garden City, New York. In addition, she has taught special education classes and has developed resource room programs at the secondary level, both publicly and privately. Ms. Bossis is presently a doctoral student and has received her M.A. and Ed.M. degrees from Teachers College, Columbia University.

RUTH GOLD is an associate professor of education at Adelphi University, Garden City, New York, and coordinator of special education programs. She received her doctorate from Teachers College, Columbia University, New York City. Dr. Gold has taught special education at the elementary level in the public schools. At present she is the chairperson of the Professional Advisory Board of the Nassau County (New York) Association for Children with Learning Disorders and is on the advisory boards of the Adelphi program for learning disabled college students and the Preschoolers Workshop in Syosset, New York. Dr. Gold is the coauthor, with Dr. Ernest Siegel, of a textbook, *Educating the Learning Disabled,* which will be published by Macmillan in early 1982.

RITA GORDON is the supervisory teacher of the Teacher-Mom Program for emotionally handicapped children in Mineola, New York. She has designed and taught an English as a Second Language Program for her school district, designed other curriculums at the elementary level, and devised and directed a program in family living for preadolescent girls. Mrs. Gordon is contributing education editor of *L.I. ALIVE,* a regional quarterly, and has been a guest lecturer at Adelphi University, Garden City, N.Y.

SHELDON HOROWITZ received his M.S. degree at Peabody College, Baltimore, Maryland, and is presently a doctoral candidate in special education at Teachers College, Columbia University. Mr. Horowitz has served as both clinic supervisor and administrative assistant to the director of the Child Study Center at Teachers College, and has worked as an adjunct instructor at both Hofstra University, Hempstead, N.Y., and Adelphi University, Garden City, N.Y. He has also been a LD resource room teacher on the junior high school level. His professional interests include clinical education practices, teacher training, and neurological and behavioral correlates in special education.

KATHLEEN JOYCE is a parttime faculty member in the education department of Adelphi University, Garden City, N.Y. She participated in the development and implementation of the Program for Learning Disabled College Students at Adelphi, and has served as its educational director. She has also taught mentally retarded, emotionally disturbed, and learning disabled children and adolescents both in New York City and on Long Island.

MARGO NEALE is the resource teacher for the primary grades at the Denton Avenue School in New Hyde Park, N.Y. As part of her resource program she has experimented broadly with ways of involving parents in a program for their children in the resource room. Ms. Neale received her M.A. from Teachers College, Columbia University, and has most recently been involved in a course in family dynamics at the Ackerman Institute in New York City.

GAIL REITER received her B.S. in elementary education from Hofstra University, Hempstead, N.Y. and her M.S. in special education from Adelphi University, Garden City, N.Y. Her professional experience includes positions as an elementary school teacher, a resource teacher on both elementary and secondary levels, and a remedial consultant for handicapped students. In addition, she has conducted workshops related to children with learning disabilities.

ELAINE SCHWARTZ is reading consultant for special education in the Half Hollow Hills Public Schools on Long Island, New York. In addition, she is head of the Reading/Learning Disability Clinic at the Huntington Center of Adelphi University, Garden City, N.Y. Dr. Schwartz also teaches graduate courses in reading and special education. She received her Ph.D. from Hofstra University, Hempstead, N.Y.

ROCHELLE SIMON is a learning disabilities resource room teacher in the Baldwin elementary schools on Long Island, N.Y. She is part of a Child Study Team that identifies, clarifies, and instructs learning disabled children. Mrs. Simon received her B.A. from Hunter College, New York City, and her M.S. in Education from Hofstra University, Hempstead, N.Y. She has taught kindergarten and first grade in the New York City public schools.

GLORIA WILSON is presently teaching as a resource room teacher for junior high school children with learning disabilities in North Bellmore, Long Island. She is also an adjunct instructor at Adelphi University, Garden City, N.Y. Mrs. Wilson is also involved in facilitating support groups for parents of exceptional children and investigating a job network for learning disabled adolescents. She has taught in a private school for children with severe learning difficulties and was a speech/language therapist for preschool and primary level children. She received her B.A. in speech therapy and her M.S. in special education from Hofstra University, Hempstead, N.Y.

JOSEPH ZACHERMAN is presently working as a supervisor of special education in the Manhattan high schools, New York City Board of Education. He is also an adjunct instructor at Lehman College, City University of New York, where he teaches courses both on the graduate and undergraduate levels in the department of specialized services. Mr. Zacherman is currently writing his Ph.D. dissertation at Yeshiva University, New York City, in the field of school administration.

BEVERLY ZIMMERMAN has completed 21 years of teaching experience from the first through sixth grades. She is presently a resource room teacher and learning disabilities consultant in the Oceanside Public Schools on Long Island, New York. In addition, Mrs. Zimmerman has been an adjunct instructor of courses on diagnosis and prescription for Adelphi University, Garden City, N.Y. She received her M.S. degree from Hofstra University, Hempstead, N.Y.